LANGUAGE IN DISPUTE: THE SUMMULAE LOGICALES

AMSTERDAM STUDIES IN THE THEORY AND HISTORY OF LINGUISTIC SCIENCE

General Editor
E. F. KONRAD KOERNER
(University of Ottawa)

Series III - STUDIES IN THE HISTORY OF THE LANGUAGE SCIENCES

Advisory Editorial Board

Volume 39

Peter of Spain

*Language in Dispute:
The Summulae Logicales*

PETER OF SPAIN

LANGUAGE IN DISPUTE

An English translation of
Peter of Spain's *Tractatus*
called afterwards

SUMMULAE LOGICALES

on the basis of the critical
edition established by

L.M. DE RIJK

by

FRANCIS P. DINNEEN, S.J.
Georgetown University

JOHN BENJAMINS PUBLISHING COMPANY
AMSTERDAM/PHILADELPHIA

1990

Library of Congress Cataloging in Publication Data

John, XXI, Pope, d. 1277.
   [Summulae logicales. English]
Language in dispute : an English translation of Peter of Spain's Tractatus, called afterwards Summulae logicales : on the basis of the critical edition established by L.M. de Rijk / Peter of Spain ; by Francis P. Dinneen.
      p.   cm. -- (Amsterdam studies in the theory and history of linguistic science. Series III, Studies in the history of the language sciences, ISSN 0304-0720; v. 39)
Includes bibliographical references.
1. Logic -- Early works to 1800. I. Dinneen, Francis P. II. Title. III. Series.
BC60.J5613   1990
160 -- dc20   89-18528
ISBN 90 272 4524 X (alk. paper)   CIP

ACKNOWLEDGEMENTS

The origin of this translation was a Christmas vacation attempt to become familiar with word-processing. It coincided with a re-reading of Bochenski's 1947 text of the Summulae, suggesting the idea that things long neglected could be refreshed while practicing the new techniques. When the outcome was proposed for publication, it was pointed out that De Rijk 1972 had outdated Bochenski 1947.

De Rijk's work is a model of careful scholarship, which this translation does not adequately reflect and occasionally may distort, given its origin and focus on linguistic challenges rather than logical rigor. The original's details are to be found in De Rijk's critical apparatus and in the 119-page Introduction to his 'Peter of Spain (Petrus Hispanus Portugalensis) TRACTATUS, called afterwards SUMMULAE LOGICALES - First Critical Edition from the Manuscripts with an Introduction' (Van Gorcum & Comp. B.V. Assen, 1972). It was soon clearly futile just to try to complement Bochenski's text (based mainly on one manuscript) by additions or corrections from De Rijk's. Acknowledgement of Van Gorcum's permission to attempt this translation is here gratefully made.

FOREWORD

"What is his noun ?" can be a poor translation of "Quel est son nom ?" but might highlight a linguist's perspective in translating an explictly logical work. There are no lexical or grammatical puzzles in "to be safe on the Fourth, don't buy a fifth on the third", but few non-Americans can 'translate' it and ordinary dictionaries won't help. Comparable cultural lapses may annoy logicians comparing this with the original, as will the fact that translation-equivalents do not rigidly follow a logical one-to-one parallel.

It seemed appropriate in translating to take account of some changes in grammatical terminology and perspective. This version seems to refer to English rather than Latin, so here, 'word-group' covers phrase, clause and sentence (oratio); 'ending' often seemed the best choice for casus; for a syntactically vs. morphologically defined unit, 'nominal' often appears for Hispanus' 'noun', as do 'verbal', 'adjectival' and other syntactically defined -al forms; where 'word' occurs, it is indicated whether it stands for Hispanus' nomen or dictio. Some of his terms have since been replaced or used for other purposes, like 'restrictive relative clause' for his (now) misleading 'implication'. 'Or' can be ambiguous, so where coordinate conjunction rather than disjunction is intended, a slanted line / links the coordinates. Instead of using 'sign' for syncategorematics like 'every', the word 'marker' was chosen. English and Latin often diverge in lexical range, so glosses rather than true translations often appear, like totus : '(the) whole (of)'. The Latin for some key words and most 'sophisms' is given, particularly in the introductory section, then wherever Latin ratio occurs, or where out of the ordinary expressions were preferred, such as 'peculiarly' for proprie. All footnotes are those of De Rijk's text except my own, initialled 'fpd'.

Since this is a work about dialectic, translation-choices made here will give ample ground for dialectical dispute. In the meantime, it is to be hoped that non-logicians, linguists and those just interested in language may find interest in reading it.

Washington, D.C., December 1988   F.P.D.

CONTENTS

INTRODUCTION

PETER OF SPAIN'S SUMMULAE, THE MODISTAE, AND LINGUISTICS

Hispanus was a contemporary of linguistic theorists called 'Modistae' after their 12th to 14th century writings entitled <u>De Modis Significandi</u>. Their concerns involved differences between the way things actually are in themselves, how we understand them, and how grammatical conventions require us to communicate about them:

modi essendi		ways things are	SO
modi intelligendi		ways of conceiving things	SEEM
	or	ways of being understood	
modi significandi		ways we must communicate	SAID
	or	ways of being REpresented	

This suggests a preference for the cognitive potential of language over its common actual role of silence-prevention. Linguists until recently have been more concerned with SAID than CIRCUMSTANCE, since SAID can be idealized as independent of the SO-ways things are, or the SEEM-ways we think about them. But that independence can only be one of degree. 'Meaning' distinguishes language from noise, and modal differences distinguish one language from another. Descriptive Linguistics allows 'meaning' a negative role (e.g. that differences between English <u>take</u> vs. <u>took</u> or tones in Chinese are distinctive). Transformational Generative Grammar attempts a less negative account of 'meaning' because of its explanatory vs. descriptive concept of an adequate grammar. In Hispanus' terms, the relation of form to matter is 'explanatory', since form determines matter much like precise questions determine what answers to them are considered apposite. What Hispanus separated as formal vs. material perspectives is what distinguishes emic Phonemics from etic Phonetics, yet both sets simultaneously define each other: without adequate phonetic description, phonological explanation is unreliable; without adequate meaning-distinctions, semantic explanations are inadequate. If its peculiar technical terms are the most precise answers to questions a discipline asks, Hispanus' work may alert us to questions modern linguistic work overlooks or confuses.

Material or etic (as in phonetics) objects of study are definable in terms of what can be called their Composition: a positive, additive list of components forming units distinguishable by the way they are distributed. Formally or emically (as in phonemics), objects with identical composition can be viewed as contrastive because of different functions they frequently serve. Of a phonetically identical high, front vowel i, we can say that in Latin it is one of five basic contrasts, but in other languages, one of three, or more than five, such oppositions. Latin i also contrasts as a syllable, morpheme, word, clause or sentence with other Latin forms. When I talk to myself about me, three emically distinct grammatical persons, but only a single real-world referent is involved, etically or materially identical in SO, functionally or formally distinct in SAID, and not much of a challenge for normals to keep distinct in SEEM.

Different modes of signifying (SAID) can refer to identical modes of existing in a real (SO) situation, as in saying (a) 'Old Sol hasn't been around much', or (b) 'The sun hasn't been rising in the morning'. While (a) ambiguously signals a State of affairs about someone, (b) ambiguously signals a personal Action or impersonal Process. We now consider (a) metaphoric, but neither an Action or a Process interpretation of (b) SAID has been thought to correspond literally to SO since Ptolemaic Astronomy was abandoned. We see this as a clear conflict among SO, SEEM, SAID - areas the Modistae assigned to modi essendi, modi intelligendi, and modi significandi. In (b), rising has an active mode of signification lacking passive contrast when the sun is involved. Similarly, we still describe people as jovial, mercurial, saturnine, choleric, phlegmatic or sanguine: in terms of astrological and physiological theories few still credit, without either lying or being deceived. Both situations involve interpretations of 'Meaning', and Hispanus provides labels for keeping separate several aspects of what that single cover term, 'Meaning', means.

SUPPOSITION and SIGNIFICATION

The tract on Supposition is the 6th of this 12-part Summary of Dialectic by Petrus Hispanus (d.1277). The Summulae's first part (I-V) introduces Aristotelian ideas familiar enough at the time to be called Old Logic; the second (VI-XII) studies properties of terms, then considered novelties of Modern Logic. The two most important properties of terms were Supposition and Signification, which contrast like meaning-as-reference (Supposition) and meaning-as-sense (Signification). Among the questions raised were how senses and referents are related: e.g., must things exist if we have words for them, or how can statements about them be labelled valid or invalid, true or false, appropriate or inappropriate, under different conditions ?

Hispanus's treatment is of current interest because identical data must be dealt with differently in related disciplines studying them (a) as natural objects and subjects, (b) to match objectivity and subjectivity and (c) to discuss the nature of subjective objects. Objective stresses extramental status, while subjective involves tests decided by individual or social values. What the Stoics called lexis, Hispanus a dictio, and Bloomfield a linguistic form, for instance, can be considered a subjective-object (because as socially constituted, it is accessible as such only to natives). But Bloomfield's phonetic form, Stoic phonē, or another use of Hispanus' dictio, is a lexical item REpresented without invoking its grammatical or semantic status. That makes it an objective-object (because neutrally accessible to native and nonnative alike), yet a quasi subjective-object (as accessible only to trained observers).

Each of those objects can be studied statically or dynamically, as end points of an action or process (**actively** thinking up terms to abbreviate how we keep things distinct from each other: meanings as senses; or the **process** of accepting terms and their senses as applying or adaptable to things: meaning as reference). Or they can be taken as a **static** table of descriptive labels: e.g., generic concepts like that of 'man', or relations such as grammatical number.

Even if, as Hispanus claimed, logical methods test the validity of how other disciplines argue to their conclusions, those methods do not endow dialecticians with a special ability to judge whether terms are appropriately defined. Still, if Dialectic is supposed to clarify conventions about how the Signification and Supposition of terms determine each other, it is not unreasonable to expect a consistent way of dealing with accounts of sense and reference in a work on Dialectic: that what Subject or Predicate mean in Logic, for instance, can be distinct from their interpretation in Grammar.

But English words like meaning and Latinate ones with an -atio suffix are as inherently ambiguous as Latin modi significandi - neutral to English 'ways of signifying' or 'ways of being signified'. In passages where Hispanus distinguishes Signification and Supposition, terms we translate as imposition, signified, acceptance, signifying, supposition and coupling are equally ambiguous. Nothing in his definitions determines whether or when, e.g., representation is equivalent to 'the act of representing', 'the process of representing', or 'the fact that a vocal expression represents' a thing by vocal expression. If exact norms could be given, their ambiguity would be systematic, and their use proportional or analogical (e.g.

how noun and verb are to be used consistently in grammar or dialectic; why indifferent use of sentence / proposition in a logical or linguistic discussion would be predictably ambiguous).

Ambiguity is more common in ordinary than in technical language. Hispanus mentions some of the differences. He says the matter Dialecticians study is only one kind of sentence and two kinds of words Grammarians predefine for them: the subset of **sentences**[1] that signify something true or false (now formally redefined as REpresentations of **Propositions**), and the subset of **words**[2] into which sentences of that sort can be resolved (logically redefined as categorematic **terms** and non-terms called syncategorematic expressions). The Dialectician studies as well two **functions** that **terms** constituting a Proposition have by serving as its logical subject and predicate. Where noun, verb and other parts of a sentence might be defined positively and independently in Grammar (e.g., by morphological shape, syntax, and meaning-type), the Dialectician's Subject and Predicate terms define each other relationally and mutually, through their functional interdependence: the matter grammar and dialectic deal with can overlap, but their formalities and functions are no more identical than those of grammar and poetry.

If words were technical terms like H_2O instead of water, they would all pair a unique Signification with a unique Referent, and violations in argumentation would be easy to identify. Hispanus calls terms like that univocal (pp. 23-27) as opposed to equivocal (identical in form, different in Signification: pp. 23, 85, 86); many words with root- or principal-Signification (p. 95) in common are called denominatives or conjugates (pp. 23, 30, 31). E.g. like univocals, grammar and grammarian have the same principal Signification, and overlap in expression (like equivocals), but differ from univocals by Consignification, and from equivocals by their form: grammar has the same principal signification as grammarian, but English derivational -ian can consignify 'person' while grammar does not: spoken /gramaH/ in English pronunciations equivocally REpresents either what writing REpresents as grandmother or as grammar). Such words occasion the kind of Ambiguity he calls **Equivocation** (p. 83).

1: Hispanus' oratio is here almost invariably translated word-group, allowing it to correspond to our sentence, phrase and clause as well.
2: Where word occurs in this translation, Hispanus' original dictio or nomen is noted.

When a construction constituted by two words like flying planes or Aristotle's book (p. 90) can principally signify more than one referent (a plane flying on its own, or one we cause to fly; the book he owns, or the one he wrote), the ambiguity involved is called **Amphiboly** (pp. 90 ff). So the kind of Ambiguity a Dialectician explains by discussing properties of terms is traceable to three linguistic sources: ambiguous words, ambiguous construction, or both.

For example, in 'The kid's study is astounding', both kid and study are equivocal (kid can be child or goat; study the result of being studied or the activity or result of studying something), so the expression is ambiguous from both points of view: (1) it is ambiguous in as many ways as the terms kid and study are **equivocal**; (2) it is as ambiguous as the **amphibolous** construction (involving active or passive study). Each interpretation of kid's study involves different sets of significations and objects, characters or scenarios, but the signification of proper names like Aristotle (if they have any) cannot dictate that term's supposition in the same way as the various significations of kid do, (lots of things can be called kids, but only one is Aristotle), while either interpretation of Aristotle's book has the same cast of characters signified by those two terms, but in different roles (Aristotle as author, or Aristotle as owner).

Hispanus deals with facts like these in several ways. He says (1) that a singular term signifies, supposes for, and summons (has Appellation for) the same thing, while suppositions of common terms can vary (pp. 175 ff.); (2) **being** this or that kind of a thing is not a matter of language, while **being signified** this or that way can be exclusively a linguistic modality (p. 69); (3) functions like subject-as-subject or predicate-as-predicate must be distinguished from that which functions as subject or predicate (pp. 187, 169), just as grammatical nouns or verbs can be considered as REpresenting terms in logical propositions, and logical terms as REpresenting subjects and predicates of judgements (pp. 2 ff); (4) while a morphological Nominative often coincides with the semantactic role of Agent, the mode of Agent can be superimposed on a syntactic Patient role or Patient mode on a syntactic Agent role: in 'Aristotle is being struck', a nominative has a Patient mode, and in 'Aristotle sees himself', the supposition of Aristotle and himself is identical, but himself has a coreferential Agent mode superimposed on its Patient role (p. 165).

A Dialectic equipped to deal with properties of terms like supposition vs. signification can handle sentences which are not isomorphic REpresentations of covert propositions (like the sentence man runs for the propositions man runs, or a man is running: p. 3.) A sentence using the word representation is intrinsically ambiguous; a proposition (a REpresentation of something as state, process, or action) is decidably true or false, but NOT by the overt sentence 'Signification is representation', because -ation forms of English are three-ways ambiguous (state, process, action) and therefore signs of at least nine propositions without change in expression.

Generic 'Signification' is defined as 'conventional representation of a thing by a vocal expression' (p. 69) and is made more specific in passing remarks Hispanus makes. E.g., Denominatives (like grammarian from grammar) have a common principal Signification but different Consignification (pp. 69, 179); substantival nouns both 'signify' and 'stand for' something, while verbs and adjectivals may share principal signification, but 'copulate' rather than 'stand for' (p. 179); a signification may derive from extrinsic imposition, conventional transfer (p. 93) or intrinsic similarity (p. 65). But the most important linguistic subdivision of 'signify' is the expression 'consignify'. Aristotle (On Interpretation III 16b 1 ff.) says nouns and verbs with identical lexical roots 'signify' (sēmainei) the same thing, but verbs 'consignify' (prosēmainei) time as well: the noun sign and verb signs differ in this way, although signs 'consignifies' more than just time-contrast.

So Supposition (or reference) is ambiguously (a) a psychological act of interpreting a term as referring to a thing, (b) the social process associating a definition with what it picks out, or (c) the state or fact that a term has a property consisting in its socially shared association pairing a meaning with a referent. What Supposition involves in all three can be variables, but Signification is a constant (pp. 69 ff.; 172 ff.; 177 ff.): Restriction decreases, or Extension increases, the number of things for which a term stands, while its Signification remains the same. E.g., nation can signify, stand or suppose for, and summon an individual existent thing; the term capitol signifies, supposes for, and calls up a particular kind of building, existent or not; in the unit-expression or construction National Capitol, Capitol is restricted in that it does not suppose for a State Capitol, and in that same phrase, State is restricted only to Capitol (not capital a state owns), while the signification (what they are able to pick out) of State or Capitol is unchanged. Hispanus says Restriction in such cases is both mutual and proportioned (p. 178): the less common (nation) restricts the more common (capitol), since there are more capitols than National Capitols; but the less common (nation) restricts the more common (capitol), e.g., because there are more Capitols than Nations in the United States. But the Signification of such terms is said to remain unaltered.

Similarly, <u>Circular</u> shares principal meaning with <u>Circle</u> and over-laps with that of <u>round</u>, which has many senses and functions. The Supposition of a <u>round</u> includes: circle, ring or sphere; circular, ring-shaped, curved or spherical object; rounded form; anything circular in cross section; completed course, series, or succession; completed spell of activity; series in play or sport; recurring period of time, succession of events or duties; single outburst of applause or single shot by one or many guns; ammunition charge for a single shot; single servings to everyone at a table or bar; dance moving in a ring; movement in a circle or around an axis; thigh of beef below the rump, above the leg; a Briton's slice of bread; archers' arrows shot; boxing's three-minute period; a musical canon, or order in ringing a peal of bells; completed game of golf; card player's turn to bid, bet, play a card, deal or be dealt cards; convex curve given the luff, head, or foot of a fore-and-aft sail. <u>Rounds</u> are a complet-ed course of time, series of events or operations; a going from place to place in habitual ciruit: <u>to go the rounds</u> is to be reported; <u>in the round</u> has to do with a stage surrounded by the audience or with a broad understanding; in sculpture, not attached to supporting back-ground, freestanding. To <u>make the rounds</u> is to visit routinely like actors or free-lance writers contacting producers and editors. The same principal meaning is involved adverbially or prepositionally ((a)round), and in verbs transitively (make round, plump, or free from angularity) as well as intransitively (become round, plump, or unang-ular). Construction (with predicate functions or other terms) can extend or restrict <u>round</u>'s supposition (the number of defined things the term stands for), signalled by word order (subjects precede), copular signification (adjectival, verbal, lexical) and consignific-ations of substantive terms (gender, number), as well as the consign-ifications of the terms with which it is constructed (tense of the verb or participle, lexical significations like <u>possible</u>, types of relative, (<u>which</u> vs. <u>another</u>), of quantifier (<u>such</u> <u>as</u>, <u>both</u>), of adverbial (<u>only</u>). Usage modifies standard signification/supposition interdependencies: <u>empty</u> has mostly to do with solid things, not air; <u>king</u> or <u>professor</u> are taken be ours, unless otherwise marked; words have consignifications one may not attend to when focusing on <u>principal</u> signification (e.g. grammatical 3rd person singular or plural in a <u>dictio</u> which happens to be a verb).

Significations are presented as abstract relationships speakers can understand, compared to concrete supposits they see, hear, feel, etc. when counting. Words are as abstract compared to concrete utter-ances as abstract-because-absent paradigmatic options compared to items concrete-because-present in the syntagmatic chain of speech. But REpresentations of these have yet a different status. International Signs suggest why this should be so, since they are ideographic, unrestricted by grammatical or phonetic peculiarities of a particular language. E.g., on a white field, a red circle encloses a heavy black line from which wavy lines arise, with a red line passing diagonally through the black one. This ideograph represents an idea or object rather than a locution. If an idea is a signification, and objects are what a significant term's supposition includes, the aptness of signs comes into question here in a way not mentioned in the Summulae.

Ideographs can be less determinate than linguistic formulations: as REpresenting a physical object, the international NO SMOKING sign does not portray white cigarettes, filter-tips, cigars, pipes, or hookahs. English words like 'No Smoking' are indeterminate differently: Smoking is ambiguous as to whether a state, action or process is involved, allowing dialectically-minded violators to retort 'My cigarette isn't smokimg, I am', or just as perversely, 'I'm not smoking, my cigarette is'. Besides, the signification or sense of Smoking is indifferently involved in a neutral description, exclamation, or prohibition - the relation of sign-to-signified (p. 70) may be less ambiguous if what is 'signified' is an institutionalized practice, but the 'relation of substitute to what has been substituted for' by the isolated term is not.

Some of the presuppositions behind these expressions are illustrated in Hispanus' Summulae Logicales. They involve notions of meaning, sense, reference, and modification. His mode of thinking is analogical. Comparing it with modern usage challenges us to see what, for example, mode, modality, mood, etc. now have in common for different fields.

Understanding, translating, paraphrasing or using the word mode as others do involves ideas so basic as to pose problems. Mode presupposes a determinable element, one in some way, yet aspectually different from one instance to the next: like Chopin's Waltz in A Flat in major or minor key, in 3/4 or 4/4 time; in grammatical paradigms, one graphic, phonetic, phonological, morphological, syntactic, or semantic element is taken to be so basic that forms related on one of those bases are called conjugations, declensions, inflections, determinations, or modifications of it. Conceptions of 'meaning' and its varieties need clarification. Latin and Greek words for 'signify' are clearest when taken separately for the state of a sound-sequence being, or the process of its becoming, or the act of making it, a name.

For instance, Latin consignificat (transliterated as consignifies) translates Aristotle's prosemainei in On Interpretation III 16b 1 ff. where he says the rhēma, hygiainei ('is healthy'), differs from the onoma, hygieia ('health'), because the rhēma signifies time in addition to what 'health' names. As an 'Answer', this is interdependent with an implicitly conventionalized 'Question' about what 'naming' involves, and about what sorts of 'things' can be 'named'. Linguists avoid that problem by adopting the philological tradition of objectively labelling one part of these words' composition roots (perhaps something like hygi-), and other parts of its composition affixes (like -ainei and -eia) and distinguishing inflectional from derivational affixes on formal grounds.

But words can have functions similar to those of affixes, as in Dixit Petrum solum scribere ('He said Peter only writes / only Peter writes'). Solum ('sole(ly)') either 'signifies' (functions as a categorematic expression like subject or predicate), 'couples' (as adjectival adjunct to the subject), or perhaps 'consignifies' (as adverbial modifier of the predicate). Hispanus proposed no separate technical terms for meanings of bound as well as free forms he called syncategorematics (3), both of which had the function of 'consignifying'. He took 'consignification' as a variable modification of its constant 'signification'. But for free forms he did propose a constant vs. variable distinction: only nouns 'signify', while verbs, adjectives, and forms of be 'link' or 'couple'.

THE 'SCIENTIFIC' STATUS OF HISPANUS' SUMMULAE

Latin was the one language medieval Europeans shared, the object of elementary schooling and the tool for all levels of scholarship. Knowledge of Greek, once the lingua franca of the Roman Empire, had become rare. In Hispanus' theocentric era, Latin style owed more to St. Jerome's transliteration of Koine Greek scripture than to Ciceronian polish. The certainty attributed to Christian Revelation was transferred by some for quite confused reasons to the Latinity of Jerome's deliberately literal translation.

The Summulae Logicales is also worth evaluating in the light of debate about the 'scientific' status of Linguistics. Hispanus claimed Dialectic was a study prerequisite to all others, because it shows how to test their fundamental assumptions. But he calls his study an Art, not a Science (1). Norms he proposed for this rigorous interpretation of language are public, refutable, and countable in the Summulae, all characteristics claimed for 'science'. The 12 Tracts of the Summulae deal with the following topics:

1) Propositions relating predicates and subjects are demonstrably contrary, contradictory, or equipollent in precise ways.
2) Predications assert 3 kinds of class-membership: Genus, Species and Individual.
3) There are 8 ways of 'being in' one of 3 kinds of membership.
4) Propositional elements (categorematic and syncategorematic) combine validly only in 3 figures and 19 subtypes of syllogisms.
5) Arguments (about whether propositions are true or false) derive from 21 common 'Topics'.
6) Suppositions (how terms stand for things) are of 7 types, with specific rules appropriate to each.
7) There are 13 fallacies (6 linguistic, 7 extralinguistic), based on mistakes about Suppositions, or faults of logical form.
8) The Suppositions of Relatives vary with their manner of recalling antecedents.
9) Supposition can be extended, but Signification cannot.
10) Supposition or Signification are independent of the existence of referents.   Appellation names the Supposition of a term signifying something that actually exists.
11) Suppositions can be restricted, but Signification cannot.
12) Suppositions of common terms are clarified by markers (like Negatives and Quantifiers) which distribute their membership.

The work appeared around 1300, about a generation before Thomas of Erfurt's more complete Modistic summary (Bursill-Hall, 1972). Born in Lisbon about 1215, Peter was a contemporary of Thomas Aquinas, and studied at the University of Paris (where Hispanus was first added to distinguish this Petrus from others.) His teaching at the University of Siena won Hispanus wide respect in the medical field.

His approach to language is that of Dialectic: it differed from Logic in that deductive certainty characterized 'Science', while Probability (rules for 'testability') attached to Arts. For instance, once a term like Circle is defined in Geometry (which the medievals called a 'Science'), deductions about radii, parallel lines, and right angles are demonstrable and acknowledged as certain. But words of ordinary language can base only probable inferences, not certain deductions, even though the syllogistic form of both sorts of arguments is identical.

Dialecticians have the annoying habit of arguing that if you use a word, you must mean it. They found the most serious way of 'meaning' it was to assert it truly or falsely. While that is not identical with using it in a way we would today allow as 'meaningful' or 'valid', every word can be challenged as though it were a Subject, Predicate, or a syncategorematic Operator in a syllogism.

Some dialectic rules of thumb proposed in the <u>Summulae</u> can be re-stated or reinterpreted from a linguistic point of view. E.g., in log-ical formulation, Hispanus shows how sentences contrast or are equi-pollent referentially because quantifiers like <u>every</u>, <u>no</u>, and especially <u>some</u>, make minimal pairs involving identical senses. The quantifier <u>some</u> still plagues linguistic arguments about identity or transformation of 'meaning' defined in terms of <u>truth conditions</u>. Modern disputes seem to have abandoned Hispanus' technical gradat-ion of contradiction, contrariety, subalternation, and subcontrariety. Norms now used for 'truth conditions' are objectively referential (SO), not subjectively conceptual (SEEM). Logicians are not con-vinced Aristotle (or his Medieval successors) attained to clarity about the scope of negation (i.e. how Constituents construct with a negative). But in the <u>Summulae</u> (p. 6), these relationships are assigned technical labels:

```
every                                                             no
man is                   c o n t r a r i e s                   man is
animal                                                         animal


s        C                                             Y        s
u           O                                     R             u
b              N                               O               b
a                 T                         T                  a
l                    R                   C                     l
t                       A             I                        t
e                          D                                   e
r                       A             I                        r
n                    R                   C                     n
a                 T                         T                  a
t              N                               O               t
e           O                                     R            e
s        C                                             Y       s


some man                                                    some man
   is                    s u b c o n t r a r i e s            is not
 animal                                                      animal
```

Asserting <u>some</u> anythings are whatever they are implicitly asserts as well that <u>some</u> are not, while assertions and negations quantified by <u>every</u> or <u>no</u> have quite different positive and negative implic-ations.

Propositions were related in a similar way (p. 14):

possible to be	**C O N T R A R Y**	possible not to be
contingent to be	3 is ever 4	contingent not to be
not impossible to be	in contrary	not impossible not to be
necessary not to be	order	not necessary to be

```
s                                                           s
     C                                              Y        
u        O                                   R              u
           N                              O                
b             T                     T                       b
                R             C                              
a    1st line yields    A      I         By rule to         a
        to 4th, Partic-      D              set,  lines     
l     ularly related    A      I         are fated          l
                R             C                              
t             T                     T                       t
           N                              O                
e        O                                   R              e
     C                                              Y        
r                                                           r

n                                                           n
```

not possible to be	Subcon. to you	not possible not to be
not contingent to be	lines one & two	not contingent not to be
impossible to be		impossible not to be
necessary not to be	**S U B C O N T R A R Y**	necessary to be

Labels used here derive from a technique of subcategorization called the 'Porphyrian Tree', first outlined by early Aristotelians, and
comparable in its form and reliance on a spatial analogy to 19th
century use of 'Trees' to show subclasses in Language Families, or
more superficially, to tree diagrams of Grammatical Derivation in
Generative Transformational Grammar:

SUBSTANCE

corporeal	incorporeal

BODY

animate	inanimate

ANIMATE BODY

sensitive	insensitive

ANIMAL

rational	irrational

RATIONAL ANIMAL

mortal	immortal

M A N

Socrates	Plato

This tree provided an imaginative constant for REpresenting how terms vary as 'inferiors' of others, with a 'descent' from generic, through several (sub)specific, to individual levels, when reference was 'diffuse' or 'personal'; how things were said to 'be-in' others; and how things were 'same' or 'different', with explicit technical terms labelling each difference. While TG Tree branches are read as 'both-and' Conjunctions in descending order (e.g. rewrite S as NP + VP = 'both NP and VP') Porphyrian descent is read as a Platonic 'either-or' Division until the last step, which is like TG's 'both-and': but this 'both-and' is no dichotomy - Plato & Socrates are just any two Individuals, as numerically indefinite as lexical items.

Notice that both Porphyrian and TG Trees preclude division at two points: a Supreme Genus (like S) is not REpresented as a constituent / species of a higher genus, while other constituents can be simultaneously species with respect to higher ones, and genus with respect to lower ones. But while individuals such as <u>Plato</u> and <u>Socrates</u> (like lexical items with which TG REpresentations stop) are constituents or members of the Most Specific Species <u>Man</u>, they are not species themselves. So <u>Substance</u> and <u>Individual</u> are emically primitive terms referring to the same etic things in different ways, and all intermediate ones are related to their highest and lowest instances in the way an S is related to lexical items exemplifying it. The scientific importance of Tree Diagrams is their claim to REpresent **Sentence**, not just <u>this</u> sentence; the scientific interest of TG Semantic Interpretation is concern with this <u>species</u> of Sentence, not just <u>this</u> individual sentence. That is the concern of Pragmatics.

Similarly, logical Subjects and Predicates are exocentric Constituents of a Proposition, so they mutually define each other's function, just as Grammar's S, NP and VP do. Describing what grammatical categories like Noun 'mean' (compared to subcategories like Proper or Common Noun) is different from giving an account of lexical items like <u>Plato</u> or <u>horse</u>. It is useful not to confuse names for natural objects, labels for grammatical categories, and those for ideas we have about either of them. This was an aim of Modistic theory, much of which Hispanus seemed to take for granted.

Hispanus' era is called one of <u>Terministic Logic</u>. It dealt not only with isolated PROforms for Substance, Quantified in deductive argumentation of the categorical type, but also with their Quality. This involved the <u>signification</u> of substantive terms (with a basic model in the Tree of Porphyry), as distinct from their <u>supposition</u>. An identical conceptual content (<u>signification</u>), common to the most generic and most specific terms with the same referent (<u>supposit</u>) was assumed. Another way of putting it is to say that the referents of Subjects and Predicates could be taken as materially identical, but formally distinct. Linguistic <u>modification</u> and its consequences dominates the Modistic tradition. Its setting in a contemporary sketch of how words 'mean' helps clarify its linguistic perspectives:

LEVELS AT WHICH WORD-SENSES RELATE TO COMPARABLE REFERENTS

ACTS		OBJECTS

SENSATION   (concerned with)   concrete, unique, intrinsically mutable, spatio-temporal things or events: e.g., **pies, wheels, days**

via
sensory integration

MEMORY
and
IMAGINATION

Typical concrete things or events; alone, or space-time related; contingent, so intrinsically mutable: e.g. **round things; kinds of weather**

via
Abstractive
Intelligence

INSIGHT
UNDERSTANDING

ABSTRACT, ideal, necessary UNITS and RELATIONS, inextended, atemporal, immutable, universal: e.g. **circumference; recurrence of seasons**

via
Comparison

JUDGEMENT

RELATIVE necessity of Abstractions and relations: e.g., **IF $\frac{1}{4}$ pie, THEN 90 degrees; IF 2 moons, THEN season ending**

via
INVESTIGATION of
Presuppositions

REASONING   results in   (scientific) (épistémé)

KNOWLEDGE or HYPOTHESIS **(Lunar Year; Geometry, Geocentric Astronomy)**

SENSE, REFERENCE, AND MODIFICATION

SENSE

The above basically psychological scheme can be read in a number of ways. Relating it to some elementary ideas of Predicate Logic can help grasp part of what the Modistae were doing, what Hispanus took from their work, and how it is relevant to TG's concern for Universal Grammar. It was suggested that Predicates stand for categories to which Subjects 'belong'; or that Predicates name classes, and Subjects name their members; or that a predication says that a Subject 'is' or 'is in' a Predicate. But different sorts of membership are expressed variously, depending on the grammar of the language involved. The most neutral, abstract, or formal REpresentation of all was: S = P. Logical form abstracts from grammatical quirks.

But how we verbalize the symbol ' = ' depends importantly on what the words used as subject and predicate 'mean'. Lexical senses of Subject and Predicate terms, and the relation-types into which those words enter, are interdependent. Odd words can disguise formal nonsense as easily as logical form can fail to illumine concrete expressions: 'Old Sol is the Sun' seems sensible enough, while 'Old Sol is Sun' and 'Old Sol belongs to Sun' are less acceptable, but we must know how the nominal phrase 'Old Sol' is used. Symbols like S = P for Propositions sidestep problems like that, but in Sentences, we have to know something about the word-types that can stand as REpresenting subject- and predicate-constituents in Predicate Logic. Propositional Logic focuses on how pairs of Predications relate to each other, not on how the constituent-pairs of its two Predications are related: we can compute when compounds like 'IF Old Sol is the Sun, THEN he hasn't been around much' are valid or invalid, even if the sense of Old Sol remains opaque, and even when we have no idea whether either part of the combination describes anything accurately or not, or even whether there is anything to describe.

The sketch of how concepts develop shown above suggests different levels of acquaintance with both things and words for them. Children use generic heavy grammatically but have limited experience with things adults consider heavy, while Newton would probably have been neither consciously invoking nor denying his definition of Gravity if he said his wife was getting a bit heavy. Similar divergences in match or overlap can be expected between individual and institutionalized concepts. Definitions of mode show that: few speakers are aware of all a Dictionary records, yet inclusion of words like mode in such standard works attests to their institutional stability.

REFERENCE

Speakers internalize the basic sense of mode without having to consult a dictionary, but they may or may not know that mode can be used to refer to everything included on a Webster list. They may have experienced the things, events, or aspects that fall within norms assigned by the SENSE of a term, but fail to see its relevance in particular cases, since the things involved can be materially identical (etically the same) but seen as emically or formally different: identical in composition, but regarded from a different functional perspective. Hispanus' way of contrasting these facts is to stress a **potential** aspect of sense when compared to **actual** reference (pp. 16, 189). A basic (i.e., potential) sense of mode is involved in the etic/emic appreciation of how 'the same thing' becomes a quite 'different thing' because of what we are willing to consider basic or accessory to some object that interests us.

Hispanus says Signification is the REpresentation of a thing through a conventional expression, but that 'words not signifying a universal or a particular ought not signify anything as we use **term** here.' (p. 69). Significations have to do with substantival (man) or **adjectival** (white or runs) aspects of the same thing in 'white man runs'. But being adjectivized or substantial are modes of things signified, not significations. Substantive nouns stand for, take the place of, supply for; adjective nouns and even verbs are said to link, join, or make a unit of (p. 69). **Supposition** is the acceptance of a substantive term for some thing: **Signification** is the imposition of a word to signify a thing; in 'man runs', man takes the place of, refers to, substitutes for Socrates, etc., so signification is prior to supposition; 'to signify' is the property of a word, but 'to substitute for' is the property of a term already composed of sound and signification. 'Signification' is a relation between a sign and what it is a sign of, supposition between a substitute and its referent/interpretation. **Copulation** is acceptance of an adjective term for something. (p. 70). **Restriction** narrows a common term from a larger to a lesser supposition; **Extension** increases a common term from a lesser to a larger supposition; discrete terms are neither extended nor restricted. Extensions are effected by verbs, nouns & adverbs (p. 172).

Consignifications include the 'meanings' of what we now term bound morphemes. They are logically accidental, compared to the substantive meaning of roots, but neither Hispanus nor any of the Medievals were able to sort them out on a formal linguistic basis. They are treated in his sections on Equivocation and Amphiboly:

'urine is healthy' is ambiguous since healthy is said of an animal as
of a subject, of urine health's sign, of food as its efficient cause; of
a diet as of one observing it. All of these work in different ways according to different significations (p. 83). Aristotle's three common
modes of equivocation and amphiboly: (1) words (dog) or phrases
(Aristotle's book) signifying several things; (2) metaphorical use of
words (equivocation) and phrases (amphiboly) (3) compounds (immortal) signify several, simple expressions (mortal) only one (p. 93).

MODIFICATION

Modification has a clear relational interpretation within an
Aristotelian substance/accident framework applied to Grammar, but
even there it depends on the selection of, and consistent adherence
to, the criteria on which things are selected as basic. At different
times, for different reasons, one and the same object can be considered as either a Constant or a Variable in a relation. Confusion here
can compound further confusions: e.g., inflection and derivation can
be seen to semantically 'modify' roots and bases; adjectives and
adverbs to 'specify' nouns and verbs; phrases and clauses to 'restrict'
nominals and verbals, and subordinate sentences to 'qualify' superordinate ones. But both phonetic as well as syntactic norms were
inexplicit in medieval works.

For these 'modifications' are in different media, at different levels,
with different effects. One could argue about whether inflection in
rex ('king') and regis ('of king') shows nominative modification by the
genitive, or of genitive by the nominative (or what the Medievals
were unable to do, modification of a root by both). Extension or Restriction of word-meaning is a type of 'modification' for Hispanus
where signification is unaffected, but the supposition of naming-
expressions can be extended, restricted or qualified in various ways,
by different parts of speech or by grammatical accidents like
person, number, gender, tense, etc. He calls the meaning of such
'accidents', consignifications.

In Thomas of Erfurt's developed Modistic tract, each subdivision in
the traditional Porphyrian Tree corresponds to Modes distinguished
as most generic, generic, subaltern, special, and most-special.
Hispanus says things 'differ' in three ways: Commonly (Socrates
sitting, standing, or compared to Plato), Properly (being snub-
nosed) or Most-Properly (man from horse by 'rationality': p. 20).

Since the kind of argumentation Hispanus examines is Categoric,
how Subjects are asserted to 'be-in' Predicates is the main concern

of Hispanus' third Tract 'On Predicaments'. He distinguished a triple mode of predicating: **equivocal** (live vs. pictured 'animal') **univocal** ('animal' of man and cow) and **denominative** ('grammarian' from 'grammar'); then some things are said with construction ('The man runs') some without ('man' or 'runs' alone). So he distinguishes eight Modes of **Being-In,** e.g. (1) Integral Part in its Whole, (wall in house); (2) Integral Whole in its Parts (house in wall, roof, and foundation); (3) Species in Genus (man in animal: any inferior in its superior) etc. (pp. 2-9, 26).

Syllogisms have three terms and two propositions (Major and Minor) with a Conclusion. But two propositions can only be made from three terms by taking one twice: as subject in first, predicate in second, predicate in both, or subject in both: the term taken twice before the Conclusion is called the Middle Term. Since there are three possible orderings, there are three figures (pp. 39 ff).

Just as Geometry is developed from axioms (self-evident, indemonstrable propositions from which theorems can be deduced), Dialectic identifies a number of popular propositions called 'Topics', of which all arguments are only lexically different versions: '... in the entire Tract, there are only 21 Topics, of which 11 are intrinsic, 7 extrinsic, and 3 mediate' (pp. 55 ff.).

The truth of propositions is decided on the basis of whether things asserted or denied are actually related just as they are REpresented in propositions. So the distinction of signification (norms for locating an instance of a term) from supposition (what things are substituted for by a term) is needed. Categorial meanings logically antecede construction (pp. 69 ff.): a term signifies Substance, Quality, Quantity, or one of the other ten Predicaments, a conventional representation of a thing by a locution. Words signifying neither a universal nor a particular are not technically terms. Signification is **substantival** (like man) or **adjectival** (like white or runs), or more exactly, something signified substantively or adjectivally, because Adjectivation or Substantiation are modes of things signified, not Significations.

Signification is imposition of a locution upon a thing to be signified, so it differs from supposition (acceptance of that term, already signifying a thing, for something). In 'Man runs', man stands for Socrates, Plato, etc. So Signification is prior to Supposition: 'to signify' pertains to a word, 'to stand for' pertains to a term already made up of a word and its signification; 'signification' is a relation of a sign to what has been signified, but Supposition is not a sign-to-signified relation, but one of a substitute-to-what-has-been- substituted for. **Coupling** (copulatio) is acceptance of an adjectival term for something.

The Dialectician looks for what invalidates an otherwise plausible argument: there are 13 Fallacies, 6 linguistic (Equivocation, Amphiboly, Composition, Division, Accent, and Fallacy of Word Figure), 7 extralinguistic (Accident, Simply or After-a-Fashion, Ignoring the Refutation, Search for Principle, Non-cause as Cause, Consequent, and Many Questions as One) (pp. 76 ff.).

But factual arguments cannot be settled by words. Of themselves, they have only properties conferred by use, but when they combine with other words, there is a double source of deception possible: equivocation based on isolated words, and amphiboly resulting from misinterpretations of construction (pp. 166 ff.).

The number of things for which a term may stand can be increased or restricted in different ways: in 'a white man is running', white restricts man to standing for whites; in 'a man can be the Antichrist', man stands not only for those who exist, but is extended by can to those who will exist. Discrete terms are neither restricted nor extended (pp. 172 ff.).

Since objects for which terms can stand may be in the realm of SO or SEEM, a subcategory of Supposition is Appellation: acceptance of a term for things that exist. Signification/Supposition indifferently concern existents and non-existents. Common terms like man are not like singulars which stand for and summon the same thing by signifying an existent like Peter. A common term's appellation for the **thing-itself-in-common** is not its inferiors, when it has Personal Supposition, as in 'man runs': man does not then signify, stand for, or summon the same thing, it **signifies** man-in-common, **stands for** particular men, and **summons** particular, existent men (pp. 175-76).

Conventions of ordinary usage also determine interpretation: terms have signification or supposition, not intrinsically, but instrumentally, as determined by their users: we usually say 'there is nothing in the box' although the box is full of air because nothing customarily supposes for solid things (p. 184).

What a term stands for is also determined by the mood of syllogisms (indicated by markers like every), and conclusions can be true or false, depending on quantification: in 'every man runs', man - is distributed for any inferior by every. But a singular term cannot be distributed, so 'every Socrates' is incongruous. But if a marker like every signifies neither a universal nor a particular thing, does it signify anything ? (pp. 186 ff.) Every does not signify a universal, but quantity universally, that a common term is taken for any of its inferiors, as in 'every man'. Thing is ambiguous, and what every signifies is a different kind of thing (i.e., the disposition of a thing capable of being a subject or predicate: p. 187).

Genus, Species and Individual, as Porphyry's Tree suggests, label aspects of solidary experiences to which we may or may not attend. Most people are capable of doing that even when they actually do not, but infants or those with some disabilities cannot. So Helen Keller's grasping that water is sometimes generic, sometimes specific, or at other times this individual thing at this particular time, at this particular place, can be described as part of the process of socialization, or the emergence of intelligence. When learning to communicate, we have to learn to attend to (among other things) what our language forces us to notice.

This involves questions for linguists, and indirectly for Linguistics, about language, meaning and use, and the status of abstractions like word. In what sense is meaning determinate (in Competence) before use (Performance) ? Could one suspect that different uses of the 'same word' were involved without that prior determination ? Having distinguished sorts of meanings from actual use, what is the status of the those sorts, independent of use?

The Medievals progressed from what they called Logica Antiqua to Logica Moderna by refining relations between two of Aristotle's Categories, Substance and Quantity: other Categories (e.g. Quality and Relation itself) were explicitly added. Part of the groundwork was laid in Priscian's definitions of the parts of speech in categorial terms, and in the commentaries on Priscian that became required at the University of Paris. 'Linguistic' progress consisted in refining the kinds questions that could be asked about language.

INTUITIVE CLASSIFICATION

Classifications recorded by Hispanus became part of Western traditional education. His Summulae was widely required as a text for generations, and later texts borrowed, amended, rejected, or extended parts of it without mentioning his name, perhaps even in ignorance of his identity: that was common in periods less concerned with personalities than with ideas. What he reported and refined were contrasts constituting the tacit conventions of communication in speech and writing. Fortunately, those conventions based on how things have been described and talked about have not kept the imaginative from proposing new ways, even if they have to deform the older conventions a bit.

That these distinctions should be called 'intuitive' is relevant the distinction between Description and Explanation: without accurate description, no need for explanation arises. One can just accept facts stoically with a 'That's just the way things are' attitude that takes any anomaly in stride. But if we share the ancient Analogists' expectation that the lot ought to make some kind of sense, we construct hypotheses about how to transform a jumble of Variables into patterns predictable from hypothetical Constants.

Ancient astronomy did that with evidence anyone can verify empirically: the sun rises and sets as anyone can see (and we still say). It seemed to make sense to take the Earth as the Constant, and planetary movements as Variables. The evidence was overt, and Ptolemaic Astronomy provided fairly reliable predictions of solar eclipses. Similar observations allowed a year 360 revolutions, defined Circle from that, and founded a Geometry still basic for our carpenters and architects.

Today's space flights provide empirical evidence for what once could only have been a geometrical flight of fancy, not an alternative design for an experienced world: many things are even more variable than supposed, but seem equally systematic. Modern grammars can simply presume facts about both the variability and constancy of linguistic structures unthinkable to older workers, and have available tools comparable in refinement to other objective methods of observation in science. But refined description is still not refined explanation.

References

Aristotle, 1955. The Organon: The Categories, On Interpretation (Cooke) and Prior Analytics (Tredennick). Loeb Classical Library, London: Heinemann.

Bochenski, Innocentius M., O.P., 1947. Petri Hispani Summulae Logicales quas e codice manu scripto Reg. Lat. 1205 edidit. Rome: Marietti.

Bursill-Hall, Geoffrey L., ed. 1972. Thomas of Erfurt, De modis significandi sive grammatica speculativa. London: Longmans.

De Rijk, Lambertus M., ed., 1972. Petrus Hispanus Portugalensis, Tractatus, called afterwards 'Summulae Logicales'. First Critical Edition from the Manuscripts with an Introduction. Assen: van Gorcum.

TRACT I
ON INTRODUCTORY NOTIONS
On Dialectic

1 **Dialectic** is the art facilitating an approach to principles of all methods. So in acquisition of sciences, Dialectic should be first.

This art is called **'dialectic'** from **'dia'** which means **two** and **'logos'**, which means **discourse** (<u>sermo</u>), or from **'lexis'**, which means **reasoning** (<u>ratio</u>), suggesting the **discoursing or reasoning of a pair,** an opponent and a respondent in disputing. But since disputation cannot be held without discourse, nor discourse without vocal expressions, since every expression (<u>vox</u>) is a sound, we must therefore start with sound as from what is prior.

On Sound

2 Sound is whatever is peculiarly perceived by the sense of hearing. I say **'peculiarly'** (<u>proprie</u>) since, though both man and bells may be heard, this is only through sound. Sounds are either vocal or non-vocal.

Vocal expression is sound produced from the mouth of an animal, formed by natural instruments. Those are called natural instruments by which vocal expression is formed: the lips, teeth, tongue, palate, throat and lungs.

A sound is non-vocal which is generated from the coming together of inanimate bodies, as in trees cracking or the sound of footsteps.

On Vocal Expression (Vox)

3 Some expressions are significative and others are not. It is
called significative if an expression represents something when you
hear it, like 'man' or the groans of those who are ill. A non-significative expression is one that represents nothing when heard, like
'buba'. Some significative expressions are such by convention, others
by nature.

A naturally significative expression is one that represents the
same thing to everyone, like groans of the sick or dogs' barking.

A conventionally significative expression is one that represents
something, depending on its inventor's choice, like 'man'. Some conventionally significant expressions are simple or uncomplex, like
noun and verb,   while others are constructed or complex, like a
word-group (oratio).

On the Noun (Nomen)

4 A Noun is a conventionally significative vocal expression
without tense, no separate part of which signifies definite things, in
the nominative case. 'Vocal expression' is put into the definition of
noun as its genus; 'significative' to differentiate nouns from non-
significative vocal expressions; 'conventionally' to distinguish it
from a naturally significant expression; 'without tense'   to
distinguish it from the verb, which signifies with tense; 'no part of
which, etc.' to distinguish it from a word-group, the parts of which
are separate signs. 'Definite' is included to distinguish the noun
from a nonfinite noun like 'non-man': this is not a noun for a
dialectician, but a nonfinite noun. 'In the nominative' (recta) is put
into the definition to distinguish it from oblique cases like 'of
Cato', 'to Cato' (Catonis, Catoni) and so on, which are not nouns
for a dialectician, but nominal cases or obliques. So only a
nominative or casus rectus is said to be a noun.

On the Verb (Verbum)

5 The verb is a conventionally significative vocal sound, with
tense, no part of which is separately significative, finite and in the
present tense. 'With tense' is included in the definition of verb in
distinction to a noun, which is a sign without tense. 'Finite' is used
to differentiate it from a nonfinite verb like 'not-run', which is not
a verb for the dialectician, but a nonfinite verb. 'Present tense'
(recta) is put into the definition to set the verb off from oblique

verbs like 'was running', 'ran' and 'will run'. The dialectician does not call these just 'verbs' but 'oblique verbs'. Only when it is in the present tense, indicative mood, is it said to be a verb, but other verbs of the same mood and other grammatical accidents are called 'oblique verbs'. All other differences are put there for the same reason as in the noun.

So it is worth noting that the dialectician posits only two parts of speech: noun and verb. The rest he calls sincategor-ematics, that is, 'consignificatives'.

On the Word-Group (Oratio)

6 A word-group (oratio) is an expression significative by convention, the parts of which signify separate things. All of 'the parts of which signify separate things' is put there to distinguish it from the noun and verb, and the rest is included on the same grounds as for the noun and verb.

A word-group is either complete or incomplete. A perfect or complete word-group generates complete sense in the mind of the hearer, like 'the man is white'; incomplete or imperfect is one that generates incomplete sense in the mind of the hearer, like 'white man'.

A complete word-group is either indicative, like 'the man is running', imperative, like 'make a fire!', optative, like 'would that I were a good cleric', or subjunctive, like 'if you come to me, I'll give you a horse'. Of all these word-groups, only the indicative is said to be a proposition.

On the Proposition

7 A Proposition is a word-group signifying something true or false, like 'man runs'. Propositions are categoric or hypothetic. A categoric is a proposition whose subject and predicate are its principal parts, as in 'man runs'. In this proposition, the noun 'man' is subject, the verb 'runs' is predicate, and what conjoins the pair is a linker (copula), which is clear by analyzing this way: 'man runs' : 'man is running'. The noun 'man' is subject, 'running' is predicated, and the verb 'is' links the one with the other. And it is called 'cathegoric' from 'kathegorizo:', -zas, which is the same as 'predico, -cas ('I predicate, you predicate'). A subject is that about which something is said; a predicate, what is said the other.

On the Categoric Proposition and its triple division

8 Categoric propositions are universal, particular, nonfinite or singular.

A Universal Proposition is one in which a common term is subject, determined by a universal marker (signum), as in 'every man runs'; or: a Universal Proposition is one that signifies something as belonging to all or to not a one of something else.

A Common Term is one that is naturally apt to be predicated of many subjects, like 'man' of Socrates, Plato and of each and every one of the rest of men.

Universal Markers are: 'every' (omnis), 'not a (one)' (nullus), nothing' (nichil), 'any one at all' (quilibet), 'both / either' (uterque), 'neither' (neuter) and their like.

A Particular Proposition is one in which a common term is subject, determined by a particular marker, as in 'some man runs'. Particular Markers are: 'some (one)' (aliquis), 'a certain (one)' (quidam), 'the (first) one' (alter), 'the other (one)' (reliquus) and their like.

A Nonfinite (indefinita) Proposition is one in which a common term is subject without a marker, as in 'man runs'.

A Singular Proposition is one in which a singular term is subject, or a common term constructed with a demonstrative pronoun is, as in 'Socrates runs' or 'that man runs'. A Singular Term is one that is naturally apt to be predicated of one only thing.

9 Again: Categorematic Propositions are affirmative or negative. An Affirmative is one in which the predicate is affirmed of the subject, as in 'man runs'. A Negative is one in which the predicate is removed from the subject, as in 'man runs not'.

10 Now that a Proposition has been divided three ways, it is worth knowing that there is a triple question-form by which we ask questions, namely: 'what ?' (que), 'what kind ?' (qualis), and 'what number ?' (quanta). 'What questions the substance of the proposition, so that to the question put by 'what ?', one must answer 'categoric' or 'hypothetic'. To 'what kind ?', one must answer 'affirmative' or 'negative', since 'what kind ?' asks about the quality of a proposition.   To **'what number ?'**,   one must answer **'universal'**, **'particular'**, **'nonfinite'** or **'singular'**,   since **'what number ?'** asks about the Quantity of a proposition.   So we have this mnemonic:[1]

> <u>What</u> is CataHype,
> <u>Kind</u> is AffirNeg,
> and <u>Quant</u> is UnParInSin

11 Again: some Categoric Propositions share both terms, as in **'a man is an animal'** - **'a man is not an animal'.** Others share only the one, as in **'a man runs'** - **'a man disputes'.** Others share no term, as in **'a man runs'** - **'a horse is moved'.** Again: some propositions sharing each term do so in the same order, as in **'a man is running'** - **'a man is not running'**, some in converse order, as in **'a man is an animal'** - **'an animal is a man'.**

12 Again: propositions sharing both terms in the same order are either Contraries, Subcontraries, Contradictories or Subalternates.

Contraries are a universal affirmative and a universal negative proposition of the same subject and the same predicate, like **'every man runs'** - **'no man runs'.**

Subcontraries are a particular affirmative and a particular negative proposition of the same subject and the same predicate, like **'some man is running'** - **'some man is not running'.**

Contradictories are a universal affirmative and a particular negative proposition, or a universal negative and a particular affirmative proposition of the same subject and the same predicate, as in **'every man is running'** - **'some man is not running'** or **'no man is running'** - **'some man is running'.**

Subalternate propositions are a universal affirmative and a particular affirmative, or a universal negative and a particular negative of the same subject and the same predicate, as in **'every man is running'** - **'some man is running'** or **'no man is running'** - **'some man is not running'.**

1:   **que ca vel ypo**
    qualis ne vel aff
    un quanta par in sin.

This is made plain in the figure below:

every
man is   **c o n t r a r i e s**   no
animal   man is
animal

```
s      C                                           Y   s
u          O                                    R       u
b             N                            O            b
a                T                    T                 a
l                   R              C                    l
t                      A        I                       t
e                        D    A                         e
r                        A    D                         r
n                      R        I                       n
a                   T              C                    a
t                N                    T                 t
e             O                            O           e
s         R                                    R       s
s      C                                           Y   s
```

some man   some man
   is   **s u b c o n t r a r i e s**   is not
animal   animal

On the Triple Matter of Categorics

13 The Matter of Propositions is of three kinds: Natural, Contingent, and Remote.

Matter is Natural in which the predicate is of the being of the subject or a peculiarity (<u>proprium</u>) of it, as in **'man is animal'**, or **'man is risible'**.

Contingent Matter is that in which the predicate can be present or absent to the subject, as in **'a man is white'**, **'a man is not white'**.

Remote Matter is that in which the predicate is incompatible with the subject, as in **'a man is an ass'**.

On their Equipollences

14 By the Law of Contraries, if one contrary is true, the other is false, but not the converse (since both may be false in Contingent Matter, as in **'every man is white'** - **'not a man is white'**). In Natural Matter, it is always the case that if one is true, the other is false and the converse (as in **'every man is an animal'** - **'not a man is an animal'**) as well as in Remote Matter (as in **'every man is an ass'** - **'not a man is an ass'**), and in Contingent Matter, when an inseparable accident is predicated (as in **'every crow is black'** - **'not a crow is black'**). But in a separable accident, both can be equally false. So it is not always the case in Contingent Matter that both are false at the same time.

By the Law of Subcontraries, if one is false, the other is true, but not the converse, (for both can be true in Contingent Matter). So the Law of Subcontraries is related to the Law of Contraries as a Contrary.

By the Law of Contradictories, if one is true, the other is false and the converse. For in no Matter can they be true or false at the same time.

By the Law of Subalternates, if the universal is true, the particular is true and not the converse; for the universal can be false, while its particular existent is true. And if the particular is false, its universal is false, and not the converse.

On Triple Conversion

15 Then: Propositions sharing both terms in converse order have a three-way Conversion: Simple, by Accident, and by Contraposition.

Simple Conversion is making a predicate out of a subject and the converse, with Quantity and Quality remaining identical. This is how the universal negative and particular affirmative are converted: 'not a man is a stone' - 'not a stone is a man'; 'some man is an animal' - 'some animal is a man'.

Conversion by Accident is making a predicate out of a subject and the converse, with Quality remaining identical, but with changed Quantity. So a universal affirmative proposition is converted into a particular negative, as in 'every man is an animal' - 'some animal is a man', and a universal negative into a particular negative, as in 'not a man is a stone' - 'some stone is not a man'.

Conversion by Contraposition is making a predicate out of a subject and a subject out of a predicate, with Quality and Quantity remaining identical, but with definite terms changed into nonfinite terms. In this way a universal affirmative and a particular negative are converted, as in 'every man is an animal' - 'every non-animal is a non-man'; 'a certain man is not a stone' - 'a certain non-stone is not a non-man'.

One should know that if there is a marker in the subject of a proposition to be converted, whatever it may be, it should have the whole predicate in its scope and reduce the whole to subject.

On the Hypothetic Proposition and its Division

16 Next on the Hypothetic Proposition. This is one that has two categorics as its principal parts, like 'if man runs, man is moved'. It is called 'hypothetic' from <u>hypos</u>, which means 'under' and <u>thesis</u>, which means 'position', suggesting 'suppositive (to)', because one part is sub-posed to the other.

Hypothetic Propositions are Conditional, Copulative or Disjunctive.

A Conditional is that in which two categorics are linked by the conjunction 'if', like 'if man runs, man is moved'. The categoric to which the conjunction 'if' is immediately joined, is called the 'antecedent', the other the 'consequent'.

A Copulative is that in which two categorics are linked by the conjunction 'and', like 'Socrates runs and Plato debates'.

A Disjunctive is that in which two categorics are linked by the conjunction 'or', as in 'Socrates runs or Plato debates'.

On the Truth of Hypothetics

17 For the truth of a Conditional it is demanded that the antecedent cannot be true without the consequent being true as well, as in 'if it is a man, it is an animal'. So it follows that every true Conditional is necessary, and every false Conditional impossible. For it to be false, it is enough that the antecedent could be without a consequent, as in 'if Socrates is, something white is'.

For the truth of a Copulative, each part must be true, as in 'man is an animal and God is'. For it to be false, it is enough that one or the other part be false, as in 'man is an animal and a horse is a stone'.

For the truth of a Disjunctive, it is sufficient that one or the other part be true, as in 'man is an animal or a horse is an ass'. It is tolerated that each part be true, but not so peculiarly (proprie), as in 'man is an animal or a horse can whinny'. For it to be false, each part should be false, as in 'a man is an ass or a horse is a stone'.

On their Equipollences

18 Rules like the following are assigned concerning Equipollences:

if a negation is preposed to any
marker, it is equipollent to its
its own contradictory.

So these are equipollent: 'not every man runs' (non omnis homo currit) - 'some man does not run' (quidam homo non currit); and so on for others.

The second rule is:

> if a negation is postposed to any
> universal marker, it is equipollent
> to its own contrary.

as in **'every man is not an animal'** (<u>omnis</u> <u>homo</u> <u>non</u> <u>est</u> <u>animal</u>) –
'not a man is an animal' (<u>nullus</u> <u>homo</u> <u>est</u> <u>animal</u>); or: **'not a man
runs'** – **'every man runs'**; and so on for other universal affirmative
and negative markers.

The third rule is:

> if a negation is preposed and postposed
> to a universal and particular marker, it
> is equipollent to its own subalternate.

like: **'not every man does not run'** (<u>non</u> <u>omnis</u> <u>homo</u> <u>non</u> <u>currit</u>) – **'a
certain man runs'** (<u>quidam</u> <u>homo</u> <u>currit</u>); so too: **'not a certain man
does not run'** – **'every man runs'**. And so of any other marker.

From these rules there follows another such rule:

> if two universal negative markers
> are positioned in the same word-group,
> such that the one is in the subject,
> the other is in the predicate – the first
> is equipollent to its contrary, the
> second to its contradictory.

So: **'nothing is nothing'** is equipollent to **'anything at all is something'**, since by the second rule; **'not anything at all'** (<u>quidlibet
non</u>) and **'nothing'** (<u>nichil</u>) are equipollent, for just as **'not every
(one)'** (<u>omnis</u> <u>non</u>) and **'not a (one)'** (<u>nullus</u>) are equipollent, so too
'mot anything at all' and **'nothing'** and by the first rule, **'not
nothing'** (<u>non</u> <u>nichil</u>) and **'something'** (<u>aliquid</u>) are equipollent. So:
'nothing is nothing' is equipollent to **'anything is something'**,
because **'not nothing'** and **'something'** are equipollent.

Let this be enough to say on equipollents.

On Mode

19 A **Mode** (<u>modus</u>) is an adjacent determination of a thing. It arises through something-adjoined (<u>adjectivum</u>). But thing-adjoined (adjective) is ambiguous: one is a sort of nominal adjective, like **'white'** or **'black'** and their like, the other is a sort of verbal adjective, like an Adverb. According to Priscian,[2] an Adverb is a sort of Verbal Adjective, - so for that reason, mode is ambiguous: one mode is nominal, which arises through nominal adjectives, the other adverbial, which arises through verbal adjectives, as in **'a white man runs swiftly'**.

Again: Some adverbs determine a verb in terms of composition as these six do: **'necessarily'**, **'contingently'**, **'possibly'**, **'impossibly'**, **'truly'**, **'falsely'**. Others determine a verb in terms of the verb's sense (<u>res</u>), as in **'he acts firmly'**, **'he runs swiftly'**. Others determine a verb by reason of tense, as temporal adverbs do; others by reason of mood (<u>modus</u>), as adverbs of wishing or commanding do, and so on of the others. On that basis, mode is taken in multiple ambiguity through adverbs.

On Modal Propositions

20 Leaving aside all other modes determining composition, it must be said that there are these six: **'necessarily, 'contingently'**, etc. When one says **'a man necessarily runs'**, it is signified that this composition is necessary. But in **'man runs well'**, or **'swiftly'**, it is signifed man's running is good or swift. So in the latter example the verb's sense (<u>res</u>) is determined, in the former, it is the verb's composition. That is how it is to be understood of the other adverbs mentioned. So only that mode which determines composition makes a proposition Modal, and that is the only one we have in mind here.

21 One should know that these six modes are at times taken adverbially, at times, nominally. Adverbially, like **'necessarily'**, **'contingently'**, **'possibly'**, **'impossibly'**, **'truly'** and **'falsely'**; nominally, like **'necessary'**, **'contingent'**, **'possible'** and **'impossible'**, **'true'** and **false'**.

A Modal Proposition is one determined by one of those six modes, like **'that Socrates run** (<u>Socratem</u> <u>currere</u>) **is possible'**, **'that Socrates run is impossible'**.

2: <u>Inst.</u> <u>gramm.</u> II 16, p.54.11.

22 Notice too, that in modals, the verb[3] should be its subject, mode its predicate. All other propositions are said to be **About Being-in** (de inesse). Propositions modified by the modes **'truly'** and **'falsely'** are left aside for now, because Opposition is taken in them the same way as in these About Being-in, as is their Consequence. But in the other four modes, Opposition is not taken that same way, as will be clear later.

23 Note that each of the four modes makes four Propositions. Since there are four modes, there will be four times four, so sixteen propositions. For example, if the mode **'possible'** be taken without negation, it makes a single proposition like **'that Socrates run is possible'** (Sortem currere est possibile). If taken with negation preposed to the verb, it makes another, like **'that Socrates not run is possible'** (Sortem non currere est possibile). A third proposition is taken when negation is placed next to the mode, like **'that Socrates run is not possible'** (Sortem currere non est possibile). A fourth proposition is taken with double negation, one placed at the verb, the other at the mode, like **'that Socrates not run is not possible'** (Sortem non currere non est possibile). This way, for each of the other modes, four propositions are taken.

On their Equipollences

24 The equipollences of those four propositions are known by four rules.

The first rule is:

to whatever affirmed dictum **'possible'** is attributed, **'contingent'** is as well, and **'impossible'** removed from it, and from its contradictory opposite, **'neccesary'** is removed.

The second rule is:

to whatever negated dictum **'possible'** is attributed, **'contingent'** is as well, and from that same dictum, **'impossible'** is removed, and from its contradictory opposite, **'necessary'** is removed.

3: Manuscript Vaticanus Reginensis 1205 (early 14th c.) has dictum ('what is said') for verbum, which suits **24** below well. [fpd]

The third rule is:

> from whatever affirmed dictum 'possible'
> is removed, from that same dictum,
> 'contingent' is as well, and 'impossible' is
> attributed to it, and to its contra-
> dictory opposite, 'necessary' is attributed.

The fourth rule is:

> from whatever negated dictum 'possible' is
> removed, from that same dictum, 'conting-
> ent' is as well, but to it, 'impossible' is
> attributed, while 'necessary' is attributed
> to its contradictory opposite.

This is clear in the following figure or ordering:

I	II
It is possible to be	It is possible not to be
It is contingent to be	It is contingent not to be
It is not impossible to be	It is not impossible not to be
It is necessary not to be	It is not necessary to be

III	IV
It is not possible to be	It is not possible not to be
It is not contingent to be	It is not contingent not to be
It is impossible to be	It is impossible not to be
It is necessary not to be	It is necessary to be

All propositions in the first line are equipollent by the first rule and are converted reciprocally; those in the second line are equipollent by the second rule and convert reciprocally; those in the third by the third rule, and those in the fourth line by the fourth rule.

Again: Consequence and Equipollence of Modals can be grasped by this rule:

all propositions about **possible** and **impossible** are equipollent, the verb being similarly, the mode dissim- ilarly related.

And all about **impossible** and **necessary** are equipollent, the verb and mode being dissimilarly related.

And all about **impossible** and **necessary** are equipollent, the verb being dissim- ilarly, the mode similarly, related.

A mode is to be understood as 'similarly' and 'dissimilarly related' on the basis of affirmation and negation. So a mode is to be called 'similarly' related when the mode is affirmed in both, or negated in both, but 'dissimilarly' when affirmed in one and negated in the other. It is to be understood the same way of the verb as for mode. Note that in the previous rule, no mention is made of contingent, because 'contingent' is converted with 'possible'. So the same decision is made about propositions of both. Examples should be sought in the figure above in the first, second, third and fourth Order, because the rule is general for all.

On their Opposition

25 Again: Modal Propositions are Contrary, Subcontrary, Contradictory or Subalternate. **Contraries** are propositions in the third and fourth Order, or propositions in the fourth and third line. So we have the verse:

Order three to four is order e'er Contrary

(Tertius est quarto semper contrarius ordo)

Subcontraries are first and second Order. So the verse:

Subcontraries to you are e'er lines one to two

(Sit tibi linea subcontraria prima secundae)

Likewise: first order contradicts the third, and second the fourth.

So the verse:

Lower III's destroy the I's on top
IV's contradict II's without a stop

(Tertius primo contradictorius ordo
Pugnat cum quarto contradicendo secundus)

Likewise: the first line is subalternate to the fourth and the second to the third. So the verse:

First line bows to fourth, Particularly related,
By this rule to the set a line to line is fated.

(Prima subest quarte, vice particularis habens se
hac habet ad seriem se lege secundum sequentem)

or:

Let order subaltern take first or second turn

(ordo subalternus sit primus sive secundus)

All this is obvious in the following figure:

possible to be	**CONTRARY**	possible not to be
contingent to be	3 is ever 4	contingent not to be
not impossible to be	in contrary	not impossible not to be
necessary not to be	order	not necessary to be

```
s                                                                 s
      C                                                  Y
u        O                                          R       u
            N                                    O
b              T                            T               b
                 R              C
a   1st line yields   A      I      By rule to          a
    to 4th, Partic-        D         set,  lines
l   ularly related    A      I      are fated           l
                 R              C
t              T                            T               t
            N                                    O
e        O                                          R       e
      C                                                  Y
r                                                                 r

n                                                                 n
```

not possible to be	Subcon. to you	not possible not to be
not contingent to be	lines one & two	not contingent not to be
impossible to be		impossible not to be
necessary not to be	**SUBCONTRARY**	necessary to be

TRACT II

ON PREDICABLES

On Predicable

1 'Predicable' is sometimes taken peculiarly (proprie); so only what is predicated of several things is called a predicable. When taken commonly, what is predicated either of several things or of one is called a predicable. So 'predicable' properly taken is the same as 'universal', but they differ because a predicable is defined by being said, a universal just by being. A predicable is what is naturally apt to be said of several things. A universal is what is naturally apt to be in several things.

Predicable or Universal divides into genus, species, difference, peculiarity (proprium) and accident, and here we take up only these five.

On Genus

2 'Genus' is said in three ways. First, as a collection of many things related in some way to each other and to a single source (principium), like the set of those of the same parentage descended from a single ancestor. Second, that is called a genus which is the source of each generation (like father and fatherland). Third, that is called a genus to which a species is subordinated. That last way is how Genus is taken here. It is defined as follows: Genus is what is predicated of several specifically different things, with respect to what a thing is essentially (in eo quod quid); as animal is predicated of a man, horse and lion, which differ in species.

3 To get to know this part of the definition (i.e. 'specifically different'), one should be aware that 'different' is said in as many ways as 'same', and that 'same' is said in three ways: same in Genus, same in Species, same in Number. Things contained under the same genus are generically the same (like man and ass under animal). Things under the same species (like Socrates and Plato under man) are specifically the same. But 'numerically same' is

said three ways: first, same in name or definition, second, same by peculiarity, and third, same by accident. Things materially single (res una) but with several names (like 'Marcus-Tullius') are said to be nominally the same. When one is the definition of the other (like 'rational mortal animal is of 'man'), they are said to be same by definition. When one is a peculiarity of the other (as 'risibility' is of 'man'), things are said to be same by peculiarity. Accidentally the same are those where one is an accident of the other, like Socrates and the whiteness in him.

4 'Generically different', 'specifically different' and 'numerically different' are used in a similar way. Generically different are things under different genera (like **man** in the genus **animal** and **tree** in the genus **plant**). Specifically different are things of different Species (like Socrates and Brunellus). Things that can be counted are numerically different (like Socrates and Plato).

5 To be 'predicated with respect to what' is said of what is responsive to the question put by **'What ?'**. When asked, **'What is a man ?'**, a suitable answer is **'an animal'**. So **animal** is predicated of **man** 'with respect to what' (in quid),

6 Genus is defined another way, as follows: genus is that to which species is subordinate.

7 Genus is divided into Most Generic and Subalternate Genus. Most Generic Genus is what has no higher genus above it, like substance. Or: Most Generic Genus is one that, being a genus, cannot be a species.

It has ten divisions: Substance, Quantity, Relation, Quality, Action, Passion, Location, When, Where, Costume. These ten are called Most Generic Genera because they have no genus above them. Though **'being'** is predicated of these ten, it is said equivocally or in multiple ambiguity of them and for that reason, being is not a Genus. We will not say anything about these ten now, but they will be discussed later under **Predicaments**.

A Subaltern Genus is what, though genus, can still be a species, as **animal** is a Genus of **man** and a Species of **animate body**.

On Species

8 Species is what is predicated of several numerically different things as to 'what (essential) kind' (in eo quod quid est). But in this definition, the verb **'predicated'** means aptitude, not actuality - as

in others - the way **man** is predicated of Socrates, Plato and other particular men who are several yet numerically different, as was clear above. It is predicated of them as to 'what kind'. When asked **'What is Socrates** ? or **Plato ?'**, a suitable answer is: **'a man'**.

Species is also defined as follows: a species is what is put under a genus. Or: a species is that of which genus is predicated, as to 'what kind'.

9 It is divided into Most Special and Subaltern Species. A Most Special Species is one that, though species, cannot be a genus, (such as **man** and **horse** and their like). Or: a Most Special Species is one below which there is no lower species.

A Subaltern Species is one which, though a species, can still be a genus. So whatever lie between a Most Generic and a Most Special Species are genera and species, taken from alternative points of view. They are genera with respect to inferiors, and species with respect to superiors.

To make this clearer, take an example in a single predicament: Substance is First Genus; below that is Body; below Body is Animate Body; below that is Animal; below Animal, rational Animal; below that is Man; below Man are Individuals, like Socrates and Plato and Cicero.

10 Individual is what is predicated of only one.

11 All this is clear in the figure called the tree of Porphyry:

SUBSTANCE

corporeal   incorporeal

BODY

animate   inanimate

ANIMATE
BODY

sensitive   insensitive

ANIMAL

rational   irrational

RATIONAL
ANIMAL

mortal   immortal

M A N

Socrates   Plato

On Difference

12 'Difference' is said three ways: Commonly, Peculiarly (proprie), or More Peculiarly. A common difference is when one differs from another by a separable accident (like Socrates sitting differs from himself not sitting or from another). An inseparable accident is like being snub-nosed or aquiline. A more peculiar difference is when one differs from another by a specific difference (like man from horse by rationality). It is in that last way that 'difference' is taken here.

It is defined as follows: Difference is what is predicated of several specifically different things, with respect to 'What kind?'. So 'rational' is predicated of man and gods, who are rational; for we and the gods are both rational, as Porphyry has it[1], but 'mortal' added to us, separates us from them. Something is said to be predicated with respect to 'what kind' which sensibly answers the question put by 'What kind ?'. When asked: 'Of what kind is a man?', a suitable answer is 'rational'. Therefore rational is predicated of man with respect to 'what kind'.

Difference is also defined as follows: that by which species go beyond a genus, as man goes beyond animal by the differences rational and mortal.

13 One should know that the identical difference is divisive as well as constitutive, but divisive of genus and constitutive of species, as rational divides animal with a difference opposed to itself. For we say: one sort of animal is rational, another irrational; and these two differences constitute diverse species under animal. Every difference added to a genus constitutes a species, so is labelled either constitutive or specificative. 'Mortal', added to the genus rational animal, constitutes man. And that is why Boethius[2] says that only Species is defined. For a definition should consist of a genus and differences; but only species has genus and differences; therefore only species is defined.

On Peculiarity (Proprium)

14 'Peculiarity' (Proprium) is said in four ways. First, that is called a proprium (or a peculiarity) which is in a species but not in

1: cf. Boethius' translation of the Isagoge 11-12.
2: De divisionibus 886A 5 sqq., ed. Migne.

every one (being a doctor or geometrician is in man but not every man). Secondly, peculiarity is said of what is in every one but not just in a single one (being two-footed is in every man, not just one). Thirdly, proprium is said of what is in each and every one, but not always (getting gray is in each and every one, but not always, since it happens only in old age). Fourthly, a proprium (or peculiarity) called Properly Proper, is defined as follows: a proprium (or peculiarity) is what is always in each member and always only in a member. Risibility, for instance, is always in each and every man and man alone. But man is not called risible because he is actually always laughing, but because he is naturally apt to laugh.

'Peculiarity' as used in that fourth sense is one of the five predicables and defined this way by Aristotle[3]: 'proprium is what is in species alone, predicated conversely of that to which it is peculiar, and does not indicate what the essence of a thing is', as risibility does in man. 'Does not indicate what the essence of a thing is' is put into a peculiarity's description to distinguish it from a definition, which is predicated conversely of a thing and indicates what its essence is, as 'sensitive animate substance' converts with 'animal' and indicates its essence, since every definition is made through substantials; and every superior is of the essence of its inferior. As defined by Aristotle[4], 'a definition is a word-group signifying what the essence of a thing is.' - A proprium (or peculiarity) however does not signify what the essence of a thing is.

On Accident

15 An Accident is what is present or absent without its subject being destroyed, like **black, white** or **sitting**. These can be present or absent in a man without his destruction.

It is defined as follows: an accident is what is neither genus nor species nor difference nor peculiarity, yet is in a thing. Or: an accident is what just chances to be-in, or not to be-in, the same thing, like **white** or **sitting** in a man.

Of these two, Aristotle says:[5] 'the second definition is better, since to understand the first, one must already know what a genus is, what a difference is, and so on for the rest; but the second is self-contained as far as getting to know what it is that it says.'

3: Topica I 5, 102a18s.
4: Topica I 5, 101b38-102a1, and VII 3, 153a15-16.
5: Topica I 5, 102b10-15.

16 An accident is separable or inseparable: separable like **white** or **sitting** for a man, inseparable, like **black** for a crow or Ethiopian, and **white** for a swan. And though black co-occurs in an Ethiopian or a crow inseparably, this is not contrary to our definition, which says it can be present or absent without corruption of the subject, since, as Porphyry has it[6], a crow can be understood as white and an Ethopian as light in color without corruption of the subject.

Again: An accident can be common (like being white, or snubnosed) or proper (like Socrates' whiteness, or Socrates' snubness).

On Commonalities and Differences of Predicables

17 What all five predicables have in common is to be predicated of several. They differ because a genus is predicated of more than the others and thereby differs from them. Difference differs from genus, because it is predicated as to 'what kind', while genus is predicated as to 'what'. Again: Difference is distinct from species and proprium (or peculiarity), because it is predicated of several species, while species is not. It differs from accident because accidents allow of intensification and remission, but difference is not susceptible of more or less. Species differs from genus, because genus contains all species without being contained by them.

18 Species is distinct from difference, because one thing can be made up of many differences, just as the two differences **rational** and **mortal** are conjoined to constitute the species **man**. But a species is not conjoined to a species to generate another species. A particular mare is bred to a particular ass for the generation of a mule, not just mare and ass in common. Species also differs from peculiarity (or proprium) because species is naturally prior to peculiarity, and peculiarity posterior to species. Further: things whose terms or definitions are different, are themselves different; but the definitions of peculiarity and species are different; therefore they themselves are different. But species differs from accident, because species is predicated as to 'what', accident as to 'what kind', or how a thing is. And species is naturally prior to accident, since every accident is naturally posterior to its subject.

6: <u>Isagoge</u> p. 13, p. 20.

19 Peculiarity (or Proprium) differs from accident, because a peculiarity is predicated of one only species, accident of several. An accident is primarily in individuals, secondarily in genera and species. For neither **man** nor **animal** runs except insofar as Socrates or Plato runs. Peculiarity is primarily in species, then through species, in an individual. Again: Genus, species, difference and peculiarity are equally shared by all those of which they are predicated, while an accident is not, but accident is susceptible of intensity or remission. Again: Genus, difference, species, and peculiarity are predicated univocally, while accident is not predicated univocally but denominatively.

On Predication

20 To be **predicated univocally** is to be predicated according to a single name and single nature (<u>ratio</u>) taken according to that name. For instance, 'man' is predicated nominally of Socrates and Plato - as in 'Socrates is a man', 'Plato is a man' - and the nature with respect to that name is single - like rational, mortal, animal - according to which it is predicated of its inferiors, as in 'Socrates is a rational, mortal, animal', 'Plato is a rational, mortal, animal', and so of others. That is why Being (<u>ens</u>) cannot be a genus, since, though Being is predicated according to a single name of all things, it is not predicated according to a single nature. For the nature of Being, as said of a substance, is 'Being in itself' (<u>ens per se</u>); as predicated of the other nine predicaments, however, it is 'Being in another' (<u>ens in alio</u>). It is so predicated according to different natures. And for that reason it is not predicated univocally but equivocally or in multiple fashion.

To be **predicated equivocally** is to be predicated by a single name and diverse natures taken with respect to that name: like 'dog' by a single name is predicated of the barker, marine animal and heavenly body. The nature with respect to that name is not the same thing said of all, but now one thing, now another.

On Denominatives

21 Whatever differ only by some ending (<u>casu</u>) of that noun on the basis of which they have appellation, are called Denominatives, like 'grammarian' from 'grammar' or 'strong' from 'strength'. So 'grammarian', 'strong', 'white' and their like are predicated denominatively. For that reason an accident is said to be predicated denominatively.

TRACT III

ON PREDICAMENTS

On some prefatory notions

1 To become familiar with the Predicaments, prefacing a few necessary things, let us first distinguish with Aristotle[1] a triple mode of predicating: some things we say are equivocals, some univocals and others denominatives.

Equivocals are those whose name (<u>nomen</u>) is common and according to that name, the substantial nature is quite different. Though 'animal' may signify both a real and a pictured animal, the name is common to them and the substantial nature of the two according to that name is quite different.

Those are called Univocals whose name is common and substantial nature the same. The name **animal** is common to man and cow and so too its nature according to that name is the same.

Those are called Denominatives that, differing only by some ending (<u>casu</u>), have appellation based on that name, like 'grammarian' from 'grammar'. They differ by case alone, i.e. only by an ending, which is material (<u>a parte rei</u>), and have appellation based on that name. A denominative noun should therefore agree with a univocal in its beginning (<u>principio</u>), like 'grammar' and 'grammarian', and 'white' and 'whiteness'.

2 Some things said are said without construction (<u>complexione</u>) like 'man' or 'runs', some with construction, like 'a man runs'.

But before the other member of this division is subdivided, ways of **Being-in** (<u>modi essendi in</u>) must be distinguished, which are necessary for becoming familiar with the next division, and for some things which will be said later.

In the first way, something is said to be-in another as an integral part in its whole, like finger in hand or wall in house.

In the second way, something is said to be-in another as an integral whole in its parts, like house in wall, roof, and foundation.

In the third way, as species in genus, like man in animal, and in general, any inferior in its superior.

The fourth way of being-in is as genus in species, like animal in man, any defining part in its definition, and all definitions in what they define.

The fifth way of being-in is as form in matter. This fifth mode is subdivided, since one sort of form is substantial, as soul is the substantial form for a man; the other is an accidental form, like being white for a man. The first of these is said to be-in peculiarly (or properly) as form in matter, like soul in body; the other is said to be-in accidentally in a subject, like whiteness in a wall and color in a body.

The sixth way of being-in is as something in its first efficient cause, like a reign in one ruling.

The seventh way of being-in is as something in its goal (finis), like virtue in beatitude.

The eighth way of being-in is as something in a vessel and in general, as a thing located in its place.

Aristotle distinguishes these eight modes of being-in[2], but Boethius assigns nine[3], because he subdivides the fifth into two, as has just been said.

3 Some things said are said of a subject, but are in no subject, like substantial genera and species and substantial differences, all of which are called substantial universals, when the name 'substance' is extended, like **man**, **animal** and **rational**. 'To be said of a subject', as taken here, is to be said of an inferior, as animal is said of man, man of Socrates, and color of whiteness. But 'To be-in a subject' is taken the way an accident is in a subject. Some, like

1: Categ. 1, 1a1-15, transl. Boeth. p. 5.3-17, ed. Minio-Paluello.
2: Physica IV 3, 210a 14-24.

substantial individuals, are neither said of a subject, nor are they in a subject; others are said of a subject and are in a subject, as genera and species of the other nine predicaments are said of inferiors, and they are in a substance as an accident is in a subject, the way color is said of whiteness as of an inferior, and is in a body as in a subject. Others are in a subject, but they are said of no subject, as this bit of knowledge is in a soul as in a subject, and is not said of any inferior; or this color is in a subject, and is not said of a subject; for every color is in a body.

4 When one is predicated of another as of a subject, things said of what is predicated are all also said of the subject. For example, if Socrates is a man, and a man is an animal, Socrates is therefore an animal.

There are diverse species and differences of things not subalternately posited, like animal and science, which are diverse genera. The differences of animal are rational and irrational; for animal is divided by them. The differences of science are **natural, moral** and **linguistic** (sermonicialis), for science is divided by them: sciences are either natural, or moral, or linguistic.

5 Each of those said with no construction at all signifies either substance, or quantity, or quality, or to something [Relation: ad aliquid], or where, or when, or be sited [Posture: situm esse], or to have, or to do [Action: facere], or to undergo [Passion: pati]. To give examples, substance as in man and horse; quantity, in two-cubited or three-cubited; quality, in whiteness and blackness; relation, double and triple; where, as in in a place; when, in yesterday, tomorrow; posture, in to sit and to lie down; to have, in to have shoes or armor on; action, in to saw, to burn; passion / undergo, in to be sawn, to be burned.

Having dealt with these, each of the Predicaments themselves must be discussed, and Substance first of all, since it is prior to the others.

On Substance

6 Substance is divided into first and second substance. First substance is what is peculiarly / properly, principally, and maximally predicated. Or: First substance is what is neither said of a subject nor is in a subject, like a particular man or a particular horse.

3: In Arist. Categ. 172B2-C9, ed. Migne.

Second Substances are species in which first substances and genera of these species are, such as man and animal; for a given man is in man which is a species, just as man is in animal which is a genus.

Substantial individuals are called first substances since they primarily underly the others; their genera and species are called second substances, since they underly secondarily. A given man is said to be a grammarian, one running, an animal, and a substance, and for that reason man is said to be a grammarian, running, an animal and a substance.

7 Again: What are said of a subject are all predicated by name and nature (ratio), like man of Socrates. But in several of the things said of a subject indeed neither the name nor nature is predicated, like this whiteness or this white thing. Yet in some things, while nothing prevents a name from being predicated of a subject, it is impossible for a nature to be predicated. So white may be predicated of a subject, but the nature of white never is.

Again: Among second substances, species is more substance than genus is, for species is closer to first substance than genus, and also because it underlies more. For species underlies whatever underlies genus, as well as genus itself. But Most Special Species are equally substances, such as man, horse, and their like.

On Commonalities and Peculiarities of Substance

8 Now we have seen these, we must discuss commonalities and peculiarites of Substance. What every substance has in common is not to be-in a subject, since to be-in a subject only suits an accident. That is clear for first substances by its definition, for second substances, by Induction and Syllogism. Inductively as follows: A man is not in a subject, a horse is not in a subject, nor is an animal, and so on for other second substances; therefore no second substance is in a subject. Syllogistically as follows: Nothing of those that are in a subject is predicated by name and nature; but every second substance is predicated by name and nature; therefore no second substance is in a subject.

This is not a peculiarity of substance but also fits differences. This is to be understood of substantial differences. Nor is there further objection from parts of substance which are in a whole. The reason why they appear to be in a subject is because the mode of being-in as accident in a subject is one thing, the mode of being-in as part in whole another, as was clear above.

9 Again: All second substances and substantial differences are appropriately predicated univocally. For all these are predicated of first substances by name and nature, since they are univocally predicated.

10 Again: Every first substance signifies **this particular thing** (hoc aliquid : tóde ti), that is, an individual and what is numerically one. But second substance seems to signify **this particular thing** by the fact that it is in a first substance and is of its essence, yet it still does not signify **this particular thing** but rather something common. What is signified by second substance is not one just as one is signified by first substance.

11 Again: There is nothing contrary to substance. This is not a peculiarity of substance, since it fits every substance, every quantity and some others as well.

12 Again: Substance is not susceptible of more or less. I am not saying one substance does not underly more than another, but I do say that each and every substance, according to its being, is neither intensified nor diminished the way a white thing is sometimes more, sometimes less, white. Socrates is not more a man at one time than another, nor more a man than Plato.

13 Again: it is a peculiarity of substance by its own changeability (mutationem) to be susceptible of contraries, as the same man is now white, now black, hot, cold, lazy and zealous.

Nor is there a further objection from a sentence, since granted one and the same word-group like the proposition, **'Socrates is sitting'** is now true, now false, it is not that way by virtue of its own development, but from the changeability of a thing, such as Socrates getting up or running.

Notice that truth and falsity are in things as in a subject, but in a word-group as in a sign. A mode of being-in is consequently equivocated when truth and falsity are said to be-in both things and a word-group. So too **'susceptible'** is equivocated when urine is said to be susceptible of health, and an animal susceptible of health. Urine is susceptible of health because it is a sign of it, an animal because it is a subject of health. So this peculiarity does not suit a word-group but a substance alone.

4: Above, p. 25.

On Quantity

14   Quantity is either continuous or discrete. A discrete quantity is such as a number and a word-group. So there are two species of it. For there is no common term in number to which the parts of number may be joined. In ten, five and five or three and seven are not joined to some common term, but are always discrete and separate.   Number is a multitude brought together out of unities. Similarly in a word-group, syllables are not linked to some common term, but each one is separate from the other.

15 Continuous Quantities are Line, Surface, Body, Place and Time. There are consequently five species of it. That a line is a continuous quantity is clear because a line's parts are joined to a common term, that is, to a point. Parts of a surface are joined to a line, and body parts to a surface. Parts of time are joined to now, as past and future are linked to the present. Parts of place are joined to the same term to which particles of a body are.

On Commonalities of Quantity

16 Now we have seen these, Commonalities of Quantity are to be discussed. The first common property is that nothing is contrary to quantity, as there is no contrary to two cubits, three cubits and surface, because contrariety is primarily in qualities (not in all qualities, but in some of them). But quantity is not quality; which is why there is no contrariety in quantity.

Again: Quantity is not susceptible of more or less. One line is not more quantity than another line, nor is a triple less a number than a quadruple.

Again: It is a peculiarity of quantity as such to be said to be equal or unequal, as a number is equal or unequal to another number, a body to another body, and a line to another line; and so on for each.

On Compared-to-Another (Relation)

17 Those are called Compared-to-another (Relatives: <u>ad aliquid</u>) which, by the very fact that they exist, are said to be to others or somehow otherwise compared to another. Such as the double of a half is a double; half a double, a half; a father is father of a son; a son is the son of a father; something greater is greater than something less; and like is like its like.

18 Some relatives are said according to Equiparity, like those
said with the same word (nomen): like is like like, equal equals
equal, near is near near. Others according to Superior Position, like
master, double, triple. Others according to Inferior Position (sup-
positionem) like servant, half, third, for the latter are subposed to
the former and the former are superimposed upon them. For a
master is superimposed on a servant, a father on his son, a double
on a half; while a servant is subposed to a master, a son to a father,
and a half to a double.

On Commonalities of Relation

19 After these come Commonalities of Relation. The first is
that contrariety consists in relation, as virtue is contrary to vice,
since both are relative to each other. But this is not appropriate to
every relation: there is no contrary to double or triple.

Again: Relatives are susceptible of more or less, as like is said
to be more or less like, and equal the same way. But this does not
suit all relatives; double is not said to be more or less double, nor is
triple, nor is a father said to be more or less a father.

Again: All relatives are said convertibly, so if there is a
father, there is a son and the converse; if a master, then a servant
and the converse; and if a double, then a half, and the converse.

Again: Relatives seem to be naturally together: for double
and half, father and son go together.

Again: Posited relatives mutually affirm and relatives denied
remove each other. If there is no double, there is no half; if there
is no father, there is no son.

20 Again: A definition of relatives is: those are 'to another'
for which to exist is somehow to be to another. And this definition
is peculiar to relatives.

Again: It is a peculiarity of relatives that if anyone knows one
of correlatives definitively, he knows the other's definition as well.
So if one knows a double definitively, he knows how to define what it
is the double of as well. For it is necessary to use the nature of the
two in both.

On Quality

21 Quality is that on account of which we are said to be of such a kind. We are said to be white in terms of whiteness, because of color, we are said to be colored; through justice, called just.

There are four species of Quality. The first is Habit and Disposition. Habit differs from Disposition by being more permanent and lasting, like virtues and things we know (<u>scientie</u>); knowledge is difficult to displace unless there is a profound alteration from illness or something like that in the knower or the one possessing virtues. Justice and chastity are not easily changed. What are easily altered are called Dispositions, like hot and cold, illness and health, and the like. Habits may be called dispositions, but not the converse. Those who have a habit are in a way well- or ill-disposed to those things to which they are habituated. But dispositions are not habits. So Habit can be defined as follows: a habit is a quality hard to change; a disposition is a quality easy to change.

22 The second species of quality is a natural capacity or inability to do something easily, or of undergoing something easily. One is called healthy because he has a natural capacity of not suffering from any things at all that happen; one is called sickly from a natural inability to undergo anything; something hard has a natural potency of not being cut quickly. Racers and boxers are so-called not because they put those activities to use, but because they have a natural ability of doing so easily.

23 The third species of Quality is Passivity or a Quality of Being Affected (<u>passio et passibilis qualitas</u>). Examples are those qualities which effect sensory reactions such as in taste, sweetness or bitterness and their like. Or those qualities are also under this species which are generated by emotions that are stable and difficult to change. Swarthiness, whether brought on by some natural reaction, by illness or by heat, is called a quality.

24 The fourth species of Quality is Form or Shape when it concerns something stable, such as the disposition of a body like triangularity or quadrilaterality, straightness and curvature.

25 Those are called Qualitatives (<u>qualia</u>) which on this basis are predicated denominatively, like **grammarian** from **grammar** and **just** from **justice**, or which are said from some quality not nominally derived.

This arises in two ways. Some are said non-denominatively from a quality because no name was imposed on the quality itself, as a runner is not so-called denominatively because no name was imposed on that quality. Other qualitatives are said non-denominatively because they do not share the name of a quality from which they are said, even when there has been a name imposed, like **'eager'** from the virtue.

There are thus three ways of taking **'what sort of'** (<u>quale</u>) from a quality.

On Properties of Quality

26 There is contrariety in qualities, like whiteness to blackness and justice to injustice. But this is not a peculiarity of quality as such because it does not suit every quality. Shape has no contrary, nor does some middle color.

Again: If one contrary be of such a kind (<u>quale</u>), the other will be of that kind. So injustice is contrary to justice; but justice is a quality; therefore injustice is a quality; and just is 'of that kind', therefore unjust is also 'of such a kind'.

Again: Quality admits of more or less; one is said to be more or less just, and grammatical, and white. But this is not a peculiarity of quality because squared does not admit of more or less, nor does circle, nor quadrangulation, or rounding.

Again: it is a peculiarity of a quality that something is called like or unlike it on the basis of that quality. So white is said to be like white and just like just, but black unlike white.

On Action (To do : <u>facere</u>)

27 Action is that by which we are said to act on what is subjected. A sawyer is said to act because he saws. Sawing is thus an action, and by sawing, the sawyer is said to perform an act from the fact that he saws. Striking is also an Action.

It is a Peculiarity of an action to entail change (<u>passionem</u>) of itself.

To do and to undergo take contrarieties. To make something warm is what is contrary to cooling it, and to be made warm is contrary to being made cold, and being delighted to being saddened.

Again: Actions admit of more or less. To warm something is said more or less, as are to be made warm and to be delighted and to be saddened.

On Passion (To undergo : _pati_)

28 Undergoing something (_passio_) is an effect and consequence of an action, like being warmed is effected by and is brought about by warming.

It is a peculiarity of undergoing something first to be brought about by action.

Again: Undergoing something is not in an agent, but in a patient. Let what have been said before suffice for now about the rest.

On four-fold Opposition

29 One thing is said to be opposed to another in four ways. Some opposites are relatively opposed, like father and son, double and half, or master and servant. Others are privatively opposed, like privation and possession, sight and blindness, or hearing and deafness. Others are contraries, like white and black. Others are contradictorily opposed like affirmation and negation, such as 'he is sitting' and 'he is not sitting'.

What relatively opposed things are has been mentioned earlier.

Contraries are things placed in the same genus, which stand maximally apart from each other, differ from and mutually exclude each other, and alternate in the same susceptibility, except when one is in a thing naturally, like whiteness in snow and heat in fire.

Privatively opposed are those that have to do with the same thing in irreversible order, like going from possession to privation and not the converse. For it is impossible that a return be made from a privation into possession, as blindness and sight have their origin with respect to the eye, and a change from sight to blindness can occur, but not naturally the converse.

On Prior

30 Prior (prius) is said in four ways. First and properly, something is said to be prior to another in time, insofar as one is said to be more venerable and older than another, as a man of forty years is said to be more venerable and older than one of twenty.

In the second way, that is said to be prior which is not convertible on the basis of subsequence in subsisting, as one is prior to two; for two to exist is an immediate consequence of there being one; so if there are two, there is also one, but not the converse.

The third way, prior is said according to order: in disciplines, principles are prior to conclusions; in grammar, letters are prior to syllables, and in a speech, the introduction is prior to narration by order.

In the fourth way, what is better and more honorable is said to be prior; most have usually called the more honorable and esteemed the first (priores) among them.

Besides the four modes just discussed, there is another kind of priority. Among things convertibly related because of essential dependency, and one thing is somehow a cause the other exists, the former is appropriately said to be naturally prior, as when a thing is cause of the truth of a proposition or sentence made about it. For example, **'that a man runs'** (hominem currere) is converted with the sentence, **'The man is running'** (homo currit) if it is true that a man runs, and **'The man is running'** is true and the converse. For a fact (res) is the cause of a sentence truly made about it. A true sentence is not a cause that a fact exist. Depending on whether a thing exists or not, a sentence is said to be true or false·[5]

On Together

31 'Together' (simul) is said in three ways. In the first way, those are said to be together whose generation is at the same time and neither of them is earlier nor later than the other. These are said to be simultaneous (simul tempore).

5:   Arist. Categ. 5, 4b9-10, p. 54.6-7.

Second, those are said to be together that are convertibles and neither is the cause of the other's existence, like any relative, such as double and half, and so of the others.

Third, those are said to be together that divide some genus among themselves, like **man, horse, lion** and others that divide the genus **animal;** or even differences, like rational and irrational. Those latter two modes are said to be naturally together (<u>simul</u> <u>natura</u>) the former to be simultaneous (<u>simul</u> <u>tempore</u>).

On Change (<u>Motus</u>)

32 There are six species of Change: Generation, Corruption, Increase, Diminution, Alteration, and Locomotion.

Generation is a process of going from non-being to being. Corruption is one of going from being to non-being. Increase is an addition of a pre-existent quantity. Diminution is a decrease of a pre-existent quantity. Alteration is a change from one contrary quality into its contrary or into its intermediary quality, as when one changes from whiteness to blackness or into intermediate colors. Locomotion is a change from one place to another.

Locomotion has six species or differences: upwards, downwards, ahead, back, rightwards, leftwards; for toward all these parts, there is a change of place.

On Possession (<u>Habere</u>)

33 'To Possess / have' is said in many ways. First, one is said to possess a quality, like learning or virtue.

Second, 'to have' is said of what has a certain size, like two cubits and three cubits.

Third, 'to have' is said of things about the body, like having clothing or a coat, or having something on a body part, like a ring on the finger.

'To have' understood this third way is one of the ten Predicaments. It is defined as follows: habit or costume (<u>habitus</u>) has to do with bodies and those things next to it, like armor and footwear. In the same way names are invented in other things, and depending on proximity, some things are said 'to have', others, 'to be had'.

Fourth, 'to have' a member, like a hand or foot.

Fifth, 'to have' something contained, as a flask has wine or a bushel has grains of wheat.

Sixth, 'to have' a possession like a house or a field.

Seventh, 'to have' a wife: of this last, Aristotle says[6] that mode is furthest from the one which is **possession** (habere). And he says[7] that there will perhaps come to light other uses of 'to have', but the usual ones have almost all been enumerated.

6: Categ. 15, 15b28-30, p. 79.6-7.
7: ibid. 15b31-33, p. 79.9-10.

TRACT IV

ON SYLLOGISMS

On the Proposition

1 A Proposition is a word-group affirming or denying something of another. A Term is what a proposition analyzes into, like subject and predicate. **To be predicated universally** (<u>dici</u> <u>de</u> <u>omni</u>) is when there is nothing to take under the subject about which the predicate may not be said, as in **'every man runs':** here running is said of every man, and there is nothing to take under the subject about which running would not be said. **To be negated universally** (<u>dici</u> <u>de nullo</u>) is when there is nothing to take under the subject from which the predicate would not be removed, as in **'no man runs';** here running is removed from any man at all.

On the Syllogism

2 A Syllogism is a word-group in which, once some things have been posited, something else necessarily happens through what have been posited, Like

	'every	animal	is	a substance,
	every	man	is	an animal,
therefore	every	man	is	a substance'.

This whole is a sort of word-group in which, once some things have been posited (i.e., the two premised propositions), something else necessarly follows through them, (i.e., the conclusion).

Every Syllogism consists of three terms and two propositions. The first of these propositions is called the Major, the second the Minor. But two propositions cannot be made from three terms, unless one is taken twice; that term is then either made subject in the one proposition and predicate in the other, or it will predicated in both or made subject in both. One of these terms is called the Middle, another is called the Major Extremity, another the the Minor Extremity. The middle is the the term taken twice before the conclusion. The major extremity is the term taken in the major proposition with the middle. The minor extremity is the term taken in the minor proposition with the middle.

On Mood and Figure

3 For a Syllogism, Mood and Figure are required. Figure is the ordering of the three terms as to which is made subject and which predicate. As was said,[1] the ordering is done in three ways. On that basis, there are three figures.

The First Figure is when what is subject in the first proposition is predicate in the second, like

| 'every | animal | is | a substance |
| every | man | is | an animal'. |

The Second Figure is when the same thing is predicated in both, like

| 'every | man | is | an animal |
| no | stone | is | an animal'. |

The Third Figure is when the same thing is subject in both, like

| 'every | man | is | an animal |
| every | man | is | risible'. |

Mood is the ordering of the two proposition in the due quality and quantity.

On universal Rules

4 So universal rules like these are given for any figure:

a syllogism cannot be made from solely particulars, nonfinites or singulars.

So one of the propositions ought to be universal.

1: Above, p. 38.

Again:
in no figure can a syllogism be made
from nothing but negatives.

Consequently, one of the premises should be affirmative.

Again:
If one premise is particular, the
conclusion must be particular,
and not the converse.

Again:
If one premise is negative,
the conclusion is negative
and the converse.

Again:
If one premise is particular, the
conclusion must be particular as
well, and not the converse.

Again:
The Middle Term must never be
put into the conclusion.

On the First Figure

5 The First Figure has nine Moods, the first four concluding
directly and the next five indirectly. To conclude directly is for the
major extremity to be predicated of the minor extremity in the conclusion. To conclude indirectly is for the minor extremity to be
predicated of the major in the conclusion.

Again: The Rule for the four moods concluding directly is:

if the minor is a negative
existential, nothing follows.

Again: under the same conditions:

if the major is a particular
existential, nothing follows.

On its Moods

6 The First Mood of the First Figure consists of two affirmative universal propositions concluding to an affirmative universal. Like

	'every	animal	is	a substance
	every	man	is	an animal
therefore	every	man	is	a substance'.

The second consists of a universal negative and universal affirmative concluding to a universal negative. Like

	'no	animal	is	a stone
	every	man	is	an animal
therefore	no	man	is	a stone'.

The third consists of a universal affirmative and a particular affirmative, concluding to a particular affirmative. Like

	'every	animal	is	a substance
	some	man	is	an animal
therefore	some	man	is	a substance'.

The fourth consists of a universal negative and a particular affirmative, concluding to a particular negative. Like

	'no	animal	is	a stone
	some	man	is	an animal
therefore	some	man	is not	a stone'.

The fifth consists of two universal affirmatives concluding indirectly to a particular affirmative. Like

	'every	animal	is	a substance
	every	man	is	an animal
therefore	some	substance	is	a man'.

It is proven through the first mood of the first figure, which concludes to a universal affirmative, convertible with a particular affirmative, the particular conclusion in this fifth mood.

The sixth consists of a universal negative and a universal affirmative concluding indirectly to a universal negative. Like

	'no	animal	is	a stone
	every	man	is	an animal
therefore	no	stone	is	a man'.

It is reduced to the second Mood by simple conversion of the con-clusion.

The seventh consists of a universal affirmative and a particular affirmative concluding indirectly to a particular affirmative. Like

	'every	animal	is	a substance
	some	man	is	an animal,
therefore	some	substance	is	a man'.

It reduces to the third mood by simple conversion of the conclusion.

The eighth consists of a universal affirmative and a universal negative concluding indirectly to a particular negative. Like

	'every	animal	is	a substance
	no	stone	is	an animal
therefore	some	substance	is not	a stone'.

This is reduced to the fourth figure by converting the major by accident and the minor by simple conversion and transposition of the premises.

The ninth consists of a particular affirmative and a universal negative concluding indirectly to a particular negative. Like

	'some	animal	is	a substance
	no	stone	is	an animal
therefore	some	substance	is not	a stone'.

It is reduced to the fourth mood of the first figure by simple conversion of the major and minor and by transposition.

On the Second Figure

7   Next, on the Second Figure, for which there are these rules:

In the Second Figure, if the
Major is a particular existential,
nothing follows.

Again:
>   In the Second Figure, from affirm-
>   atives alone, nothing follows.

Again:
>   In the Second Figure, the Conclusion
>   is always negative.

This third rule can be understood through the second.

On its Moods

8 The Second Figure has four Moods. The first consists of a universal negative and a universal affirmative concluding to a universal negative. Like

	'no	stone	is	an animal
	every	man	is	an animal
therefore	no	man	is	a stone'.

This is reduced to the second mood of the first figure by simple conversion of the major.

The second consists of a universal affirmative and a universal negative concluding to a universal negative. Like

	'every	man	is	an animal
	no	stone	is	an animal
therefore	no	stone	is	a man'.

It is reduced to the second mood of the first figure by simple conversion of the minor and conclusion, and by transposition.

The third consists of a universal negative and a particular affirmative concluding to a particular negative. Like

	'no	stone	is	an animal
	some	man	is	an animal
therefore	some	man	is not	a stone'.

It is reduced to the fourth mood of the first figure by simple conversion.

The fourth consists of a universal affirmative and a particular negative concluding to a particular negative. Like

	'every	man	is	an animal
	some	stone	is not	an animal
therefore	some	stone	is not	a man'.

It is reduced to the first mood by Reduction to Absurdity (<u>per</u> <u>impossibile</u>).

On Reduction through the Impossible

To Reduce to Absurdity (<u>reducere</u> <u>per</u> <u>impossibile</u> : Contradiction) is to infer from the opposite of the conclusion with one of the premises, the opposite of the other premise. Take the opposite of a conclusion like: **'every stone is a man'** with the major premise of this fourth mood, and a syllogism will be made in the first mood of the first figure as follows:

	'every	man	is	an animal
	every	stone	is	a man
therefore	every	stone	is	an animal'.

This conclusion is opposed to the minor premise of the fourth mood. This is to prove through Reducing to Absurdity (<u>probare</u> <u>per</u> <u>impossibile</u>).

On the Third Figure

10 Next on the Third Figure. The third figure is where the same term is made subject in both premise. Rules for which are:

In the Third Figure, nothing
follows if the Minor is
an existential negative.

Again:
In the Third Figure, the Conclusion
can only be particular.

On its Moods

11 The Third Figure has six Moods. The first consists of two universal affirmatives concluding to a particular affirmative. Like

	'every	man	is	a substance
	every	man	is	an animal
therefore	some	animal	is	a substance'.

It is reduced to the third mood of the first figure by converting the minor by accident.

The second mood consists of a universal negative and a universal affirmative concluding to a particular negative. Like

	'no	man	is	a stone
	every	man	is	an animal
therefore	some	animal	is not	a stone'.

It reduces to the fourth mood of the first figure by conversion of the minor by accident.

The third consists of a particular affirmative and a universal affirmative concluding to a particular affirmative. Like

	'some	man	is	a substance
	every	man	is	an animal
therefore	some	animal	is	a substance'.

It reduces to the third mood of the first figure by simple conversion of the major and conclusion and through transposition.

The fourth consists of a universal affirmative and a particular affirmative concluding to a particular affirmative. Like

	'every	man	is	a substance
	some	man	is	an animal
therefore	some	animal	is	a substance'.

It reduces to the third mood of the first figure by simple conversion of the minor.

The fifth consists of a particular negative, and a universal affirmative concluding to a particular negative. Like

	'some	man	is not	a stone
	every	man	is	an animal
therefore	some	animal	is not	a stone'.

It reduces to the first mood of the first figure by Reduction to Absurdity. Take the opposite of the conclusion with the one premise and infer the opposite of the other premise, like

'every   animal   is   a stone
every   man   is   an animal
therefore   every   man   is   a stone'.

This conclusion made in the first mood of the first figure contradicts the major premise of the fifth mood.

The sixth consists of a universal negative and a particular affirmative concluding to a particular negative. Like

'no   man   is   a stone
some   man   is   an animal
therefore   some   animal   is not   a stone'.

It reduces to the fourth mood of the first figure by simple conversion of the minor.

On some Rules

12 A rule like this for syllogisms concluding to a particular negative indirectly is given:

no syllogism concluding indirectly to a negative particular can conclude to it directly, and none concluding to it directly can conclude to it indirectly.

Again:

The First Figure includes every kind of Proposition, that is, universal and particular, affirmative and negative. The Second includes the universal and particular negative. The Third includes the particular affirmative and negative, but not the universal.

13

BARBARA   CELARENT   DARII   FERIO   BARALIPTON
CELANTES   DABITIS   FAPESMO   FRISESOMORUM
CESARE   CAMESTRES   FESTINO   BAROCHO   DARAPTI
FALAPTO   DISAMIS   DATISI   BOCARDO   FERISON

In these four verses, there are nineteen words (<u>dictiones</u>) representing nineteen Moods of the three Figures in such a way that in the first word, the first Mood is understood, in the second word, the second Mood, and so on. So the first two verses represent the moods of the first figure, the third (except for the last word), represents the moods of the second figure, such that the first word of the third verse represents the first mood of the second figure, the second word the second mood, and so on for the others. The last word of the third verse with the other words of the fourth represents the moods of the third figure through its order.

Notice that by the vowels A, E, I, O, the four kinds of propositions are understood: by A the universal affirmative is to be understood, by E the universal negative, by I the particular affirmative and by O, the particular negative.

Again: In any word there are three syllables. Anything left over is superfluous, except for M, as will soon² be clear. By the first of those three syllables is understood the major proposition of a syllogism, by the second the minor, and by the third the conclusion. For example, the first word BARBARA has three syllables, in each of which there is an A. By A being put there three times, it is signified that the first mood of the first figure consists of two universal affirmatives concluding to an affirmative universal. That is how the rest of the words are to be understood, depending on the vowels used in them.

Again: Notice the first four words begin with the consonants B, C, D, F, as do all other words following. By this it is to be understood that all moods understood through a word beginning with B should be reduced to the first mood of the first figure; all moods signified by a word beginning with C to the second; with D to the Third, and with F to the Fourth.

Again: Wherever S is put in these words, it means that the proposition understood by the immediately preceding vowel it is to be simply converted. P means a proposition should be converted by accident. Wherever an M occurs, it means there should be transposition in the premises (to transpose is to make a minor out of the major and vice versa). When C occurs, it means the mood understood by that word is to be proven by Reduction to Absurdity.

2: Below, p. 47-48.

On unusable Connexities (conjugatio)

14 Since Aristotle shows in Prior Analytics[3] connexities in which a conclusion will not follow from premises are useless, by finding terms in which pairing of this kind does not hold, a discovery of terms like that is useful for that reason.[4]

So wherever an unusable pairing is made contrary to the syllogistic rules assigned above, further objections are to be sought by taking two species with a single genus, (like **man, ass** and **animal**); or two species with a peculiarity of one of them (like **man, ass, risible**); or one species with its genus or peculiarity (like **man, ass, risible**). For in these, an instance will be found.

To find further objections is to accept terms in which the premises are true and the conclusion false, while the propositions remain identical in quantity and quality. For example, this is an unusable conjugation:

	'no	man	is	an ass
	no	stone	is	a man
therefore	no	stone	is	an ass'.

Against this useless pairing a further objection is inferred this way:

	'no	ass	is	a man
	nothing	risible	is	an ass
therefore	nothing	risible	is	a man'.

Here the premises are true and the conclusion is false, with the propositions remaining identical in quantity and quality in both false syllogisms.

3: Anal. Priora I 27, 43a20ff., p. 58ff.
4: i.e., terms technically labelled in quibus non.

TRACT V

ON TOPICS

On the multiple ambiguity of Ratio

1 'Ratio' is used in several ways. In one, it means the same as definition or description, like: 'univocals are those with a name in common and the same substantial definition (ratio) according to that name.'[1] In another, ratio ('reason') is the same as a kind of mental ability. In another, it is the same as a word-group demonstrating something, like the reasons debaters advance. In another, ratio ('design') is the same thing as a material's form: in a knife, for instance, iron is the material while its form is the shape put into the iron. In another way, ratio ('nature') is the same as a common essence predicable of many things, like the essence of a species, or genus, or difference. In another way ratio ('reason') is the same as a middle term inducing a conclusion, and it is in this last way that ratio is taken here in the definition of Argument, as follows:

On Argument and Argumentation

2 An Argument is a reason grounding conviction in debatable matter, that is, a middle term testing a conclusion to be confirmed by an Argument. The conclusion to an argument or arguments is an attested proposition. Before it is tested, it can be doubted. It is then the same thing as a question. Question is defined as follows: a question is a proposition which may be doubted. A middle term is what has two extremes.

Argumentation is the explication of an Argument by a word-group, that is, a word-group that makes an argument explicit. But an argument differs both from a middle term and from argumentation, since a middle term is called that because it has two extremes, while an argument adds to a middle term the power of testing the conclusion (so in order for there to be an argument, there must be a

---

1: Arist. Categ. I 1a8-9.

middle term and it must have the power of testing the conclusion).
But the whole word-group, consisting of premises and conclusion, is
called Argumentation, and in it, the power of an argument is
revealed.   One sort of whole word-group can induce a universal
affirmative, another only a universal negative, another only a
particular negative.

On the Species of Argumentation

3   There are four types of Argumentation: Syllogism,
Induction, Example and Enthymeme. A definition of syllogism was
given above.

Induction is progression from particulars to the universal. For
example:

'Socrates	runs,	
Plato	runs,	
Cicero	runs,	
		and so on of individuals
therefore every man	runs'.	

An Enthymeme is an imperfect syllogism, i.e., a word-group in
which, without positing all its propositions, a precipitate conclusion
is inferred. For example:

'every	animal	runs
therefore this	man	runs'.

In the argumentation cited, the proposition **'every man is an animal'**
is understood and not put in there, for if it were, it would be a
perfect syllogism.

Notice that every enthymeme should be reduced to a syllogism.
Therefore in any enthymeme there are three terms just as in a
syllogism. Two of those terms are put into the conclusion and they
are the extremes, the other one is the middle term and that is never
put into the conclusion. One extreme is used twice in an enthymeme, the other once only. From the extreme taken once, together
with the middle term, a universal proposition should be made in the
required mood, and that way a syllogism will result. For example, in
this enthymeme:

'every animal	runs
therefore every man	runs'

the extremes are 'man' and 'runs', and the middle term is
'animal'. The extreme 'man', is taken once; and from that and the
middle, a universal proposition is made as follows: 'every man is an
animal'; then the syllogism is complete, as follows:

'every animal   runs
every man   is   an animal
therefore every man   runs'.

    The form of Argumentation called Example is when through
one particular, another particular is tested because of some likeness
found in the pair, for example:

'It is bad for Leonese to fight Astorgans;
therefore   it is bad for Astorgans to fight Zamorans';

On Topic in General

    4 An Argument is confirmed by a Topic (<u>Locus</u>), so a definit-
ion of Topic must be given as taken here. A Topic is the basis of an
argument, or that from which a suitable argument is derived for a
proposed question. We have already said what a question is.[2]

    One should know that proposition, question, and conclusion are
substantially identical but differ formally; as was clear above,[3]
they have distinct <u>rationes</u> ('functions / senses') or definitions. As
something doubted, it is a question; as already tested by an argument, a conclusion; as posited for another in order to test it, it is a
proposition. So a proposition is so-called as what is put into the
premises to test a conclusion.

    Topic divides into Maxim Topic, and Topic Differential of
Maxim. A Maxim Topic is the same as the maxim itself - a proposition compared to which no other is more basic, i.e., better known.
For example 'every whole is greater than its part', 'whatever a
definition is predicated of, the thing defined is as well', 'whatever a
species is predicated of, its genus genus is as well'.

    A Topic Differential of Maxim is that by which one maxim
differs from another. For instance, these two maxims: 'whatever a
definition is predicated of, the thing defined is as well', and
'whatever a species is predicated of, its genus is as well' differ
through the terms constituting them, one by 'genus' and 'species',
the other by 'definition' and 'defined'. So these simple terms are

called maximal differences.

Both a Maxim Topic and a Topic Differential of Maxim are called 'Topic', since both give solidity to an argument. So **Topic** (locus) is taken here proportionally to a natural Place (locus), since place in nature provides firm ground to natural things and keeps them in being, while here a Topic confirms an argument.

A Topic Differential of Maxim is divided into Intrinsic, Extrinsic and Middle. It is intrinsic when an argument is taken from what are substantive of a thing, as from a definition. It is extrinsic when the argument derives from things completely separate from a thing's substance, as from opposites; like querying whether Socrates is white, and concluding: **'Socrates is black; therefore he is not white'.** A Topic is Middle when an argument is taken from things partly agreeing with the terms posited in the question and partly differing, like univocal and denominative terms, which are called conjugates. An example would be querying whether justice is good, and concluding: **'a just thing is a good thing, therefore justice is good'.**

ON INTRINSIC TOPICS

An Intrinsic Topic can be divided into a Topic from Substance and a Topic from Concomitants of Substance.

On the Topic from Substance

5 A Topic from Substance is when an Argument is taken from the substance of terms posited in the question. It subdivides into a Topic from Definition and from Description, and into a Topic from Nominal Interpretation.

On the Topic from Definition

6 A Definition is a statement signifying a thing's essence (quid est esse). The Topic from Definition is the relation between a definition and the thing defined. It contains four arguments and four maxims. First, making the definition subject of an affirmation; second, predicating the definition affirmatively; third, making it subject of a negation; and fourth, predicating it negatively.

2: Above, p. 49.
3: Above, p. 38, p. 49.

Examples of all are: **'a rational, mortal, animal runs, so man runs'.**
The Topic here ? From Definition. The Maxim:

anything predicated of a definition
is predicated of the thing defined
as well.

Second: **'Socrates is a rational, mortal, animal; therefore Socrates
is a man'.** The Topic here ? From Definition. The Maxim:

anything a definition is predicated of,
the thing defined is as well.

Third: **'a rational, mortal, animal is not running; therefore a man is
not running'.** The Topic here ? From Definition. The Maxim:

anything removed from a definition is
removed from the thing defined as well.

Fourth: **'a stone is not a rational, mortal, animal; therefore a stone
is not a man'.** The Topic here ? From Definition. The Maxim:

from whatever a definition is removed,
so is the thing defined

On the Topic from the Thing Defined

7 The Topic from the Thing Defined is a relation between a
thing defined and its definition. It likewise contains four arguments
and four maxims.

First, by making the thing defined subject of an affirmation, as
in **'a man runs, therefore a rational, mortal, animal runs'.** The Topic
here ? From the Thing Defined. The Maxim:

anything predicated of the thing defined
is predicated of its definition as well.

Second, by predicating it affirmatively, as follows: **'Socrates is a
man, therefore Socrates is a rational, mortal, animal'.** The Topic
here ? From the Thing Defined. The Maxim:

whatever the thing defined is predicated of, so too is its definition

Third, by making the thing defined subject of a negation, like **'a man**

is not running, therefore a rational, mortal, animal is not running'.
The Topic here ? From the Thing Defined. The Maxim:
anything removed from the thing defined
is removed from its definition as well

Fourth, by predicating it negatively, as follows: 'a stone is not a
man, therefore a stone is not a rational, mortal, animal'. Whence
the Topic ? From the Thing Defined. The Maxim:

from whatever the thing defined is
removed, the definition is removed
as well.

Note that in all of these, Topic is denominated from what
causes inference, not from what is inferred. So when definition is
the cause, the Topic is from definition; when the thing defined is
the cause, the Topic is from the thing defined. Why ? Because a
Topic or Differential Maxim should be denominated from what
causes an inference, and not from what is inferred.

On the Topic from Description

8 A Description is a word-group signifying the being of a thing
through accidentals, as 'risible animal' is a description of man. Or
as follows: a Description is a word-group consisting of genus and
peculiarity, for example: 'risible animal'.

The Topic from Description is the relation of Description to
Thing Described. It contains four arguments and four maxims just
like the Topic from Definition. Arguments and Maxims are formed
in the same manner here as there, except that 'Description' is substituted for 'Definition'. Similarly for Thing Described.

On the Topic from Nominal
Interpretation

9 There are two kinds of Interpretation. One is not converted,
like 'hurting the foot' (ledens pedem), an interpretation of what I
say as stone (lapis). The other is converted, like 'lover of wisdom',
an interpretation of what I say as 'philosopher' (philosophus). That
is how 'interpretation' is taken here. It is defined as follows:
Interpretation is exposition of one word (nomen) through some other.

The Topic from Nominal Interpretation is a relation between
interpretation and the thing interpreted. It contains the same

number of arguments and maxims as the ones mentioned before. For example: 'a lover of wisdom runs; therefore a philosopher runs'. The Topic here ? From Nominal Interpretation. The Maxim: anything predicated of an interpretation is predicated of the thing interpreted.

So too on the side of a predicate. The Maxim:

anything an interpretation is predicated of, the thing interpreted is as well.

Negatively: 'a lover of wisdom is not envious; therefore a philosopher is not envious'. The Maxim:

anything removed from an interpretation is removed from the thing interpreted.

Similarly in a Predicate. The Maxim:

from whatever an interpretation is removed, the thing interpreted is as well.

On the Topic from Concomitants of Substance

10 Now about the Topic from Concomitants of Substance: that is when an argument is taken from what follow upon terms posited in a question. It divides into Topics from Whole, Part, Cause, Generation, Corruption, Uses and from the Commonly Occurring.

On the Topic from Whole

11 The Topic from Whole divides like a whole. That can be the sort of whole that is universal or integral, in quantity or in mode, in place or in time. The Topic from Whole is divided like that, since a universal whole is other than an integral whole, and so for the others.

On the Topic from Universal Whole or Genus

12 A Universal Whole, as taken here, is something superior and substantial. A Subjective Part is something that is an inferior under a universal.

The Topic from a Universal Whole or Genus is a relation between a universal whole or genus itself and its part or its species. It is always destructive. For example: 'a stone is not an animal; therefore a stone is not an animal'. The Topic here ? From Genus. The Maxim:

whenever Genus or Universal Whole is removed, Species or a Subjective Part is removed as well.

On the Topic from Species or Subjective Part

13 The Topic from Species or Subjective Part is a relation between a thing itself and its genus or whole. It is always constructive. It contains two Arguments. First, by making species subject, for example: 'a man runs; therefore an animal runs'. The Topic here ? From Species or Subjective Part. The Maxim:

anything predicated of Species is predicated of Genus as well.

Second, by making species predicate, as follows: 'Socrates is a man; therefore Socrates is an animal'. The Topic here ? From Species. The Maxim:

anything a Species is predicated of, its Genus is as well.

On the Topic from an Integral Whole

14 An Integral Whole is what is composed of parts having quantity and a part of it is called integral. The Topic from Integral Whole is a relation between a thing itself and its part. It is always constructive, for example: 'there is a house; therefore there is a wall'. The Topic here ? From an Integral Whole. The Maxim:

given an Integral Whole, any part of it is given as well.

The Topic from Integral Part is a relation between a thing itself and its whole. It is always destructive. For example: 'there is no wall; therefore there is no house'. The Topic here ? From an Integral Part. The Maxim:

given rejection of an Integral Part,
its Whole is rejected as well.

On the Topic from a Whole in Quantity

15 A Whole in Quantity is a universal taken universally, for
example: 'every man', 'no man'. The Topic from Whole in Quantity
is a relation betweem a thing itself to its part. It is both constructive and destructive. For example: 'every man runs; therefore
Socrates runs'. The Topic here ? From a Whole in Quantity. The
Maxim:

anything predicated of a Whole in Quantity is predicated of any Part of it.
or:
if the universal is true, any singular
of it at all will be true as well.

Destructively: 'no man is running; therefore Socrates is not
running'. The Topic here ? From a WHole in Quantity. The Maxim:

anything removed from a Whole in Quantity is removed from any Part of it.
or:
if the universal is true, any singular
of it will be true as well.

The Topic from a Part in Quantity is a relation of parts in
quantity all taken together in relation to their whole. It is both constructive and destructive. For example: 'Socrates runs, Plato runs,
(and so on for individuals); therefore every man runs'. The Topic
here ? From Part in Quantity. The Maxim:

anything predicated of all Parts in
Quantity taken together is predicated
of its Whole as well.
or:
if any singular at all is true,
its universal is true as well.

Negatively: 'Socrates is not running, Plato is not running, (and so on
for individuals), therefore no man is running'. The Topic here ?
From Parts in Quantity. The Maxim:

anything removed from all Parts in
Quantity taken together is removed
from its Whole as well.
or:

   if any singular at all is true,
   its universal is true as well.

On the Topic from a Whole in Mode

16 A Whole in Mode is a universal itself taken without determination. Because all arguments and maxims are formed in this whole and in its part in exactly the same way as in genus and species, examples are omitted.

On the Topic from a Whole in Place

17 A Whole in Place is a word (<u>dictio</u>) embracing every place adverbially, like **'everwhere'**. A Part in Place is a word embracing one place adverbially, like **'here'**. The Topic from a Whole in Place is a relation between a thing itself and its part. It is both destructive and constructive. For example: **'God is everywhere; therefore God is here'**; **'Caesar is nowhere; therefore Caesar is not here'**. The Topic here ? From a Whole in Place. The Maxim:

whatever suits a Whole in Place, suits
its Part as well.
or:
anything removed from a Whole in Place
is removed from any Part of it as well.

   The Topic from a Part in Place is a relation between a thing itself and its whole, for example: **'Caesar is not here; therefore Caesar is not everywhere'**. The Topic here ? From Part in Place. The Maxim:

to whatever a Part in Place is unsuited,
its Whole is unsuited as well.

On the Topic from a Whole in Time

18 A Temporal Totality is a word (<u>dictio</u>) embracing every time adverbially, for example: **'always'** and **'never'**. A Temporal Partial is a word signifying a bit of time adverbially like **'now'**, **'then'**, **yesterday**, **today** and **tomorrow**. Examples of this should be taken just as in a Whole in Place.

On the Topic from Cause

19 A Cause is that upon whose being something else naturally follows.   It divides into Efficient, Material, Formal and Final Cause.   Efficient Cause is that from which a beginning of change (<u>principium</u> <u>motus</u>) comes, as a house-builder is the principle changing and working so that a house comes into existence, and the smith, that there be a knife.

The Topic from Efficient Cause is a relationship between a thing itself and its effect. It is destructive and constructive. For example: **'the builder is good; therefore the house is good';** or: **'the smith is good; therefore the knife is good'.** The Topic here ? From Efficient Cause. The Maxim:

> that is good whose efficient cause
> is itself good as well;

or:

> given an efficient cause, its effect
> is immediately given as well.

The Topic from Effect of Efficient Cause is the converse of this.

20 Matter is that from which one thing is made along with another. There are two sorts of matter: permanent, like iron in a knife, and transient, like flour and water in bread, or straw and fern in a field. Matter is defined as: Matter is what is in potency only.

The Topic from Material Cause is a relation between a thing itself and its effect.   It is both constructive and destructive. Constructive, for example: **'there is iron'**, or **'flour'; therefore there can be iron weapons',** or **'bread'.** The Topic here ? From Material Cause. The Maxim:

> given a material cause, it is possible
> for a materialized thing to be given.

It is destructive in permanent matter as follows: **'there is no iron; therefore there are no iron weapons'.** The Topic here ? From a Material Cause. The Maxim:

> if a permanent material cause is re-
> moved, its effect is removed.

From its Effect (constructively) as follows: **'there are iron weapons;**

therefore there is iron'. The Topic here ? From the Effect of a Material Cause. The Maxim:

given effect of a permanent material cause, permanent matter is itself given.

From the Effect of transient matter: **'there is a field,** or **bread; therefore there was fern,** or **flour'.** Transient Matter is not stable but is completely changed into another nature. The Maxim:

given effect of transient Matter, it must be that transient matter itself pre-existed.

21 Form is what gives being to a thing and keeps it in being. The Topic from Formal Cause is a relation between a thing itself and its effect. Constructively as follows: **'there is whiteness; therefore there is something white'.** The Topic here ? From Formal Cause. The Maxim:

given formal cause, its effect is given as well.

Destructively: **'there is no whiteness; therefore there is nothing white'.** The Topic here ? From Formal Cause. The Maxim:

if a formal cause is removed, its effect is removed as well.

The Topic from its Effect will be the converse.

22 Final Cause or Purpose (finis) is that for the sake of which something is done. The Topic from Final Cause is a relation between a thing itself and its effect. As in **'beatitude is good; therefore virtue is good'.** The Topic here ? From Final Cause. The Maxim:

if its purpose is good, a thing itself is good as well.

Or: **'suffering is evil; therefore sin is evil'.** The Topic here ? From Purpose. The Maxim:

if its purpose is evil, a thing is itself evil as well.

The Topic from Effect of Final Cause is the converse.

On the Topic from Generation

23 Generation is a progression from non-being into being. The Topic from Generation is a relation between itself and what is generated. For example: **'development of a home is good; therefore a home is good'**. The Topic here ? From Generation. The Maxim:

anything whose generation is good, is itself good as well.

and:

anything whose generation is evil, is itself evil as well.

The Topic from thing generated will be the converse. The Maxims are these:

if a thing that is generated is good, its generation is good as well.

and

if a thing that is generated is evil, its generation is evil as well.

On the Topic from Corruption

24 Corruption is progression from being into non-being. The Topic from Corruption is a relation of corruption to the thing corrupted. For example: **'corruption of the home is bad; therefore the home is good'**; or **'corruption of the Antichrist is good; therefore the Antichrist is evil'**. The Topic here ? From Corruption. The Maxim:

if a thing's corruption is evil, it is itself good;

and

if a thing's corruption is good, it is itself evil.

The Topic from Thing Corrupted will be the converse.

On the Topic from Uses

25 Use, as understood here, is the operation or employment of a thing, like cutting with axes or riding a horse. The Topic from

Uses is a relation of an operation to what its working or employment is. For example: 'horseback riding or splitting is good; therefore a horse is good or using axes is good'. Whence the Topic ? From Uses. The Maxim:

if a thing's use is good, it is itself good as well.

Or: 'killing is evil; therefore a killer is evil'. The Topic here ? From Uses. The Maxim:

if its use is evil, it's evil itself as well.

On the Topic from Things Commonly Co-occurring

26 **'Things Commonly Cooccurring'** is taken in two ways. There are things which sometimes do or do not cooccur, for example, being **suave** and an **adulterer**. Only a sophistic Topic, not a dialectic one is taken from them. There are others where one thing always follows the other, as **regret** follows upon **failure**. From these a dialectical Topic is taken. For example: **'he has regrets; therefore he has failed'**. The Topic here ? From Things Commonly Cooccurring. The Maxim:

if the second of things commonly co-occurring is there, so is the first.

Destructively: **'he has not failed; therefore he has no regrets'**. The Topic here ? From Things Commonly Occurring. The Maxim:

if the first of things commonly co-occurring is not there, neither is the second.

ON EXTRINSIC TOPICS

27 What an Extrinsic Topic is was already mentioned. Among Extrinsic Topics are ones from Opposites, from Greater, from Less, from Likeness, from Proportion, from Transfer, and Authority.

On the Topic from Opposites

Again: There are four kinds of Opposition: Relative Opposition, Contrariety, Privative Opposition and Contradiction. Things that are just not found without each other are relatively opposed, like father and son. Contrariety is the opposition between Contraries like white and black. Privatively oppposed are those having to do with the same thing, like sight and blindness for the eye. Contradiction is an oppposition in which, as such, there is no middle ground: there is nothing intermediate between being and not-being.

On the Topic from Things Relatively Opposed

28 The Topic from Things Relatively Opposed is the relation of one correlative to another. It is both constructive and destructive. For example: **'there is a father; therefore there is a son'**, and conversely; **'there is no father; therefore there is no son'** and the converse. The Topic here ? From Things Relatively Opposed. The Maxim:

given one correlative, the other is given as well.

and

when one correlative is rejected, the other is rejected as well.

On the Topic from Contraries

29 Some Contraries are mediate, like black and white, between which there are intermediate colors; others are immediate, like healthy or ill for an animal. The Topic from Contraries is a relation between one contrary and another. Constructively, we have: **'an animal is well; therefore it is not sick'**, or **'this body is white; therefore it is not black'**. The Topic here ? From Contraries. The Maxim:

if we posit one contrary, that excludes the other.

It holds destructively for immediate contraries only for as long as its subject is stable, as in **'this animal is not well; therefore it is ill'**. The Topic here ? From Immediate Contraries. The Maxim:

if one immediate contrary is eccluded, we must posit the other if its subject persists.

On the Topic from Privative Opposites

30 What Privatively Opposed Things are was discussed above.[4] The Topic from Privative Opposites is a relation between

Privation and Habit or between Habit and Privation. For example:
'he is sighted; therefore he is not blind'; or 'he is blind; therefore
he is not sighted'. The Topic here ? From Privative Opposites. The
Maxim:

> given one of opposed privations, the
> other is removed from the same thing.

This does not hold destructively without stability in a subject and a
time span naturally set. Calves are neither called blind nor sighted
before the ninth day, nor children toothed or toothless before a set
time.

On the Topic from Things
Contradictorily Opposed

31 The Topic from Contradictory Opposites is a relation of
one thing contradictorily opposed to another, for example: 'that
Socrates is sitting is true; therefore that he is not sitting is false'.
The Topic here ?   From Things Contradictorily Opposed.   The
Maxim:

> if one contradictory opposite is true
> the other is false, and the converse.

On the Topic from the Greater and
on the Topic from the Lesser

32 Greater as taken here is what surpasses another in power
and ability, Lesser as what is surpassed by it. The Topic from the
Greater is a relation between more and less. It is always destructive. For example: 'a king cannot take the camp; therefore neither
can a soldier'. The Topic here ? From the Greater. The Maxim:

> if what seems to be greater is not so,
> neither is what seems to be less.

The Topic from the Lesser is a relation between less and more. It is
constructive. For example: 'a soldier can take the camp; therefore
a king can too'. The Topic here ? From the Lesser. The Maxim:

> if what seems to be lesser is so,
> then so is what seems to be greater.

4:   Above, p. 63; cf. p. 32.

On the Topic from Like

33 The Topic from Like is a relation between one like thing and the other. As in **'as risibility is in a man, whinnibility is in a horse; but risibility is a Peculiarity of man; therefore whinnibility is a Peculiarity of a horse'.** The Topic here ? From Like. The Maxim:

like is judged by like.

Destructively: **'the way risibility is in a man, whinnibility is in a horse; but risibility is not peculiar to a man as a genus; therefore neither is whinnibility in a horse as a genus'.** The Topic here ? From Like. The Maxim:

if one of likes is present, the other is present as well.

or:

if one of likes is absent, the other is absent as well.

On the Topic from Proportion

34 The Topic from Proportion is a relation between one proportional and the others. For example **'a ship's pilot (<u>rector</u>) is to a ship as an academic rector is to schools; but for sailing ships a pilot is chosen for skill, not by lot; therefore for running schools, a rector should be chosen for skill, not by lot'.** The Topic here ?
From Proportion. The Maxim:

Proportionals are judged proportionally.

This Topic differs from the Topic from Like, because in the latter, comparison is based on an inherent likeness, as in **'as risibility is in a man, whinnibility is in a horse'**; but in the Topic from Proportion, a comparable relation rather than inherent likeness is attended to, for example: **'a sailor is to his ship, as a teacher is to his classes'.**

On the Topic from Transfer

35 There are two sorts of Metaphor or Transfer. One where a name or word-group signifying one thing is transferred to signify something else through a likeness, as **laugh** is transferred to **bloom** when we say **'a meadow laughs'.** A word-group is transferred when we say **'you are ploughing sand'** for **'you are wasting your labor'** of somebody who works in vain. That sort of transfer pertains to sophistics, not dialectics.

Another sort of transfer is when a better known expression (<u>nomen</u>) is taken for one less well known. As in proving a philosopher does not envy others, a transfer be made to **'a wise man does not envy others'**. This sort pertains to dialectics.

The Topic from Transfer is a relation between one transferred thing and something else, for example: **'a wise man does not envy others; therefore a philosopher does not envy others'**. The Topic here ? From Transference. The Maxim:

what suits something under a familiar name suits it under a less familiar one as well.

This Topic differs from that of Nominal Interpretation, because in the latter, one accepts a word's (<u>nomen</u>) definition or description or exposition, as **'philosopher'** is expounded by what I say in **'lover of wisdom'**; but in the Topic from Transference, no exposition of a word is sought: for a less familiar word, a better known one is taken, or something else by which the proposal is easily proven.

On the Topic from Authority

36 Authority, as taken here, is the judgement of an expert in his field.   So this Topic is commonly called the Topic from Judgement of Fact.

The Topic from Authority is a relation betweem authority and what is proven by it, as in **'astronomers say the heavens are changeable; therefore the heavens are changeable'**. The Topic here ? From Authority. The Maxim:

all experts are trustworthy in their own field.

ON MEDIATE TOPICS

37 Now about Mediate Topics. It has already been said what a Mediate Topic is.[5]   One is from Conjugates, another from Case-forms, a third from Division. Conjugates and case-forms differ because a univocal / an abstract / a base (<u>principale</u>) form (which are the same thing) is said to be conjugate with its denominative,

5: Above, p. 52.

like 'justice' and 'just' (justitia et justum). Those deriving from a base form are called case-forms, like just and justly [justum et juste]. This difference is assigned by Aristotle in Second Topics".[6]

On the Topic from Conjugates

38 The Topic from Conjugates is a relation between one conjugate and another, for example: **'justice is good; therefore something just is something good'.** The Topic here ? From Conjugates. The Maxim:

what inheres in one conjugate is in the other as well.

or

if one conjugate is inherent, the other is as well.

On the Topic from Derivates (casibus)

39 The Topic from Derivates (case-forms) is a relation between one derivate and another. For example **'what is just, is good; therefore what is justly done, is well done'**, and the converse. The Topic here ? From Derivates. The Maxim:

what suits one derivate suits the other as well.

On the Topic from Division

40 One sort of Division is by negation, For example **'Socrates is either a man or he is not a man; but he is not a non-man, therefore he is a man'.** The Topic here ? From Division. The Maxim:

if a pair equally divide something, given one, the other is removed.

or:

if one is removed, the other is given.

A second kind of Division is not by Negation. This come about in six ways: three as such (per se) and three by accident. First, a division of genus into species, for example: **'some animals are rational, some irrational'.** Second, a division of a whole into its

6: Topica II 9, 114a 27-34.

integral parts, For example **'one part of a house is a wall, another the roof, another the foundation'.** Third, a division of an expression into its Significations, for example: **'dog means the barker, or a fish, or a celestial body'.** Of the three accidental divisions, the first is that of a Subject into its Accidents, for example: **'some animals are well, some are sick'.** Second, a division of an accident into its Subjects, for example: **'one healthy thing is a man, another is a brute animal'.** Third, a division of an accident into accidents, for example: **'one healthy thing is hot, another is cold'.**

The Topic from Division is a relation between one exclusive term and another, for example: **'if Socrates is an animal, he is either rational or irrational; but he is not irrational; therefore he is rational'.** The Topic here ? From Division. The Maxim is the one mentioned above.

In any other sort of Division, an Argument may be formed constructively or destructively in similar fashion.

TRACT VI

ON SUPPOSITIONS

1 Some things are said with construction and some without. **'A man runs'** and **'a white man'** are said with construction; **'man'** is not: by itself **man** is an unconstructed term.

Each unconstructed term signifies either substance, or quality, or quantity, or relation, or action, or passivity, etc.

On Signification

2 The Signification of a term, as taken here, is the conventional representation of a thing by a vocal expression (<u>vox</u>). As a result, since every thing is either a universal or a singular, words (<u>dictiones</u>) not signifying a universal or a particular ought not signify anything. So they will not be terms as **'term'** is taken here, any more than universal and particular markers (<u>signa</u>) are not terms.

One sort of signification is that of a substantive thing and it is effected by a substantival noun like **'man'**. Another is that of an adjectival thing and it is effected by an adjectival noun or a verb, like **white** or **runs**. As a result, signification is not properly substantival or adjectival: something is signified substantively and something adjectivally, since being adjectival or substantive are modes of things that are signified, not modes of signification.

While substantive nouns are said to stand for (<u>supponere</u>), adjectivals as well as verbs are said to couple (<u>copulare</u>).

On Supposition and Copulation

3 Supposition is the acceptance of a substantival term for something. Signification and supposition differ because signification is through the imposition of a vocal expression upon a thing to be signified, while supposition is the acceptance of a term itself, already signifying a thing for someone, as in **'a man runs'**, where

the term 'man' stands for Socrates, or Plato, and so on. As a result, signification is prior to supposition. Nor do signification and supposition have to do with the same things, because 'signify' has to do with a vocal expression, while 'stand for' has to do with a term already composed, as it were, of a vocal expression and a signification. Therefore Supposition is not Signification.

Copulation is acceptance of an adjectival term for something.

On the Division of Supposition

4 Supposition is either common or discrete. Common supposition is what is effected by a common term, like 'man'. Discrete supposition is what is effected by a discrete term, like 'Socrates' or 'this man'.

Again: Common suppositions are either natural or accidental. Natural supposition is acceptance of a common term for everything it is naturally apt to take part in: 'man' taken as such, naturally stands for all men who were, are, and will be. But accidental supposition is acceptance of a common term for those things for which it demands something added. In 'man exists', the term **man** stands for present men; in 'man existed', for past men, and in 'man will be' for future men. So 'man' has diverse suppositions depending on the diversity of what are added to it.

5 Accidental suppositions are either simple or personal. Simple supposition is acceptance of a common term for a universal thing signified by it. In 'man is species' or 'animal is genus', the term 'man' stands for man-in-general and not for one of its inferiors, and the term 'animal' stands for animal-in-general and not for one of its inferiors. So too for any other common term, as in 'risible is a peculiarity', 'rational is a difference', 'white is an accident'.

6 Again: Simple suppositions include that of a common subject term, as in 'man is a species' or that of a common term put in an affirmative predicate, as in 'every man is an animal'. The predicate term 'animal' has simple supposition, since it only stands for the nature of a genus. Or that of a common term put after an exceptive word (dictionem), as in 'every animal except man is irrational'. Here the predicate term 'man' has simple supposition. So this does not follow: 'every animal except man is irrational; therefore every animal except this man'; it is a Fallacy of Word Figure, shifting from simple to personal supposition. So is 'man is a species; therefore some man is a species'; and 'every man is an

animal; therefore every man is this animal'. In all these a shift from simple to personal supposition is made.

That a common predicate term is to be taken simply, is clear in 'study about all contraries is the same study'. If the term study did not have simple supposition, it would be false, since no particular study is about all contraries. Medicine is not about all contraries, only about the sick and well, and grammar is about the congruous and incongruous, and so for the others.

7 Personal supposition is acceptance of a common term for its inferiors. In 'a man runs', the term 'man' stands for its inferiors.

8 Again: Personal suppositions are either determinate or diffuse (confusa). Determinate supposition labels what a common term has when taken indefinitely or with a particular marker, as in 'man runs' or 'some man runs'. Each of these is called determinate, since though in each, the term 'man' stands for every man running or not, they are true only if one man is running. To stand for is one thing, to make a locution true for something another. In the examples above, as said, the term 'man' stands for every man, running or not, but it makes the utterance true for one man running. That each is determinate is clear, because in 'Socrates is an animal, Plato is an animal, Cicero is an animal', etc.; therefore every man is an animal', there is a Fallacy of Word Figure, shifting from many determinates to a single one. That way a common term, taken indefinitely, has determinate supposition; so too does one with a particular marker.

9 Diffuse supposition is the acceptance of a common term for several things by means of a universal marker. In 'every man is an animal', the term 'man', by means of the universal marker, is taken for several, since for any one at all, of its supposits.

Again: Diffuse supposition is either diffuse by demand of marker or mood or else by demand of fact. In 'every man is an animal' by marker demand, the term man is diffused or distributed for any of its supposits. Since each man has his own essence, the verb 'is' is taken by factual demand for as many essences as 'man' is for men. Since his own animality is within each man, 'animal' is taken by factual demand for as many animals as 'man' is for men, and for as many essences as the verb 'is'. That is why the term 'man' is said to stand for things diffusely, mobilely, and distributively. It 'stands for' diffusely and distributively, since taken for every man; mobilely, since descent can be made from it to any supposit, like **'every man; therefore Socrates'** or **'every man; therefore Plato'.** The term **'animal'** is said to be diffused immobilely, since descent below it is not allowed, as in **'every man is an animal; therefore every man is this animal'.** There supposition shifts from simple to personal. So too in **'man is the most noble of creatures; therefore a particular man';** and **'roses are the most beautiful of flowers; therefore a particular rose'.** These differ in that the latter has simple supposition in the subject, the former in the predicate.

Doubts

10 It would not seem to be contrary to have said that in **'every man is an animal',** the predicate term **'animal'** has simple supposition, though it was earlier said it has diffuse supposition. As genus is predicated there of species, the term **'animal'** is taken for the common thing genus itself and so has simple supposition. But as the common nature of genus itself is multiplied through supposits of man, it is said to have diffuse supposition, not mobilely, but immobilely. Mobilely diffuse supposition cannot coexist with simple supposition, neither as to the same thing nor as to different things. But diffuse supposition immobilely can coexist with simple supposition, not as to the same thing, but as to diverse ones, as was said.

This way the contrariety perceived by those holding a predicate term would have simple supposition, and would be diffused immobilely when there is a universal affirmative subject marker (as in **'every man is an animal'**), should disappear.

11 I believe it to be impossible that a common predicate term is diffused immobilely or mobilely when there is an affirmative universal marker in the subject, as in **'every man is an animal'** and others like it[1]. As Porphyry has it, everything predicated of another is either greater than or equal to it. He means this of predication as such. In **'every man is an animal',** there is predication as such and an equal is not predicated; therefore something greater is predicated; not an accidental; therefore a substantial or essential; therefore genus or difference; not difference; therefore genus. But the nature of genus, multiplied mobilely or immobilely, is no longer genus. Therefore, in **'every man is an animal',** since genus is predicated there, it is impossible that a common term signifying the

---

1: <u>Isag.</u> p 7.4-6, Boethius' translation, p. 13.5-7.

nature of a genus be multiplied immobilely or mobilely; for it would not even be a genus, just as, if man is diffused mobilely or immobilely, it will not be species.

Again: The same seems to be Aristotle's view in First Topics[2]. He says it is necessary that everything predicated of another be either predicated conversely or not; if conversely, it is a definition or peculiarity; if not conversely, it either falls within the thing's definition or it does not; if within the definition, it is genus or difference.   Aristotle there intends this to be predication in the nominative case with species as subject, as such, or as multiplied. But in **'every man is an animal'**, there is predication in the nominative and neither equal nor accident is predicated; therefore genus or difference is; not difference; therefore genus. So this comes back to the same thing as before: for which reason it is not possible that a common predicate term be diffused mobilely or immobilely.

Again: Universal whole which is genus and whole in quantity are opposed.   But whole in quantity is ambiguous: one whole is complete, as wherever a common term is diffused mobilely;   the other is incomplete or diminished, as wherever a common term is diffused immobilely. For that reason if a common term is multiplied simply, a whole in quantity results simply; if multiplied somehow or other, a whole in quantity results somehow or other. Therefore if it is impossible for a whole in quantity to be genus precisely as genus, it is not possible that a common predicate term be diffused, as they were saying.

Again: The pairing (comparatio) by which inferiors reduce to their superior is opposed to that by which a superior reduces to its inferiors. By the first, **'common'** is taken as formally common. That way common itself contains all beneath it.   By the second, it is taken as **'multiplied'** or **'diffused'**, whether the common term is multiplied for all or for some inferiors. If therefore genus stands as such as formally common, it is impossible that it be multiplied precisely as such.

We concede all these points.

2: I 8, 103b 7-17.

Solution

12 The argument that convinced them is readily solved. They say that in **'every man is an animal'**, since each and every man is matched with his own essence and animality (it being impossible to be a man without being an animal) - therefore the term **'animal'** will be taken for as many animals as **'man'** is for men. We say this argument lacks all plausibility. When I say **'every man is white'**, or **'every man is black'** (it being impossible to be a man without being an animal), it is necessary that as many animals or animalities be understood in the subject as there are men for whom the term **'man'** is taken.

Yet it is fatuous to say that the multitude of those animalities comes from multiplication by a predicate, when **'white'** or **'black'** is predicated. So I say that since man is constituted (logically, not naturally speaking) of **'rational'** and **'animal'**, that is why **'man'** of itself contains **'animal'**. So when **'man'** is multiplied, it has in itself a multitude of those animalities. As when I say **'every man is white'**, or **'every man is black'**, man no way has these animalities from a predicate.

So too in the proposal when genus is predicated, as in **'every man is an animal'**. In this proposition, **'man'** is subject, in which a multitude of those animalities is understood, as was said, and the genus **'animal'**, is predicated, which is in no way diffused, mobilely nor immobilely, but stands there for the common generic essence itself, predicable of several. So **'animal'** is predicated and **'animal'** is understood in the subject, as in: **'every rational, mortal animal is an animal'**.

So I say in like manner that the verb **'is'** is neither diffused mobilely nor immobilely, because the fact that animal would be or exist in man, is something the subject had of itself before it was a subject of an actual or potential predicate in a proposition.

For this reason we abolish a certain previous division, namely: **diffused suppositions are either by demand of marker or mood, or else by demand of fact.** We say all diffusion is due to a demand of mood. In **'every rational mortal animal is an animal'** the term **'animal'** is taken for every animal which is man because of the marker. So too in **'every man is an animal'**: the term **'man'** is taken, not only for every man, but for every animal that is a man. It is for that reason there are as many animalities as humanities, from a natural point of view, (for humanity is identical in a logical, not a natural approach, in any individual of man); just as man-in-general is identical. That it be this or that animality is due to matter. In the course of nature, my humanity is autonomous and other than your humanity, just as my soul, through which my humanity is in me, is different from your soul, through which humanity is caused in you. And because of this marker or mood, diffusing 'man' does not diffuse 'animal', but 'animal' as contracted to 'man' through its differences.

So every diffusion is by demand of marker or mood.

TRACT VII

ON FALLACIES

INTRODUCTION

On the Definition of Disputation

1 Disputation is the activity of one person syllogizing with another as to a proposal to be demonstrated. Five things are required for a disputation: its originator, called the opponent, one with whom to dispute, called the respondent, the disputed proposal, the activity of disputing and its instrument. All five are suggested in the description of **'disputation'** just given. By the meaning of **'activity'**, the action of disputing itself is touched on. The difference **'syllogizing'** suggests that activity arises from a syllogism as the tool of disputation. By the difference **'of one'** is understood the originator of actual disputing, and by the difference **'with another'**, the person with whom one disputes. By **'as to a proposal'** is understood disputed facts, the object of the disputation.

2 To the five things singled out in this description a sixth can be added by the difference **'to be demonstrated'**. That blends the activity of disputing with its object, a union one can understand by pairing that activity with its disputed object, just as in equating the activity of **seeing** with its object, **something visible,** we grasp the union of **seeing** with **something visible** as something that is not just what can be seen, but actually is. So when the activity of disputing is unified with its object, we have not just something that can be, but actually is, disputed or delimited.

3 If one objects that since induction is the tool for disputation, a syllogism is not unique to it, there being only one tool for a given thing, - say tools for an act are of two sorts, one perfect, the other imperfect. Just as in grammar, where a simple congruous sentence is the finished tool for speaking and a figurative one incomplete, the syllogism is the perfect and complete tool for disputation, while induction is an imperfect one, as is an enthymeme or example. So

while there is one complete tool for an act, not a number of them, the incomplete ones falling short of perfection can be several.

On the Division of Disputation

4 There are four kinds of disputation: didactic, dialectical, tentative (examination-arguments) and sophistical (contentious).

5 Didactic (doctrinalis) disputation comes to its conclusion from principles peculiar to each discipline and not just from what seem true to a respondent. The tool for this type of disputation is a demonstrative syllogism. That involves reasoning from true and basic premises or from such premises as derive their principle of knowledge from them. Opposed to that is another, called a pseudo-argument, and it is taken from the same principles, but falsely.

6 Dialectical disputation is what collects contradictions from probable premises. Its tool is the dialectical syllogism, one that comes to a conclusion from probable premises.

7 Tentative disputation argues from what seem true to the respondent and anyone pretending to have knowledge must know. Its tool is a tentative syllogism, one coming to a conclusion from things that seem probable to the respondent. So if sometimes what he argues from are necessary, or false, or simply probable, this is not because they actually are that way, but because they seem probable to the respondent. Aristotle treats that at the beginning of the Topics[1], when he divides a tentative syllogism into three parts, of which he later says: 'so the first mentioned is the tentative (litigiosus) syllogism and it should be called a syllogism'.[2]

8 This shows why a question some put is invalid: since Aristotle deals in the beginning of the Elenchi[3] with tentative disputation when delimiting species of disputation, why, they ask, does he not delimit the tentative syllogism there, though he deals with other species of syllogism ? The tentative syllogism is one objectors often call materially faulty. But it is not because dialectical syllogisms start from false premises that they are materially defective (as they say), but because they offend against what counts as probable. A dialectician takes probable simply: something that is simply

1: Topica I 1, 101a 1-2, Boethius' Translation p. 6.8-977.
2: Topica I,1, 101a 1-2, transl. Boeth. p.6.
3: Sophistici Elenchi 2, 165b 4-7.

probable is what seems true to all, or most, or experts, and to these as the majority, or all, or best known. A tentative syllogism does not take probable that way, but only as what is probable to the respondent, therefore as probable after-a-fashion (secundum quid). So it offends against what counts as probable.

9 Sophistical disputation syllogizes from what seem probable but are not. Its disputation-tool is the sophistical syllogism, one that seems to be, but really is not, a syllogism, the one of which the Elenchi[4] says that one sort is litigious, which is a syllogism, though seemingly unsuited to the facts. That is a tentative syllogism, which we have just discussed.

10 Notice that 'disputation' is said proportionally or analogically of these four, as is the description of disputation given above. That is why Aristotle does not define, but divides, disputation in the Elenchi[5]. A definition is of something said univocally, not analogically. Yet a description of what is said analogically can be validly given, which may be said analogically just like the thing described by it.

11 If asked which of the four disputations mentioned is called 'disputation' as prime analogate and secondary analogates, say that if differences put in the above description are inspected, it is easy to see. Taking 'disputation' from the perspective of the difference 'of one with another', (since we understand opposing disputants by it, there being a greater opposition between a sophistical opponent and a respondent), 'disputation' taken that way is said primarily of sophistical, then of tentative (where there is still opposition but not as great), then of dialectical (where opposition is less), and lastly of didactic disputation (since that does not question but assumes what it demonstrates). All the others question it. Taking 'disputation' from the persepctive of syllogistic activity, everything reverses: didactic disputation is the prime analogate and its secondary analogates are dialectical, then tentative, and lastly sophistical. So too if we take 'disputation' from the perspective of its object (the proposal to be demonstrated), because the didactic more truly demonstrates and tests, the dialectical less than didactic, the tentative less than dialectical, and the sophistical less than the others.

12 Again: Didactic disputation is either mathematical or scientific (naturalis) and each of these has several species. The demonstrative syllogism is divided similarly.

4:   Soph. El. 11, 171b 16-21.
5:   Soph. El. 2, 165a 38-b8.

Again: There are three basic species of dialectical disputation. One is for distinctions (obviationes) called discriminative; another for practice, called exercitative disputation; the third for disciplines discussed according to a philosophy. Similarly, there are three kinds of dialectical syllogism. The third of these has four kinds. The first is to establish or refute an accident, the second a genus, the third a peculiarity, and the fourth a definition. Similarly, taken that third way, there are four kinds of dialectical syllogism.

Again: There are two basic kinds of tentative disputation. The first argues from commonalities to commonalities, as one argues provisionally in dialectics or sophistics. The other is from commons to peculiars, as one who argues hypothetically in special disciplines like geometry, arithmetic or medicine. Similarly, there are two basic kinds of tentative syllogism; one from commons to commons, the other from commons to peculiariarities.

On Sophistical Disputation and its Ends

13 There are five kinds of Sophistical disputation. They derive from the ordering of sophistical disputation to five goals or special ends: Refutation, Falsity, Paradox, Solecism, and Trivialization.

14 Refutation is denial of what was conceded, or concession of what was denied in the same disputation by the force of argumentation.

15 'Falsity' is said two ways, one a sort of contradictory falsity like 'Socrates is running and not running', the other, propositional, like 'an Ethiopian is white'. The first is the clearest of all falsities and pertains to refutation. The second pertains to the goal of falsity when it is obvious. So Falsity as a goal is manifest propositional falsity demonstrated by disputation. For even if a sophistical opponent leads a sophistical respondent to a covert falsity - as that the earth is larger than the least of visible stars - he does not thereby attain his goal, since the falsity of this proposition is not manifest but covert. Or if he willingly concedes a proposition manifestly false, and is not forced to do so by some truly or apparently inferring middle term, the opponent still does not attain his goal.

16 Paradox (inopinabile) is what is contrary to the opinion of all, or of most, or of experts, and of these as of all, or of the majority, or of the best known. So Paradox and the Improbable are

substantially the same but differ formally since the Improbable is so-called with respect to overtly opposed concepts. Paradox is so-called because the mind is unwilling to take it in or agree to it, but rejects it and disagrees.

17 Solecism is a fault made in putting parts of a word-group (partes orationis) together contrary to rules of the art of grammar, like 'whites man' or 'men runs'.[6]

18 Trivialization (nugatio) is useless repetition from the same part of a word-group like 'man man runs' or 'rational man'. I say 'of the same part of a word-group', for if the same thing is posited in different parts, it is not trivializtion, like 'a man is a man' or 'a man is rational'. It is called useless repetition, since if the same thing is repeated for greater expressivity, it is not trivialization, as in 'God, my God'.

19 Therefore sophistical disputation leading to refutation is the first species of sophistical disputation. The second is sophistic disputation leading to Falsity, the third to Paradox, the fourth to Solecism, the fifth to Trivialization. Similarly, there are five species of sophistical syllogism taken in the same way.

20 One must know that species are set up under a genus in two ways. In one, a formal difference added to a genus constitutes a species, as 'rational' and 'mortal' added to 'animal' constitute 'man'. In the other, final differences adjoined to a genus constitute a species under a genus. It is in that second way that species of sophistical disputation are set up. Aristotle notes this in the Elenchi[7], when after dividing disputation simply taken into four species, he adds those five goals by which sophistical disputation is again subdivided into the five species he studies, as was said.

21 Now that disputation has been divided into four species and any of those subdivided into their basic species, and sophistical disputation so divided into the five species mentioned above (which are perfected and constituted by the ordering of sophistical disputation to five goals or ends, as was said) - since those five ends or goals are not the proximate ends of sophistic disputation but species of it, as shown by what was said above, next comes the proximate goal of sophistic disputation, apparent wisdom. Sophists prefer to seem wise and not be, rather than be wise yet not appear to be. So in every sophistical disputation, apparent wisdom is intended as a sort of proximate and principal end of sophistical disputation in itself.

On the thirteen Fallacies

22 Once the end of sophistical disputation is known, fallacies that lead to it must be considered. Ends are always earlier in intention, later in execution: we first think of a house, then lumber, walls, and mortar. In execution it reverses: first come walls and mortar, then lumber to make its parts, and finally there is a house. So too in sophistical disputation: we first think of the principal end, then of what lead to it, but when finally we get to disputing, it reverses. So we must know that just as opinion, the end in dialectic, is acquired through arguments derived from dialectical Topics, similarly, apparent wisdom, sophistical disputations' end, is acquired through arguments taken from sophistical Topics.

23 Sophistical Topics in general are thirteen fallacies, six linguistic (in dictione) and seven extralinguistic (extra dictionem). First we must discuss the linguistic ones.

ON LINGUISTIC FALLACIES

24 Six fallacies are made linguistically (in dictione): Equivocation, Amphiboly, Composition, Division, Accent and Word Figure (figura dictionis). That there are six linguistic ones, Aristotle tries to prove inductively and syllogistically[8]. Inductively: The Fallacy of Equivocation is made in one of these six ways; so too, Amphiboly is made in one of these six ways, and so of the others; therefore every linguistic fallacy is made in one of these six ways. Syllogistically:

> Every deception made because we do not signify the same thing with the same words (nominibus) or word-groups (orationibus) is made in one of these six ways;
>> but every linguistic fallacy is made because we do not signify the same thing with the same words and word-groups;

6: Hispanus' examples: vir alba and homines currit. [fpd]
7: Soph. El. 3, 165b 12ff.
8: Soph. El. 4, 165b 27-30.

therefore every linguistic fallacy is made by one of
those six ways.

The syllogism is in the First Mood, First Figure. Proof of the
major:

All polysemy (multiplicitas dictionis) arises in one of
these six ways;
  but every deception made because we do not
  signify the same thing by the same words and
  word-groups is made from polysemy;
therefore, every deception made because we do not
signify the same thing by the same words and
word-groups is made in one of those six ways.

This was the major. Proof of the minor:

Every linguistic fault (malitia dictionis) arises
because we do not signify the same thing by the same
words and word-groups.
  but every linguistic fallacy is from a linguistic
  fault;
therefore every linguistic fallacy is made because we
do not signify the same thing by the same words and
word-groups.

This was the minor and the two syllogisms are in the First Mood of
the First Figure.

25 It should also be known, as Alexander in his commentary on
Sophistical Refutations has it, that polysemy (multiple ambiguity)
occurs in three ways, one actual, the second potential, the third
imaginary. Actual polysemy occurs when a simply identical word
(dictio) or a simply identical word-group signifies several things, as
will be clear in Equivocation and Amphiboly, where there is actual
polysemy. What concerns potential and imaginary polysemy will be
clear in their proper places. Since the nature of polysemy is more
truly realized in actual than in potential polysemy, and more truly in
potential than in imaginary polysemy, we must therefore first speak
about fallacies producing actual polysemy, then about those in which
it is potential, and finally about the imaginary.

9: Cf. L. Minio-Paluello, Note sull' Aristotele Latino Medievale
    IX, 229-231 [in: Rivista di filosofia neo-scolastica 46 (1954)] and
    L. M. de Rijk, Logica Modernorum I, 100-105.

ON EQUIVOCATION

On the Definition of Fallacy

26 Now we have dealt with these, we must speak of equivocation or the Fallacy of Equivocation. Understand that **'fallacy'** is
ambiguous. One way, fallacy means deception caused in us, in
another, it means the cause or principle of that deception. It is that
second way that we have fallacies in mind here.

27 That is why one should know that in any fallacy taken that
second way, <u>principle</u> is ambiguous and so is <u>cause</u>: motive principle, motive cause or plausible cause (<u>causa</u> <u>apparentiae</u>) consequently all label an identical principle. A different principle / cause
is the principle of defect / cause of non-existence, which is the same
thing, or the cause of falsity. It is the motive principle / plausible
cause in any fallacy that moves one to believe in what is not. The
principle of defect / cause of falsity, is what makes what is believed
in something false.

Since those two principles (or two causes) are in any fallacy, it
is fitting for them to be in Equivocation. The motive principle /
plausible cause in Equivocation is the unity of a word (<u>dictionis</u>)
simply taken. I say **'simply taken'** because of accent; under accent
a word is not simply the same, as will be clear later. The principle
of deficiency / cause of non-existence / falsity in Equivocation is
the diversity of natures and of things signified.

On the Definition of Equivocation

28 So Equivocation is defined as follows: Equivocation is when
things of a different nature are subsumed under the same word
(<u>nomine</u>), taken simply. This definition uses **'thing'** indifferently for
things themselves, with respect to the double mode of things, and
with respect to their relations. An example with respect to things
themselves is the word (<u>nomen</u>) **'dog'**, which signifies an animal that
barks, a marine animal and a celestial body. **'Healthy'** is an example
with respect to the double mode of things, since in one mode the
word (<u>dictio</u>) signifies (the subject), and in another mode consignifies
its accidents. It thus always signifies the same health, that of an
animal, but by different modes. When we say, **'the urine is healthy'**,
its sense is: **'the urine is a sign of healthiness'**, but only that of an
animal. When we say **'food is healthy'**, its sense is: **'food can produce health'**, but only that of an animal, and **'a diet is healthy'**,
because it preserves animal health, and **'a drink is healthy'** because

it prepares for animal health. It is always the same health, but its modes are diverse, since 'healthy' said of an animal signifies health as the health of a subject or health in a subject. When said of urine, as of a sign of health; of food, as of what effects it; of drink, as of what prepares for it. All these modes are different. It is taken for relations of things, as in prepositions that mean different causal relations, as will be clear in paralogisms.

As for the other mode mentioned, the two principles / causes we have cited are insufficient for Equivocation, It is further required that there be in us an inability to tell different nominal natures (<u>rationes</u>) apart. So Equivocation / Fallacy of Equivocation taken this way can be defined: the Fallacy of Equivocation is the deception caused in us by our inability to distinguish diverse natures in the same word (<u>nomine</u>) taken simply.

On the Division of Equivocation

29 The kinds of Equivocation can be taken in two ways, as Aristotle seems to intend[10]: first, in itself, and secondarily, as having something in common with Amphiboly. But in either this or that way, Aristotle indicates only three kinds or modes of Equivocation.[11]

On the First Species

30 The first kind is when the same word (<u>dictio</u>) indifferently signifies diverse things, as the word (<u>nomen</u>) **'dog'** equally signifies something in the sea, in the sky, or the thing that barks. And a paralogism is formed as follows:

> **'every dog is something that can bark**
> **but a certain marine animal is a dog**
> **therefore a certain marine animal is**
> **something that can bark'.**

This does not follow since both premises are polysemous, true in one way, false in two others, since in each there is a triple sense based on the triple signification of the word (<u>nomen</u>) **'dog'**.

Or as follows:

10: <u>Soph. El</u>. 4, 165b 30-166a21.
11: <u>Soph. El</u>. 4, 165b 30-166a6.

'those who are literate, learn
the learned are literate
therefore the literate learn'.[12]

In this paralogism, the major premise and conclusion are ambiguous, since **'learn'** is equivocal as to **'understand a teacher'** and **'retain what a teacher says'**.   Some understand what their teacher says well enough but retain it poorly, while others retain well what he says, but understand it poorly.   Yet both the one and the other are said to learn.   So **'learn'** is equivocated for this pair.

On the Second Species

31   The second kind or second mode of equivocation is when the same word (dictio) signifies different things analogically (secundum prius et posterius) as the word **'expedient'** primarily signifies **'good'** and secondarily **'something necessary that happens in bad things'**.   I am not saying it means something simply necessary, but something necessary that happens in bad things; as when some great evil occurs that can only be avoided through a lesser one, that lesser evil is then called necessary with respect to the greater one.   So it is not simply necessary, but necessary with respect to a greater evil.   For example, amputation of a body part is bad; yet it is necessary lest the entire body become diseased.   A paralogism can be formed as follows:

'every expedient is a good
an evil is an expedient
therefore an evil is a good'.

Each of the premises is ambiguous, as is clear from the foregoing, since although **'expedient'** signifies **something good** and **necessary in evils,** to the extent that it signifies **a good,** the major is true, but false to the extent that **'expedient'** signifies **something necessary in bad things**.   The converse is to be said of the minor.

So too here:

'every healthy thing is an animal
urine is a healthy thing
therefore urine is an animal.'

12:   The original example is 'quicumque sunt grammatici discunt; scientes sunt grammatici; ergo scientes discunt'. [fpd]

Each of the premises is polysemous, as often said.

32 Equivocation from metaphor reduces to this second type.
For example:

'whatever laughs has a mouth
but a meadow laughs
therefore a meadow has a mouth.'

or

'whatever runs, has feet
the Seine runs
therefore the Seine has feet.'

the verbs **'runs'** and **'laughs'** primarily signify **laugh** and **run** and
secondarily **bloom** and **flow,** for the latter signify from proper
imposition and the former from customary use. So in both paralogisms each premise was ambiguous.

33 Every prepositional polysemy is also reduced to this second
species of equivocation. Any preposition entails one relationship
primarily and others secondarily. For example, the prepositional **'on**
the basis of' (secundum) primarily means a relationship of formal
cause and secondarily a relationship of efficient cause. A paralogism like this can be formed:

'it is a peculiarity of quality that something be called
similar or dissimilar on the basis of that quality
but something is said to be similar or dissimilar on the
basis of its similarity or dissimilarity
therefore similarity and dissimilarity are qualities',

which is false, for in fact they are relations. The major has a double
meaning by the ambiguity just discussed. So if the prepositional **'on**
the basis of' (secundum) means efficient cause, it is true (since two
qualities of the same species are an efficient cause of similarity, for
they make their subjects similar to each other). But if it means
formal cause, it is false. A quality is not a formal cause of similarity itself, since its form is similarity, like whiteness is the form of
something white, the warmth of something warm, or the dampness
of something damp). The converse is to be said of the minor.

Similarly, the preposition **'in'** primarily means a spatial relationship and secondarily all others, which are clear depending on the
modes of **being-in** distinguished above. That is why Aristotle,[13]
where he distinguishes those modes, says: 'one thing is simply and
properly said to be-in another as in a place'.

34 Note that the preposition **'in'** does not indifferently signify relations other than a spatial one, but primarily and secondarily, as is clear here:

> **'in whatever illness is found, that is an animal**
> **but illness is found in an imbalance of humors;**
> **therefore an imbalance of humors is an animal'.**

The major is ambiguous. If the preposition **'in'** there means a relationship of material cause as that-in-which, i.e., a relationship of something as subject, it is true. If it means a relationship of efficient cause, it is false. The converse is to be said of the minor, for while an animal is the subject of an illness, imbalance of humors is its efficient cause. That is how **'in'** is taken here according to different relations and it primarily signifies that relationship which is one of an illness itself to its subject. Secondarily, it signifies a relation of an illness to its efficient cause. Just as **'healthy'** or **'sick'** are said primarily of an animal, and secondarily of what effects or keeps it that way, the preposition **'in'** primarily means a relationship of those things to their subjects, secondarily their relationship to what they effect or conserve.

35 If you object that, since a cause is naturally prior to its effect, therefore the preposition **'in'** primarily means a relation of health or illness to an efficient cause, secondarily a relation to its subject (the opposite of what was being said) - one must say that **'primarily'** is said ambiguously. In one way it has to do with causing, and that way a cause is naturally prior to its effect. In another it has to do with the completion and perfection of its species, so we say anything completed and perfected is naturally prior to what is less so. In the latter way, we speak of what is prior in that second kind of Equivocation. Since health is not yet complete in kind when it exists only causally, but is in its complete species in an animal as in its subject, - it is in this way primarily in an animal and secondarily in what causes the animal to be that way (i.e., in its cause), since here it has more of its perfection and kind, less so there. Similarly, the preposition **'in'** first signifies the latter relation, and secondarily the former, as was said.

On the Third Species

36 The third kind of Equivocation is from diverse consignification of a word (<u>dictio</u>). As here:

13:   <u>Physics</u> IV 3, 210a 14-24, especially 210a 24.

**'whoever was being cured, is healthy
    someone suffering a disease was being cured
    therefore someone suffering a disease is healthy'.**

The minor and conclusion are ambiguous, since the participle **'suffering'** consignifies present time as well as imperfect past. So **'suffering'** consignifies **suffering then** as well as **suffering now.** If the minor is taken for **suffering then,** it is false, since one would be both healthy and suffering from a disease at the same time which is false. If taken for **suffering now,** it is true, since one can be suffering now and could have been cured then. The converse is to be said of the conclusion.

So too here:

**'whoever was getting up, is standing
    the one sitting was getting up
    therefore the one sitting is standing';**

the minor and conclusion are ambiguous just as in the preceding paralogism. Thus Aristotle says in the Elenchi:[14] 'for that a sick man is doing something or other or having something or other done to him, has not one meaning only'. That is, if **'suffering'**, or any other present tense participle is adjoined to a verb signifying activity or passivity, they do not signify one thing, as in **'the one suffering runs'** or **'sees'** or **'is weighed down',** the sense is: **the one suffering now runs** or **sees** or **is weighed down,** or **the one suffering earlier.**

On the three species

37 Aristotle assigns these three kinds or modes of Equivocation in the Elenchi,[15] first by giving one paralogism based on equivocation of the verb **'learn',** secondly by another involving the nominal **'expedient',** and thirdly, a pair of them based on the polysemy of the participles **'suffering'** and **'sitting'.** There is another mode distinguishing consignifications of common modes of equivocation and amphiboly as will be clear later.[16]

38 Some assign a different reason for the diversity and order of these equivocation modes. They say that in the first mode an

14: Soph. El. 4, 166a 2-3.
15: Soph. El. 4, 165b 30-166a6.

equivocal word (dictio) is at the major extreme in the major, as shows in the paralogism effected by the equivocation of the verb 'learn'. In the second mode, the equivocal is the middle term and in the minor extreme for the third, as shows in Aristotle's paralogisms. So since the major extreme is prior to the middle because it is the major and the middle is prior to the minor extreme, that is why these modes are so ordered.

But I do not think Aristotle adverted to that, since division of Equivocation according to major, middle, and minor extremes in a paralogism would not be a division of Equivocation in itself, but only a division relative to, or in comparison with, something else. Further: the nature of being a middle, major or minor extreme is accidental to a given word (dictio), for the same one is sometimes at the middle, sometimes at the major extreme, and sometimes at the minor, whether it signifies one thing or many. Therefore the division of equivocation on the basis of its being a major, minor and middle extreme is a disivion of a subject into its accidents. Therefore the division of equivocation would not be into its subjective parts. Besides, it would be division of equivocation on the basis of an accident and not as such. All of which are drawbacks.

39 For that reason the nature of diversity and order, as we have suggested, lies in this, that an equivocation arises in three ways. That a word (dictio) signifies several things derives either from its signification or its consignification, for a word is not so much a sign of many things as a sign of signification or consignification. If it derives from signification, then those things which are signified are either signified on a par by a word or analogically; if on a par, it is the first mode; if analogically, the second; if from consignification, the third. And that way there are three modes. They are ordered this way since the nature of equivocation or definition is better preserved where many things are equally signified than where one is primarily signified and the rest secondarily. In both those modes, it is better preserved than in the third, since each of the others arises from the side of signification, in which diversity of the things signified is expected. The third is from the side of consignification, in which the diversity expected is not of the things signified, but of the modes of being signified.

16: Below, p. 90-91.

ON AMPHIBOLY

On the Definition of Amphiboly

40 'Amphiboly' is used ambiguously. Sometimes it names a principle of deception existing in a word-group that is simply identical. That deceptive principle is composed of a motive principle and a deficiency principle. But sometimes it names the deception caused in us by that principle. It is taken here the first way.

41 The cause of amphiboly's plausibility (apparentia) / motive principle is the simple unity of the same word-group. Its cause of nonexistence / the principle of amphiboly's deficiency is the diversity of the same word-group.

42 Amphiboly is the principle of deception from a word-group that is simply one, yet signifies several things. In this definition, both principles mentioned are touched on. I say **'a word-group simply one'** to put aside composition and division, since in them, there is no word-group that is one simply, but only one after-a-fashion.

43 One should know that just as **'amphiboly'** is said two ways, **'fallacy of amphiboly'** is ambiguous in the same way. **'Fallacy of amphiboly'** sometimes names the principle of deception itself, on the basis of which amphiboly is defined. Sometimes it names the deception caused in us by that principle. This distinction is general for any kind of fallacy.

44 **'Amphiboly'** comes from **'amphi'**, which means a doubt, and **'bole'**, which means a judgement, - or **'logos'**, which means a speech, suggesting **'dubious judgement'** or **'dubious speech'**.

On the first species

45 There are three kinds of Amphiboly. The first derives from the fact that a word-group principally signifies more than one thing, like **'Aristotle's book'.** This is ambiguous, since in one way, **'Aristotle's book'** is the same as **'the book edited (or made) by Aristotle'**, in another, **'(the book) owned by Aristotle'**.

So a paralogism is formed this way:

'whatever is Aristotle's is owned by Aristotle
   this book is Aristotle's
therefore this book is owned by Aristotle'.

Both premisses are doubly interpretable by the ambiguity mentioned.

On the second species

46 The second kind of amphiboly comes from transfer of a word-group. This is when a word-group properly signifying one thing is transferred to signifying another through some sort of likeness, as when **'ploughing sand'** is transferred to **'wasting labor'**.

So a paralogism is formed this way:

> **'whatever is ploughed is broken up
> sand is ploughed
> therefore sand is broken up'.**

The Minor is ambiguous because **'plough sand'** properly signifies **'break up earth'**, but by transfer, **'waste time'**. The likeness lies in the fact that anyone who ploughs sand squanders his labor and works in vain.

On the third species

47 The third kind of Amphiboly comes from the fact that some word-group signifies several things, while each part taken by itself signifies only one, as in **'knowing age'**.[17] This is ambiguous, for it signifies both that someone knows the age and that the age has knowledge of something. This is because **'age'** can be subject to or object of to the verbal **'knowing'**. This is like it: **'that someone sees that he sees'**[18], since the second word (<u>dictio</u>) **'that'** can be subject to or object of the verb **'sees'**. So is this: **'that someone knows that he knows'**[19]; the second word **'that'** can be subject to or object of the verb **'knows'**. And: **'I would like fighter acceptance'**.[20] This can be paraphrased as:

17:   The Latin text has a finite construction: <u>scit saeculum</u> ('the age knows' or 'he knows the age'). [fpd]
18:   'quod quis videt, hoc videt' is not as ambiguous as the English version. [fpd]
19:   'quod quis scit, hoc scit'.
20:   'vellem me accipere pugnantes': Hispanus says the ambiiguity (paraphrased, not translated in English) is in the fact that "the accusative <u>me</u> can be subject or object of <u>accipere</u>". [fpd]

'whoever I want acceptance from, I wish they would
   accept me
I want fighter acceptance of me
   therefore I want fighter acceptance.'

Both premises are doubly interpretable by the ambiguity mentioned.
This is similar:

'quod quis videt, hoc videt   what one sees, sees this
   videt autem columpnam   but he sees a column
ergo columpnam videt'.   therefore one sees a column

The major is ambiguous, as has been said. This is like it:

'quicumque sunt episcopi   whoever are bishops
   sunt homines   are men
isti asini sunt episcopi   those asses are the bishop's
ergo isti asini sunt homines'   therefore those asses are men

Both premises are ambiguous, because the word episcopi can either
be in the nominative or genitive case.

48 It is clear that deception from diversity of case produces
amphiboly rather than equivocation, because case is assigned a word
(dictioni) so that one can be ordered to another word. Therefore
deception from diversity of case is a deception from the ordering of
one word to another; therefore it has to do with word-groups;
therefore it is not a matter of equivocation. Again, it is clear that
deception from diversity of case produces amphiboly rather than
equivocation through Aristotle's forming amphibolous rather than
equivocal paralogisms on the basis of case-diversity.[21]

On Modes Common to
Equivocation and Amphiboly

49 Since Aristotle puts modes common to both after Equivocation and Amphiboly in the Elenchi[22], we will put the common
modes of both after those two sophistical Topics, following his
example. There are therefore three modes common to equivocation
and amphiboly.

21: Soph. El. 4, 166a 9-14.
22: Soph. El. 4, 166a 14-21.

The first mode common to both is when a word (<u>dictio</u>) or word-group principally signifies more than one thing. Notice that as far as a word (<u>nomen</u>) is said to signify more than one thing, that first mode comes under equivocation, like 'fish' and 'dog': both these words principally signify more than one thing. As for a word-group being said to signify more than one thing principally, that first mode pertains to amphiboly, as in the word-group, **'Aristotle's book'.**

The second mode common to both comes from what we become accustomed to say, when using a word or word-group metaphorically, for example. Such word-(<u>nomen</u>) transfer belongs to equivocation, as when the verb 'laugh' is transferred to 'bloom', as was clear before[23]; in a word-group, transfer is part of amphiboly, as was clear in the example **'ploughing sand'.**[24]

The third mode common to both is when a composite word (<u>nomen</u>) signifies several things, but a separate thing simply, that is, it signifies only one thing. An example of equivocation is in the words (<u>nomina</u>) **'immortal'** and **'incorruptible'.** In one way, '**im- mortal'** is the same as **'not able to die'**, and **'incorruptible'** the same as **'not able to be corrupted'.** In another, **'immortal'** is the same as **'able not to die'** and **'incorruptible'** the same as **'able not to be corrupted'.** This is clear in Adam's case: before sinning, he was immortal (i.e., able not to die). If he did not sin, he would never die. So he was able not to die, since it was possible that he would not sin and so would not die. But he was not immortal in the other signification, **'not able to die'**, for then the possibility of dying and sinning would be denied him, which is not true. This is the same as the fact that the word (<u>nomen</u>) **'immortal'** in one way does away with the potency of dying and in another, with the act of dying, by positing the potency for the same act.

It is better expressed this way than before because it is clearer. Yet each is true and comes to much the same thing. Since it has this capability from its composition, it is therefore said that a composite signifies several things, but only a single thing when taken apart, that is, analyzed into its parts, capable of the prior sense. Then neither part signifies several things, but only a single thing.

50 If one objects that parts of a word (<u>nomen</u>) signify nothing separately, as the beginning of <u>Peri Hermenias</u>[25] has it, answer that parts of a composite word are compared both to the significate (<u>significatum</u>) they had before being put together and to the signific- ate the same word has as a composite. A composite's significate is constituted from the partial concepts of those same parts. As far as the first significate is concerned, parts of a composite word do signify; as far as the second significate is concerned - the one constituted from the first two - those parts signify nothing as distinct.

51 Note too that the concept of a composite word (<u>nomen</u>) is simple compared to the composite word that signifies it, and so is indivisible. But the same concept compared to the partial concepts of its own parts is divisible, since it is made up of them. The concept of a simple word, however, is not divisible in any way. So it is necessary that the parts of a composite word, to the extent they exist in their own whole, would have more the nature of what is to be signified than the parts of a simple word. This is what Aristotle says in the beginning of Perihermenias,[26] that in simple words, a part is not significative in any way, though some can mean something in composites, but of nothing separate, that is, is the concept of nothing discrete, and that because it exists within its whole.

52 An example of amphiboly is found in the word-group **'knowing age'**. Granted that while neither word (<u>dictio</u>) **'know'** and **'age'**, signifies several things, the word-group they constitute does, as was clear in the third mode of amphiboly. That is how a composite signifies several things, while as a separate item, a composite means only one thing, as far as amphiboly is concerned.

Doubts

53 Evidence for the major of the three modes just discussed can be doubted. First, because the division of those three modes is incorrectly given by Aristotle. Every correct division is made through opposites; but the division of those three modes is not through opposites; therefore the division of those three modes is incorrect. This is a syllogism in the Fourth Mood, Second Figure. The major is clear because in it, **'opposite'** is taken commonly for 'opposites' as any genus of opposition and for disparates. The minor is clear, since the first mode in terms of equivocation arises from the fact that a nominal (<u>nomen</u>) principally signifies several things; but a nominal taken in the third mode in terms of equivocation, like **'immortal'**, principally signifies several things; therefore the third mode of equivocation is contained under the first. But not a single

23: Above, p. 101.
24: Above, p. 107.
25: De interp. 2, 16a 20-21; Boethius' Translation p. 6.
26: ibid. 16a22-25, p. 6.7-9.

disparate thing or true opposite is contained under the other; therefore the division of those three modes is not made through opposites.
This is the minor.

Answer that this division is correct and is made through opposites. And that the foregoing syllogism is valid, though its minor is
false. To the objection made in testing it, answer that 'to principally signify several things' is found in a nominal (nomen) from two
causes. One is conventional imposition of a name (nomen), the
other, composition of the nominal itself. The first of these causes
pertains to the first mode, the second to the third mode. So though
'immortal' may principally signify several things, this is not due to
conventional imposition upon this or that thing, but to the nature of
its composition, since the prefix 'in' can only do away with the act
of dying, or the potency antecedent to that act, and so consequently
with the act itself. Thus the fact that it may signify several things
is not based on the whim of the one coining an expression.

If it be objected that every word (nomen) signifies conventionally, therefore this one does too, - answer that the nominal (nomen)
'immortal' and almost all composites signify by convention in one
way and by a kind of necessity in another. As to their remote cause,
all names (nomina) signify by convention but there is necessity as far
as their proximate cause is concerned. That the two words (dictiones) 'horse' and 'wild' are put together has choice as a source,
but once a word like 'wildhorse' ('mustang': equiferus) is a sort of
composite out of them, it must have the sort of significate it does.
So in 'wildhorse', composition is the proximate cause of its signification, the choice to put them together its remote cause. So it does
signify by free choice as far as its remote cause is concerned, but as
to its proximate cause, its composition, it signifies of necessity. In
simple words (nominibus) like 'horse', choice is proximate cause.

Just so in equivocal words (nominibus), since in simple ones,
imposer's choice is the proximate efficient cause that it principally
signify several things, as in the word 'dog'. In equivocal composite
words, the putting together itself is the proximate cause that they
signify several things, and choice of such putting together is the
remote cause. Since those modes are distinguished wholly in terms
of proximate rather than remote causes, it is obvious the three are
opposed and one is not contained under the other. It is also clear
from this how in the third mode a word may principally signify
several things conventionally, as well as how it does so of necessity.

54 Again: Since Aristotle puts an example in the first mode of
Equivocation and not of Amphiboly, conversely in the third mode,
but of neither in the second, he does not make those modes very
clear.

Reply to this by saying that to signify several things principally
is more appropriate to a word (<u>nomini</u>) than a word-group and it is
therefore found primarily in equivocation rather than in amphiboly.
That is why he gives an example of equivocation instead of amphiboly in the first mode, to thereby signify that this mode primarily
suits equivocation rather than amphiboly. It is the converse for the
third mode, since for a composite to signify several things, while
separately only one, primarily suits a word-group, secondarily a
word (<u>nomini</u>). Parts of a word-group, when in their whole, not only
constitute the significate of the word-group, but also each and every
one of its parts retains its proper significate, discrete and separate
from the significate of another. In a composite word, it is not the
case that its parts are parts as such, retaining their significate
discrete and separate from the significate of another ---[27] - but as
said before[28] in the division of modes. That is why he gives
examples in the third mode of amphiboly rather than of equivocation, thereby signifying that the third mode primarily suits amphiboly
rather than equivocation. In the second mode, he gives neither
examples of equivocation nor of amphiboly, since, though metaphor
occurs in all of them, it does not occur identically in all. So he
exemplifies neither, since in a science, determination should not be
made except for those which are the same for all.

Or it should be said, and more aptly, that proper signification
of a word (<u>dictionis</u>) is said to be what usage commonly accepts.
What is now meant by a word metaphorically will later be signified
properly when usage has become set. Then the word will be equivocal as to the first mode. And because it so happens that a
signification which is not proper but metaphorical at one time later
becomes proper through frequent use, he thus did not have to put
examples in the second mode, since in an art, that should only be
made determinate which always stays the same.

55 Again: It still seems division of those modes is not
correctly made, since equivocation from consignification is not
contained under any of them. This is clear inductively for any of

27: the text has a gap here.
28: p. 93 ff.

them, since a word (dictio) signifies its accidents neither principally nor metaphorically. So it is equivocation from consignification in neither the first nor second mode, nor even in the third, for in that mode, equivocation is solely in composite words (nominibus), while equivocation from consignification is not only in composites but in simple forms as well.

Answer that the principal signification of a word (dictionis) has a double opposition: it is opposed both to consignification and metaphoric signification. So when it is opposed to the one, it removes the other; when opposed to the former, it removes the latter. That is why 'to principally signify several' is taken here in opposition to metaphoric signification, This way, it does not exclude consignification. So what is here labelled peculiarly as 'principal signification', is anything signified by a word (dictionem) as commonly used, in such a way that its proximate cause is choice. That I say 'by common use', excludes the second mode; that choice is proximate cause of that signification removes the third. Then equivocation from consignification is contained under the first mode, since in common use, grammatical accidents are represented both by a word (dictionem) and by choice, for whoever imposed a word to signify a given sort of thing, simultaneously did so to signify in a given gender and number, as the word (nomen) 'stone' was imposed to signify a given sort of thing under a given sort of accidents.

56 Again: It is asked why deception from some grammatical accidents produces equivocation, as in the word 'suffering', while deception from other accidents results in amphiboly, as it does in deception based on diversity of case.

Solution: Some grammatical features are not attached to words (dictio) absolutely but only as relatable to others. Take endings (casus): case-ending is a noun's accident insofar as activity or passivity emanates from a noun, e.g. a nominative, or as activity or passivity pass into a noun (e.g. oblique cases), and similarly as case-ending is a noun-accident compared to a verb. So case-ending is a relational accident - a disposition of a substance in respect of an act - and through such accidents, words are ordered to each other. It is a mistake to say 'man's runs', since the ending (casus) needed is not there. So deception from grammatical accidents like that is deception from word-ordering, so deception in word-grouping, resulting in amphiboly, not equivocation. There are other absolute accidents attached to a word (dictio) as such, like tense. Words are not ordered to each other through accidents like those: we can

equally well say   'the man runs', 'the man has run', 'the man will
run', 'I see the man', 'I have seen the man', or 'I will see the man'.
Though tense changes, the noun-verb construction stays the same,
both before and after, so it is not constructed with tense mediating
with what is its subject or object. So deception from accidents like
those is not a matter of word-grouping but one of words (dictio): so
equivocation rather than amphiboly is found there. Say in brief that
deception from accidents that are absolutes produces equivocation,
but deception from accidents that are respective produces
amphiboly.

ON COMPOSITION AND DIVISION

On Potential Polysemy

57 Composition, Division and Accent produce potential polysemy according to the Commentator, as noted above[29]. Potential
polysemy is when an identical word (dictio) or word-group signifies
different things depending on different perfections. For example,
the verb 'pendere' has a one perfection in the second and a
different one in the third conjugation, since they are thereby two
specifically different verbs. That is why it is necessary that they
have different perfections, yet it is the identical verb materially,
since it is composed of the same letters and syllables. That way one
has material identity and diversity of perfection and on the basis of
diversity of perfection there is a diversity of significates. So too in
a word-group: when it is composite, it has one perfection and it has
a different one when divided. Like this word-group: 'two and three
are five' when composite is categoric with a coordinate subject;
divided, as in 'two are five and three are five', it is copulative.
Obviously a copulative and a categoric proposition have different
perfections.

So too every word-group taken as composite or divided: some
difference is always to be found on the side of perfection and
thereby, of significates. Since in these a word (dictio) or a word-
group is capable of being transmuted from one perfection into another, and through this capability, a diversity of significates is
found, it is thus called a potential polysemy. In equivocation and
amphiboly, since a word or a word-group still existing under the
same perfection signifies different things, an actual polysemy is said

29: but inaccurately: see p. 82 ff.

to be there since it is polysemous on the basis of the same actuality or same perfection. For a perfection is called an actuality.

Objections

58 An objection to what was said is that since the word-group **'bread eating dog'** (panem comedere canem)[30] may be one thing or another, depending on whether the accusative **'bread'** is subject to the verbal **'eating'**, or that same accusative is put next to that same verbal --; but this example is not one thing or another materially, since it consists of the same letters, syllables and words; therefore it is materially identical. Therefore while it may be one thing or another simply, a word-group should be one or another specifically. On that basis, it signifies different things. Therefore the word-group **'bread eating dog'** existing identically as to matter, and diversely as to its diverse perfections, signifies diverse things. Therefore there is a potential polysemy here, since the definition of potential polysemy given above suits it. Since only amphiboly is found there, amphiboly then will produce a potential polysemy. Which is contrary to what was said.

Say that in the word-group **'bread eating dog'** there is no potential polysemy, only an actual one, since it is a specifically identical word-group, as will be clear. To the objection that it is one thing or another specifically, though identical materially because it is composed of the same letters, syllables and words, say polysemy consists of both identity and diversity in a word-group, since word-group identity is ambiguous as to identity of perfection or identity of material. Both those identities are in the word-group **'the man runs'**, since there we have one and the same perfection - hence identity of perfection - and since it is composed of the same letters, syllables and words having always the identical material ordering, material identity is also there; that way material identity is also found there.

59 Again: **'diversity of word-group'** is said in many ways. One is based on species - **'two and three are five'** differs specifically from **'two are five and three are five'** -, another is material difference. That too is ambiguous, since a word-group can either be composed of different letters, syllables and words, like **'Plato runs**

30: The translation substitutes an English participle for the Latin infinitive. Both subject and object of comedere must be in the accusative case. [fpd]

and Socrates disputes', or of the same elements variously ordered.
That is ambiguous as well, since it is either a word-group of
identical words arranged differently as to the same perfection, or
there is a material difference in word-group from words variously
ordered as to different perfections. This last way, a word-group is
one thing or another as to composition or division. In the next to
last way, a word-group is one or another on the basis of amphiboly.
For example, in **'bread eating dog'**, no matter which accusative is
subject or object, the word-group is always identical on the basis of
its perfection, since this word-group is completed by the inflection
found there, even though the inflection is infinitival [in Latin fpd.].
Just as an indicative word-group is completed by its peculiar inflection, and the imperative from its own proper inflection, so too this
infinitival word-group is perfected in its own way by infinitival
inflection, even though it is not a simply perfect sentence. So the
word-group mentioned is identical specifically and one thing or
another materially, depending on whether one of those accusatives is
subject or object; and similarly of the rest.

This can be illustrated by a natural similitude: one now a boy,
then youth or old man, is still the same person, though his physique
is not the same but changes from this to that. Not skinny, because
plump at one time and slim at another, but still the same person.
Just as material parts are so transmuted, yet one's human species
remains the same, so there is material diversity within yet specific
identity, - so too in the word-group **'bread eating dog'** there is
diversity of matter in the way discussed, but identity of species.

60 Again: If asked whether amphibolous word-groups participate equally in word-group identity, say one way, yes, another way,
no. As is clear from the above, word-group identity is ambiguous: -
one material, the other specific. Speaking of material identity, a
given amphibolous word-group is always the same, like **'Aristotle's
book'**; the next is one thing or another like every word-group that is
amphibolous because a particular case-form can be subject or object
of the same verb. Speaking of specific identity, every amphibolous
word-group is equally the same: it has no specific difference in its
parts, since each and every word-group in and of itself has its proper
perfection by which it is always perfected. So for that reason each
and every amphibolous word-group is simply identical in itself by
identity of species.

On Composition

61 Having said all this, composition must now deal specially
with composition. But first one must see when a word-group is said

to be composite or divided. We must therefore know that a word-group cannot be called composite or divided unless a different position [or arrangement: <u>situm</u>] can be found in it with respect to which parts can be variously ordered. When words (<u>dictiones</u>) are ordered according to their most due position [or arrangement] in a word-group, it is said to be composite. If removed from that position [or arrangement] and placed in a less appropriate one, the word-group is divided. Take a word-group example: **'whatever lives always is'** (<u>quicquid</u> <u>vivit</u> <u>semper</u> <u>est</u>) can be [construed either as] composite or divided. Since the unit **'whatever lives'** is the subject and the verb **'is'** the predicate, the verb **'is'** is the principal [verb] and the verb **'lives'**, is not the principal [verb] since it is included in the subject.

Proof: A verb is what consignifies time and is always the sign of what are predicated of something else[31]. Therefore that verb actually predicated, actually shares the nature of verb simply taken; what is not actually predicated, does not participate in the nature of verb simply taken. Therefore, since the verb **'is'** actually is predicated, it will actually share the nature of verb simply taken, and since **'lives'** is not actually predicated, but is bound to the subject (which is contrary to the nature of verb-as-verb), it will not actually share the nature of verb simply, though both is a verb simply according to its potential, since each has in itself the aptitude of being predicated. Thus each is potentially a verb simply, but not each is actually a verb simply. So one is a principal member and the other is not, as was said. Therefore, since an adverb of its nature has to modify a verb, it will then more directly modify the more principal verb than a less principal one, and so is located in its more due position [or arrangement]. For that reason, when the word (<u>dictio</u>) **'always'** modifies the verb **'is'**, the word-group is composite, as follows: **'whatever lives, always is'**; and if it is separated from that, it will be divided, as follows: **'whatever lives always, is.'** All others are to be understood similarly depending on the nature of the words used.

32. So too of this word-group: **'I have set you slave being free'**.[32] Since signs as signs ought to suit and contrast by reason of their significates, for words (<u>dictiones</u>) are signs of things, if things could be ordered more suitably, so too should signs, - then when ordering of things is more suitable, ordering of signs will be too. When ordering of things is less suitable, that of words will as well. Since it is a more suitable status for human nature to leave slavery behind for freedom than to fall into slavery from it, the participle **'being'** is better construed with the noun **'slave'** than with the

nominal **'free'**. That way it is composite and its sense is: **'you being a slave I have set free'** that is, **from you a slave I have made a free man**. The other way, it is divided, and its sense is: **'you being a free man I have made a slave'** that is, **'of you, a free man, I have made a slave'**.

63 Notice Aristotle puts this word-group among paralogisms of division.[33]   Also that wherever composition, division, or accent is found, a word-group need not be true in one mode and false in another: it can be that it is true or false in either sense, as in **'I touch the one struck manually'**. Assume someone had been struck with a hand and I touch him with mine. The first version is then ambiguous, since the ablative **'manu'** (**'manually'**) can determine the verb **'touch'** or the participle **'struck'**, This is true in both senses. But this would be false in both: **'I touch the one struck with a stick'**, its position [or arrangement] remaining the same. It is like that in equivocation. The sentence **'every dog is substance'** can have three senses and be true in any, while **'every dog is whiteness'** is false in any sense. So too for amphiboly.

All this shows that they are not telling all who say a word-group is taken as composite when false in a composite sense, and as divided when false in a divided sense, since this is not true in all of them, as was said. But this is true, that if a paralogism is made on the basis of composition, its solution will be in division, and if on the basis of division, the solution will be in composition. The second answer is held by Aristotle[34], not the first.

On Causes of this Fallacy

64 The cause of plausibility / motive principle of composition is unity of a word-group as to its species caused by composition. I say 'caused by composition' since, from the fact that a word-group is so composite or divided, its species and truth vary accordingly. The principle of compositional deficiency is the possibility of different significates for the same word-group. I say this because even though a word-group is composite and so may stand under one species in that composition, it is still possible for it to have another species or

31:   Aristotle, De interp. 3, 16b 6-8.
32:   'ego posui te servum entem liberum'
       'free(,) I have made you(,) a slave
33:   Soph. El. 4, 166a 36-37.
34:   Soph. El. 20, 177a 33-35.

another perfection than it can have through division. For that reason it is possible for it to have diverse significates. All this was clear in the word-group used earlier:[35] **'whatever lives always is'.** So the potential a word-group has for diverse species, which derives from its expression (<u>vox</u>) side, is ordered to its potential for diverse significates derived from the factual side. (<u>a parte rei</u>)

65 Some say a composite's cause of plausibility is composition itself, while the cause of its nonexistence is a word-group's division. Others say the cause of plausible composition is the truth of the composite word-group, while the cause of its nonexistence is the falsity of that same word-group when divided. For they say the truth of a composite word-group motivates belief in its truth when divided, since the motive principle always produces belief in the opposite by the principle of deficiency.

66 That these objectors poorly distinguish such principles of this sophistical Topic is clear first in that all linguistic fallacies differ from nonlinguistic ones because the motive principle of the former's fallacies comes from the expression or sign side, while their principle of deficiency comes from the factual side. But nonlinguistic fallacies take both principles from the factual side. Therefore their first judgement cannot stand, since it holds both those principles are from the expression or sign side. Composition or division of a word-group itself is expected on the basis of expression or sign.

Again: Nothing changes except into something simply or partially like it. So it is not possible for one contrary to change into another. Composition therefore does not become division nor the converse. Through the first of these reasons the falsity of the second position is clear, which posits both principles of composition from the factual side, since there is no truth in a word-group except on a factual basis.

Again: In equivocation, the motive principle derives from linguistic unity (<u>unitate dictionis</u>), its principle of deficiency from things signified. It is the same in amphiboly and like that in accent, as will later be clear[36], as well as in the fallacy of word-figure. So it is fitting that it occur the same way in composition, or there will not be six linguistic fallacies. Aristotle taught the opposite by induction and syllogism[37]. Therefore it is fitting to posit the motive

35: Above, p. 100 ff.
36: Below, p. 109.

principle of composition from the expression side and the principle of deficiency from the factual.

67 That is why we said the motive principle of composition is word-group unity based on its species caused by composition, while the principle of deficiency is the potential for different significates for the same word-group. Unity of a composite word-group motivates belief in one significate without the possibility of another. That is how a motive principle moves to an opposite by the principle of defect, as in other sophistical Topics.

On its modes

68 Two modes of composition can be assigned. Aristotle seems to hint at them in his chapter on composition.[38]

On the first mode

The first mode comes from the fact that a **dictum** ('something said') can stand for itself or part of itself as subject to some verb, as in: **'to one sitting walking is possible'** (<u>sedentem</u> <u>ambulare</u> <u>est</u> <u>possibile</u>). A parologism is formed as follows:

**'it happens that anyone who can walk does walk
    but one sitting can walk
therefore it happens that one sitting walks'.**

(<u>quemcumque</u> <u>ambulare</u> <u>est</u> <u>possibile</u>, <u>contingit</u> <u>quod</u> <u>ipse</u> <u>ambulet</u>
    <u>sed</u> <u>sedentem</u> <u>ambulare</u> <u>est</u> <u>possibile</u>
<u>ergo</u> <u>contingit</u> <u>quod</u> <u>sedens</u> <u>ambulat</u>)

The minor is ambiguous, since if the dictum **'to one sitting-walking'** (<u>sedentem</u> <u>ambulare</u>) is itself made subject to the predicate **'is possible'**, its sense is single. The word-group is false in that sense, since then the opposed actions **'walk'** and **'sit'** are joined together. This is as false as **'the one sitting is walking'** (<u>sedens</u> <u>ambulat</u>) But if that dictum is subject of the predicate mentioned as for part of itself (i.e., for the subject of the dictum), then the sense would be like: **'the one sitting has in himself the power of walking'** and in this sense, the minor is true. This is to be distinguished the same way: **'that one not writing is writing is possible'** (<u>non</u> <u>scribentem</u> <u>scribere</u>

37: Above, p. 81 ff.
38: <u>Soph. El.</u> 4, 166a 23-32.

est possible). A paralogism is to be formed the same way. These word-groups and their like are composites in that an entire dictum stands for itself, and divisives when the dictum stands for part of itself, since a predicate is attributed more appropriately to an entire dictum than to a part of it, even though the dictum is always subject.

69 There is consequently nothing to the objection of those who say that if it is true on the basis of the mode just mentioned, the possibility of walking is now attributed to the entire dictum, now to a part, the one I say as **'one sitting'**, therefore the accusative **'one sitting'** (sedentem) is subject to **'it is possible for one sitting to walk'**. This is awkward, since the word-group would be incongruous; [in Latin: fpd] an accusative cannot be subject to a third-person verb. So the distinction mentioned is null.

The solution is plain from what was said, since a dictum as a unit is always subject to a third-person verb, now for itself (then possibility is attributed to a dictum as a unit), now for part of itself (i.e. a dictum's subject), and then possibility is attributed to the subject of that dictum, namely to what I say as **'one sitting'**.

70 Others distinguish these word-groups saying a parallelism is implied by the participles **'sitting'** or **'writing'**, as Priscian has it,[39] since the participle was invented to imply its parallelism to the verb, as in **'I read sitting'** (sedens lego). This parallel is made explicit by the word (dictio) **'while'** or **'although'**, as in **'while I am sitting, I am reading'** or **'although I am sitting, I am reading'**. They say therefore that the word-groups cited are ambiguous since the parallelism implied by the participle **'sitting'** can be signified with respect to the verb **'walk'**. Then the sense of **'to one sitting walking is possible'** is **'while I am sitting, it is possible for me to be walking'**, which is false. Or else a parallel can be denoted with respect to the predicate. Then the sense of **'to one sitting walking is possible'**; is **'while he is sitting, he has the potency to walk later on'**, which is true.

This distinction comes to the same thing as the first, for when a parallelism is denoted with respect to the verb **'walk'**, possibility is imposed upon the dictum as a unit, which is false. But when parallelism is denoted with respect to the predicate, possibility is imposed upon the dictum's subject, and that way is true.

71 Word-groups of this sort are usually labelled de re (about a thing) and de dicto (about what was said). Word-groups are said to be **de dicto** when a dictum stands for itself. When a dictum stands for part of itself, word-groups are called **de re**. They label a dictum's own subject a **rem** (thing); but a dictum's subject is not the dictum. So even though a dictum may be a thing, it is not a thing as they take 'rem' here.

On the second mode

72 The second mode of composition stems from the fact that a given word (dictio) put in a word-group can determine different things. Take 'letters which you know how to learn now is possible'[40], where the adverb 'now' can determine the verb 'learn'; (it is false that way, since letters you know cannot be learned now, since you are in ignorance of what you learn; as Aristotle says: 'whoever is learning, is ignorant'.[41]) Or it can determine the predicate 'is possible' and so is true. Letters one knows, one can relearn now. One can forget and so now have the capacity to learn in the present.

This is similar: 'what one only can bear, can bear many'. And a paralogism is formed this way:

> 'what one only can bear, can bear many
> but what can not bear many, can one only bear
> therefore what can not bear many, can bear many'.[42]

The major is ambiguous, since if the word (dictio) 'only' determines the verb 'can', it is false; and its sense is 'what one only can bear etc.', that is, 'what only can bear one and can not bear many, can bear many'), for if it only can bear one, it therefore cannot bear many. But if the word 'only' determines the verb 'bear', it is true; and its sense is 'what can only bear one, can bear many', that is, 'what has power such that it only bears one, can bear many', for whatever can bear many also has the power to bear one alone. A ship that can carry ten men can also carry one; so that ship with a capacity of bearing only one still can carry many. So what can bear one alone can carry many.

39: Inst. gramm. XI 8, p. 552.
40: 'litteras quas scis discere nunc est possibile'.
41: Cp. Topica III 2, 117a 12, p. 53.
42: 'quod unum solum potest ferre, plura potest ferre
    sed quod non potest plura ferre, potest unum solum ferre

73 How potential ambiguity may be in a word-group, composite or divided, and when a word-group should be declared composite and when divided has become clear in what was said. Now it remains to state the principles / causes and modes of division.

On Division

74 The motive principle / cause of plausibility of division is therefore word-group unity as to its species caused by division, since it has one species when divided and another when composite. The deficient principle / cause of nonexistence of division is the possibility of different significates in the substance of a divided word-group. I say this because, though a word-group may have a single significate by the particular way it is divided, still its substance is potential with respect to composition and that way with respect to a different significate.

On the first Mode

75 There are two modes of division. The first comes from the fact that a given word (<u>dictio</u>) can conjoin terms or propositions. That is ambiguous as to whether it links or disjoins them, since 'conjoin' is common to linking or disjoining, just as 'conjunction' is common to the copulative, disjunctive, or other conjunctions. It is the genus for all. That is why conjoining terms or propositions is common to both, namely to couple or disjoin the same things. The first mode derives from that, as in 'five are two and three'. A paralogism is formed as follows:

'whatever are two and three are three
   but five are two and three
   therefore five are three'.

The minor is ambiguous. It can be divided, with the sense: 'five are two and five are three' That way it is copulative. Or it can be composite, with the sense: 'five are two and three'. It has a copulative predicate and then there is a pairing of terms. The major is ambiguous in the same way. And so is: 'five are even and odd'.

By disjunction as follows:

'every animal is rational or irrational
   but not every animal is rational
   therefore every animal is irrational'.

ergo quod non potest ferre plura, potest ferre plura'.

The major is ambiguous because it can be divided, with the sense: **'every animal is rational or every animal is irrational'**, in which case it is disjunctive, and disjunctive of propositions. Or it could be composite, with the sense: **'every animal is either rational or irrational'**, in which case it has a disjunctive predicate. It is a disjunction of terms. This is the way those word-groups are said to be composites, since conjunction is primarily disjunctive of word-group parts and secondarily disjunctive of word-groups.

So too in: **'every animal is either well or ill'**, **'every line is either straight or curved'**, **'every number is either even or odd'**, or **'every substance is either corporeal or incorporeal'**.

On the second Mode

76 The second mode of division comes from the fact that a given case-form or a given determiner can be ordered with different things, as in, **'you see the one struck with your eyes'** (tu vides oculis percussum). A paralogism is made as follows:

> **'with whatever you see one struck, he is struck by that**
> **but you see this one struck with your eye or eyes**
> **therefore this one has been struck with your eye or eyes'.**

The minor is ambiguous because the case-form or ablative **'eyes'** can be ordered with the verb **'see'** and then it signifies the instrument of sight, with the sense: **you see with your eye the one who has been struck.** It is then composite, for since that ablative is a determination of an act, and an act is more truly in a verb than in a participle, it ought for that reason primarily determine a verb and secondarily a participle. Or it could be ordered with the participle **'struck'** and then it signifies an instrument of striking. That way it is divided, with the sense: **you see the one who was struck by your eyes.**

These are like it: **'Free (,) I made you (,) a slave'** and **'goodly Achilles left fifty (and a) (of a) hundred men'.**

So is **'you know only three men are running'**,
assuming six are in the race and you only know of three;
> **'but whatever is known is true**
> **therefore that only three men are running is true'.** [43]

The major is ambiguous, since the adverb **'only'** can determine the verb **'know'**, in which case it is composite and true; but if it modifies the verbal **'running'**, it is divided and false.

Also **'you are born today'**[44]. Proof: You exist today; there-fore born or unborn; but not unborn; so you are born today. The major is ambiguous because the adverb **'today'** can determine the verb **'are'**, in which case it is composite and true; or the participle **'born'**, in which case it is divided and false.

ON ACCENT

On the Definition of Accent

77 Accent is a law or rule for raising and depressing a syllable of any one of parts of a word-group (partes orationis). It is divided three ways into an acute, grave and circumflex accent. An acute accent is one that sharpens / raises a syllable; a grave accent is one that depresses a syllable and lowers it, and a circumflex is one that sharpens a syllable and depresses it.

78 Accent, as a principle of deception, is the polysemy of a word substantively the same, caused by diversity of accents.

On Causes and Modes of the Fallacy of Accent

The cause of accentual plausibility is the unity of a word (dictio) on the basis of a one accent. The cause of accentual falsity is diversity of significates through capacities a word has from one accent to another. There are two modes of the fallacy of accent.

On the first Mode

79 The first mode comes from the fact that a given word, identical as to substance, can be dominated by a different accent. As here:

'omnis populus est arbor   every po:pulus is a tree
  sed gens es populus   but a tribe is a populus
  ergo gens est arbor'.   therefore a tribe is a tree'.

43: 'tu scis tantum tres homines currere,
         sed quicquid scitur est verum
         ergo tantum tres homines currere est verum'.
44: 'tu es hodie natus'.

The major is ambiguous, since the word (<u>dictio</u>) **'p o p u l u s'** means one thing when the first syllable is lengthened [poplar tree] and another when shortened [people]. This is like it:[45]

'omnis ara est in templo	[every sty is in the eye]
stabulum porcorum est ara	[a pigpen is a sty]
ergo stabulum porcorum est in templo'	[so a pigpen is in the eye]

so too here:

'quicquid hamatur hamo capitur	'whatever is taken is caught with a hook
sed vinum amatur	but wine is taken/loved
ergo vinum hamo capitur'	therefore wine is taken with a hook'.

'a m a t u r' means one thing without aspiration, but something else with it, and it is produced in a different way. So is this:

'iustos viros oportet pendere	'just men should hang
sed viros iustos non oportet pendere[46]	but just men should not hang
ergo oportet iustos viros pati	therefore that just men should suffer and not
et non pati idem'.	suffer is the same thing'

On the second Mode

80 The second mode comes from the fact that something can be either a word (<u>dictio</u>) or a word-group, as here:

'tu es qui es	'you are who you are
sed quies est requies	but quiet is rest
ergo tu es requies'	therefore you are rest'.

The major is ambiguous because, when I say **'q u i e s'**, it can be a word or a word-group, and correspondingly this means different things. Just as this does:

'Deus nichil fecit invite	'God did nothing unwillingly
sed vinum fecit in vite	but He made wine on the vine

45: · The English parallels, but does not translate the Latin example, where <u>ara</u> means 'altar', <u>a:ra</u> or <u>bara</u> means 'pigsty'.
46: <u>Pe ndere</u> is intransitive 'hang'; <u>pendere</u> is transitive 'hang'.

ergo vinum fecit invite'.   Therefore He made wine
                                      unwillingly'.

The major is ambiguous, since when I say **'i n v i t e'**, it can be a
word - in which case it is true -; or a word-group, and so false; it is
like that in the conclusion. This is similar:

'metuo longas pereunte noctes Lidia dormis'

what I pronounce as **'m e t u o'** can be a word or a phrase.[47]

D o u b t s

81 Doubts arise from what was said. First, how **'accent'** is to
be taken here, whether accepted on the basis of the definition laid
down at the beginning of this tract on accent, or taken commonly
for every mode of pronouncing in speech (dictio), which includes
lengthened, shortened, aspirated, unaspirated, acute, grave and the
like. That it is not to be taken here properly but commonly is seen
because some paralogisms are taken from accentual production or
suppression (as in the verb **'pendere'**, ['hang'] when the second syllable is lengthened or shortened), others from aspiration, which is
obvious enough. Therefore **'accent'** is not taken here properly, but
commonly.

That it is not to be taken commonly but properly seems to be
on the authority of Aristotle in the Second Elenchi[48] where he gives
a general solution for all word-groups according to accent, saying, 'it
is obvious how this must be solved; for the spoken word (nomen)
does not mean the same thing when pronounced with a grave or an
acute accent.'   Therefore it is taken properly, not commonly, for
grave and acute are different accents properly taken.   Again: If
'accent' were taken commonly, as used here, it would be common to
duration and breath; therefore it would be predicated of them as it
is of acute and grave.

Say **'accent'** is taken here commonly for every mode of
pronunciation, not commonly on the basis of predication, but as a

47: Horace, Carmina I 25, vss. 8-9:
          'me tuo longas pereunte noctes, // Lidia dormis ?'
          me your long perishing nights, // Lidia do you sleep ?
          m e t u o = 'I fear'.
          Cf. Arist., Soph El. 4, 166 b4-5 in Boethius' translation,
48: Soph. El. 21, 178a 2-3.

consequence. 'Common' is said two ways, predicatively and as a consequence only, such that it is not predicatively: the way surface is consequent upon white, black and all intermediate colors (it being a peculiarity of surface in the first place to be colored); - and this is to be understood in bodies composed of elements, since other bodies (like elements, the heavens, and stars) are not colored; though this is not now our concern, being part of natural science; - let it just be assumed that surface is consequent upon all the colors mentioned and that it is predicated of not a one. It is thus one way common as a consequent and not as a predicate; in another, it is common in predicating, as superiors of inferiors. On this basis, then, I say 'accent' is taken commonly here, with 'common' taken as a consequence, since upon variation or diversity of time follows diversity or variation of accent, as is clear in the word 'pendere', depending on whether the middle syllable is lengthened or shortened. Thus the solution is clear.

As to the objection to Aristotle's authority, that a word (nomen) does not mean the same when pronounced with a grave or acute accent - this happens now by accentual difference alone, now by durational diversity and variation in lengthening and shortening what is produced, upon which accentual differences follow. To the objection that accent would be predicated of time and breath, if it were common, the solution is clear from what was said: it equivocates 'common'. 'Accent' is not here common by predication, but as said, so is predicated neither of time nor breath. What is here labelled breath is according as a syllable or word (dictio) is said to be aspirated, since breath is primarily an accident of a syllable, and of the word through a syllable, as is clear in Priscian's tract on orthography,[49] where four syllabic accidents are assigned: duration, tenor, breath, and number of letters, and tenor is the same as accent. All these are primarily in a syllable, second-arily in a word (dictio). I say 'primarily' in the way that the incomplete and indistinct is prior to the complete and distinct. Indeterminate and indistinct in the syllable as such, they are determinate and distinct in a word or in a syllable as far as it is in a word.

82 Again: Since 'accent' is to be taken commonly, as was said, it is asked why that fallacy is called **according to accent** instead of **according to time** or **breath**.

49: Inst. gramm. II 12, p. 51.

Say that, as is already clear from the above, since diversity of accent follows upon them and not the converse, it is called a fallacy **according to accent,** and not **according to time** or **breath,** since the label **'according to accent'** is more common, from the fact that its diversity is more common.

ON WORD FIGURE

On Mode of Signifying in a Word (<u>dictio</u>)

83 Mode of signifying in a word (<u>dictio</u>) is ambiguous as to substantial or accidental. For example: **'quality of noun'** is accepted ambiguously as to naturally apt to be shared in by several or as naturally apt not to be shared in by several, but by one only. Taken this way, it is completive / perfective of a noun; so essential; so it is said every noun signifies substance with quality essentially. The other way, that same quality is taken as actually shared in by several, or as actually shared in by one only singular thing. Taken that way, it is an accident of a noun. It is the same thing to say **'quality of noun'** is taken one way as to its potential of being shared in by several, or being shared in by one only - so essential -, and in another as actually being shared in by several, or by one only, so accidental.

Note that each quality is divided into proper and appellative. But proper and appellative insofar as they mean a potential for being shared in by one only or by many. Taken that way, they are parts of an essential quality. As meaning the actuality of being shared in by one or several, they are parts of an accidental quality. And as parts of an essential quality, they are included in Priscian's[50] definition of noun and by Donatus.[51] As accidental parts, they are listed among accidents of a noun. For instance: **'man'** as meaning a quality naturally apt to be shared by several thus signifies an esssential quality. As meaning man is actually in this and that, it signifies an accidental quality; it is an accident for a name (<u>nomen</u>) to be actually in several things, but not an accident for it to be so potentially (<u>habitu</u>) or by aptitude, indeed it is essential to it.

84 If one ask whether that quality of man be **humanity,** say it is not, since **'humanity'** is a kind of word (<u>nomen</u>) having of itself its

---

50: <u>Inst</u>. <u>gramm</u>. II 18, p. 55 and V 22, pp. 56-57.
51: <u>Ars</u> <u>gramm</u>. I 5, p. 373.

own substance and its own quality;   this way an infinite regress would arise, which is impossible.   By the word (<u>nomen</u>) **'man'** is signified its own substance and its own quality and similarly the quality of Socrates; as naturally apt to be shared in by an individual, it is essential to it;   as that aptitude is in its actuality, it is accidental to it.

85 From what was said it is clear the mode of signifying in a word (<u>dictione</u>) is essential one way, accidental in another, depending on whether it is taken according to what it can signify or what it does signify.

86 Again: In a noun there is another accidental mode of signifying from the side of accidents such as that by which a noun signifies in masculine or feminine gender, and so of the others. Therefore there is a double mode of signifying in a noun, one substantial, the other accidental.   So too in a verb: **'act'** and **'undergo'** are taken ambiguously as to potential - that way they are essentials to a verb - or as to actuality - in which case they are its accidents.   For example: **'see'**, **'run'**, **'sit'** and **'walk'**, etc. are taken ambiguously as to potentiality or actuality.   They are taken potent- ially when we say a sleeper sees, a stabled horse runs well or walks or goes out often, and that someone standing is always sitting or sleeping.   They are taken as actual when he opens his eyes and sees things outside or when he now covers ground at top speed.   We like- wise say **'it burns'** about fire or a hot poker as of a potential, when nothing is affected or being burned up by what we say burn, that is, that they have the potential of burning.   In general: whenever we predicate a verb signifying a mode of activity of something doing nothing, we predicate potential and there, **'to do something'** is taken as a potential, as saying a knife cuts, even though no one is cutting with it.   But when we predicate a verb of the same subject because an activity is actually united with it, we predicate activity in actuality.   So too in verbs signifying passivity.   That is why we said **'act'** and **'undergo'** are taken ambiguously, i.e. as potentiality or actuality.   Taken as to potential, they are a verb's essentials, on the basis of activity, its accidentals.

So there is a double mode of signifying in a noun and a verb, namely essential and accidental.   So too in any other part of a word- group.   Therefore in a word (<u>dictio</u>) simply taken, this double mode of signifying is found.

On Figure

87 Figure is what is contained by a boundary or boundaries; one boundary like a circle within its diameter, boundaries like multilateral figures within their sides. A circle is not its circumference but a surface the circumference contains, nor are three straight lines ending at three points from each part a triangle, but the plane contained by those three lines. Figure is found primarily in natural things, then mathematical things, then subsequently in a word (<u>dictio</u>), since proportionally.

On Word-figure

88 Since every figure is an accident of what it is the figure of, if figure ought to be used proportionally of word (<u>dictio</u>), it should be taken from the aspect of what are accidental to a word. So we say word-figure (<u>figura dictionis</u>) is a mode of signifying accidentally in a word. That is why we distinguished a double mode of signifying above. The reason why figure is a word-accident like figure in the examples cited, is not a proper likeness by which this 'figure' is proportionally derived from that one, but a common likeness of the latter to the former on the basis of which each is an accident, not on the basis that each is a figure, since as accidental, it coincides with any other accident. The proper likeness by which figure is in a word, is that, just as in natural and mathematical objects, figure bounds and contains that of which it is the figure, so too in a word, an accidental mode of signifying bounds and contains it. I am not saying a word is bounded by a vowel the way **'musa'** has its **a** boundary, but by a conceptual one. Figure here is not a word's vocalic boundary, though in that vocalic boundary of a word is understood what signifies through the mode **what** or **what kind**, or in a masculine or feminine mode, and so of the others. It is clear that containment pertains to word-figure as just discussed, since what is elemental about a thing is said to bound and contain it. That is clear in figure properly taken, which bounds and contains the body it belongs to, and is an element of that body itself. Since an accidental mode of signifying should come last to a word naturally, though not temporally, it is thus last on the part of what are understood in a word. Accidental mode is, as it were, what bounds and contains a word. That is why it is called word-figure and to that extent, it is a likeness or proportion of the latter figure to the former.

89 Notice that deception is not occasioned by this figure unless the figure or mode of signifying of one word (<u>dictio</u>) is assimilated to the figure or mode of signifying of another. This figure-similarity is ambiguous in words. One way, it depends on whether a pair of words, alike in figure, have the same mode of signifying. On this figure-likeness, deception does not arise, because no defect is there, as when both are masculine or feminine gender, both signify **what** or both **what kind,** and so of the others. '**Likeness**' of one word-figure to another is taken another way when one word has but a single mode of signifying and through some overlap with another, seems to have the other word's mode of signifying when taken under that other as middle term, as will be clear in paralogisms. Since a word taken under a middle term this way has its own proper mode of signifying different from the one posited as middle term, it is therefore not simply like it, but dissimilar. It appears to be like it because taken under it, and Aristotle shows this dissimilarity in the Elenchi chapter[52] **Fallacie autem fit in hiis,** where he says: 'it is difficult to distinguish what are said similarly and diversely' that is, dissimilarly; so in one and the same word, diverse modes of signifying are implicated, one truly and the other only apparently. For that reason there is imaginary ambiguity and through that plausibility, a defect. It is a diminished and imaginary likeness. This is the way '**likeness**' of figure is taken in this fallacy and not in the first mode.

90 From all this it is already obvious what imaginary ambiguity is, and that it is not just polysemy (or multiple ambiguity) simply taken: that is conventional representation of several things in the same sign. Actual polysemy is for that reason polysemy simply taken, because that description is completely verified in it, as is clear in equivocation and amphiboly. Potential polysemy is not polysemy simply taken, since there is no sign identical because of the diverse dispositions in which it is taken, as was clear above.[53] Imaginary polysemy is when the same word (dictio) truly has one mode of signifying and seemingly an opposed one. So as far as one sign simply taken is there and that it involves several things within itself, this better suits actual than potential polysemy. To the extent that that polysemy is not one of things but of modes of signifying, it is suits actual less than potential polysemy.

On Causes and Modes of Word-figure

91 We have established which mode of signifying in a word (dictio) should be called word-figure, how '**figure**' is to be taken

52: Soph. El. 7, 169a 30-31.
53: p. 97 ff.

metaphorically in a word and what metaphorical likeness is. Also, which likeness between one word-figure and another produces a fallacy and why this polysemy should be called imaginary. So we must next discuss causes and modes of this fallacy.

The motive principle of the Fallacy of Word-figure is the likeness of one word to another in an accidental mode of signifying. Its principle of deficiency is the incompleteness or diminution of that likeness.

92 There are three modes of the Fallacy of Word-figure. A word (dictio) has a certain accidental mode of signifying which is a principle of congruity or incongruity, like masculine, feminine and neuter. Another is an accidental mode of signifying due to the thing signified, which thing is a principle of truth or falsity. This second mode differs from the first because the first derives from a thing as existing in a word from the aspect of principles of congruity or incongruity, while the second is due to a thing from the aspect of principles of truth or falsity. I say 'to a thing' universally, as 'what', 'what kind', 'what quantity', etc. The third mode of signifying in a word is that of a word signifying a single thing as 'this individual something'.[54] And on the basis of these three modes of signifying or of understanding in a word, there are three modes of the Fallacy of Word-figure.

On the first Mode

93 The first is when a masculine is interpreted as a feminine or the converse, or when there is another between those two, as in:

'omnis substantia colorata   every substance colored by
    albedine est alba   whiteness is white
sed vir est substantia   but a man is a substance
    colorata albedine   colored by whiteness
ergo vir est alba'.   therefore a man is white.

So too in:

    'omnis aqua est humida   all water is wet
       fluvius est aqua   a river is water
    ergo fluvius est humida'.   therefore a river is wet

54: tóde ti.

In both, a masculine is interpreted as a feminine. 'F l u v i u s' (river) is masculine gender and because of the compatibility it seems to have with water, in that we have here a mode of taking one thing as under another, it seems to share the same mode of signifying with water, and so is of the same gender. Understand I am not positing this plausibility because one thing is subordinate to another according to truth, but because we have here a mode of taking one thing under another. For example, this is a Fallacy of Word-figure:

'omnis **pe**tra est alba	every stoney thing is white
vir est petra	a man is a stoney thing
ergo vir est alba'.	therefore a man is white

though the minor extremity is not truly found under its middle term, we do have there a mode of taking something under the middle term, and for that reason it seems to have the same mode of signifying as the middle term aside from its proper one. So it involves different modes of signifying in itself. It is clear on the basis of what sort of compatibility it would seem to be of similar figure. That is just how it is to be understood in any other mode.

94 Notice that since likeness of word-figure arises through the way of taking something under the middle term, all paralogisms of word-figure are for that reason contrary to rules of inference, but differently. Those violating the first mode invalidate the nature of inference both in truth and plausibility, because they posit an incongruity - solecism - and in what they appear to conclude, there is neither truth, falsity, nor polysemy. There is no relationship there at all, neither a true nor a plausible one, of premises to what seems to be concluded. Since what is prior is not there, neither do its consequences exist. So they are neither syllogisms nor properly paralogisms in the first mode of word-figure, but rather incongruous sentences.

95 This is not contrary to what we said above that there is a motive principle and a principle of deficiency (so one of plausibility), because that plausibility was in the premises themselves. What we are now saying is that there just seems to be a conclusion. In other modes, truth and falsity remain, so relationships remain, and even if they are not true, they seem to be, since something posterior posits what is prior to it. Truth and falsity are posterior to relationships. For that reason, by having posited truth or falsity, dependencies true or plausible are posited. In this word-group:

'omnis homo est albus   every human being is white
    femina est homo   a woman is a human being
ergo femina est albus'.   therefore a woman is white

a feminine is interpreted as a masculine, conversely to the examples
above, because of how the middle term is taken, as was said. But in
this:

'omnis substantia animata   every animate, sensitive,
    sensibilis est colorata   substance is colored
animal est substantia   an animal is an animate,
    animata sensibilis   sensitive, substance
ergo animal est colorata'.   therefore an animal is
                                        colored

neither is interpreted as one of the others. But if a paralogism were
formed this way:

'<u>Musa</u> et <u>poeta</u> similiter   <u>Muse</u> and <u>poet</u> have the
    terminantur   same ending
  sed <u>Musa</u> est feminini   but <u>Muse</u> is feminine
    generis   gender
ergo et <u>poeta</u>'.   therefore <u>poet</u> is also
                                        feminine

there is a Fallacy of Consequent, not a Fallacy of Word-figure, since
words (<u>dictiones</u>) are not taken as signs or instruments, but as things,
since words are said to be taken as signs or instruments when we
speak about things by using them. That way they are signs of things
and an instrument of speaking. But when we are not speaking about
things by means of them, but about themselves as such, words are
taken as things, and for that reason there is deception in a thing, not
in a word. But if the paralogism were formed thus:

'qualiscumque est Musa,   of whatever sort a Muse is,
    et poeta   a poet is as well
sed Musa est feminini   but Muse is feminine
    generis   gender
ergo et poeta'.   therefore poet is feminine
                                gender as well

words are taken as we use them to speak about things, so they
function as signs and instruments. There is no Fallacy of Word-
figure here, since 'of whatever sort' is distributive of quality, and a
quality cannot be extended further than to the quality which is the

thing signified, like whiteness, knowledge and the like, and to the quality which is a mode of signifying like masculine, feminine and the like. For the thing signified by the noun **'whiteness'** is a quality which is a thing, and similarly by the noun **'color'**. But feminine gender in the noun **'whiteness'** (<u>albedo</u>) is a quality which is a mode of signifying or of understanding, as is masculine gender in the noun **'color'**. For that reason it is fitting that **'of whatever sort'** distributes for both, or for neither, or only for one, or only for the other, since it cannot be for several modes. To say it distributes for neither is fatuous, since it is distributive of quality and there is no other mode of quality other than these two. If one says it distributes for both, he validly takes it under the middle term and the syllogism is entirely valid since it subsumes the other; but the major is false, since this way its sense would be: **whatever quality this thing has, or that thing, and under whatever mode of signifying this or that thing is understood;** and each part of that copulative is false, so the major is false. But if one says it distributes only for the quality which is a mode of signifying, then he again takes it validly under the middle term and the syllogism is valid, since it assumes some particular mode of signifying. But the major is again false, for its sense is: **under whatever mode of signifying 'Muse' and 'poet' are understood.** Since it is a valid syllogism, there is no Fallacy of Word-figure there. If one says it distributes only for the quality which is the thing signified, then there will be four terms, since it would assume another quality, as in this:

> **'every white man is running**
> **an Ethiopian is black**
> **therefore an Ethiopian is running':**

this way nothing is taken under the middle term, neither truly nor plausibly; for that reason, there is no Fallacy of Word-figure.

On the second Mode

96 The second mode of the Fallacy of Word-figure arises when we change one mode of a word (<u>dictio</u>) signifying a universal into another mode of a word also signifying a universal. This happens in three ways: first, a mode generally found in any predicament (as in **in what**) is changed into a mode proper to another predicament (as in **in what sort** or **in how many** or in **in relation to what**). The mode called **in what** is found in any predicament, since any genus or species is predicated **in what** of its inferiors; but **'what sort'** means the mode peculiar to Quality; **'how much'**, that of Quantity, and **'to something'**, the mode peculiar to Relation. A paralogism is formed as follows:

'whatever you saw yesterday, you see today
  but yesterday you saw white
  therefore you see white today';

'white' (album) of itself means **what sort**, even when taken absolutely; but since it is taken under a middle term meaning **what**,
because of that mode being subordinate to it, it seems to signify
what. So 'white' contains within it diverse modes of signifying, one
truly, the other seemingly; that is why **what** is changed into **what
sort**.

A second way one mode of a word signifying a universal is
changed into another mode of a word signifying a universal, is when
the mode peculiar to one predicament is changed into the proper
mode of another, as **how much** changes into **what sort**. As in:

'however much you bought, you ate
  but you bought raw
  therefore you ate raw';

'(something) **raw**' (crudum) means **what sort**, and since it is taken
under **how much**, it seems to have the mode of quantity, and so has
within itself one mode truly, the other apparently. Because of this
seeming likeness, **how much** is changed into **what sort**.

The third way one mode becomes another is when the mode
peculiar to one predicament is changed into another mode of that
same predicament, as **how much** changes into **how many**, in:

'as many fingers as you had, you now have
  but you had ten fingers
  therefore you now have ten fingers';

'a ninth' and 'a tenth' predicate a discrete quantity through the
mode **what**, since they are species of number, and species means
what. But 'nine' and 'ten', which are derived from them denominatively, mean a discrete quantity and through the mode of discrete
quantity. 'As much as' (quantumcumque) says something in a mode
of continuous quantity, so when the one is taken under the mode of
the other, **how much** is changed into **how many**. This second mode
is subdivided three ways and is usually labelled predicamental commutation, not because the content (res) of one predicament is changed into the content of another, but because one mode is changed into
another mode, as we said. So here:

'whatever you saw yesterday, you see today
    yesterday you saw whiteness
    therefore today you see whiteness'

this is no Fallacy of Word-figure, since just as **'whatever'** means
what (quid) commonly in any predicament, but not substance, so
too **'whiteness'** (albedinem) means **'what'**. But if ('yesterday you
saw) **white'** (album) were assumed, it would become a Fallacy of
Word-figure because of diverse modes, as we said.

On the third Mode

97 The third mode of the fallacy of word-figure arises when
'what sort of thing' is interpreted as **'this particular thing',**[55] that
is, when a common mode is changed into a singular mode. Or the
converse, extending the label (nomen) **'common'** to simply common, like **man** or **animal,** and to common by addition of another
expression, like **'Coriscus the musician',** where the common term
'musician' is adjoined to a singular one. Aristotle says[56] this kind of
paralogism results:

'Coriscus is 'a third man' other than man
    but Coriscus himself is a man
    therefore he is 'a third man' other than himself';

'man', as Aristotle says[57] and every common term, signifies not
this particular thing but **a sort of thing** or **to something,** and so
for the other common modes. But what **Coriscus** means is **this
particular thing,** that is, a discrete thing and one signified as
singular, which cannot be in several things, but can be common. So
'Coriscus' taken simply has the mode of individuation or singularity
and as taken under **'man',** seems to contain within it the mode **a
sort of thing,** like **'man'.** This way it seems to involve several
modes, while **'man'** on the contrary is simply **a sort of thing,** since
it is simply common. This mode **what sort** is nothing other than an
aptitude for existing in several things, but since **'man'** is in this and
that singular thing, both of which are **this individual thing,** it
seems **'man'** is **this individual thing** too, and so **'man'** involves
several modes, one truly (which is **a sort of thing)** another seemingly
(namely **this particular thing).** So too any other common thing,

55: tóde ti.
56: Soph. El. 22, 178b 37-39.
57: Soph. El. 5, 166b32-33.

which is what a genus and a species is, has two modes. So when I
say: 'Coriscus is 'a third man' other than man', it is not true unless
man is a sort of thing. But if man were this individual thing, as
Socrates is and other individuals are, it would not be predicated of
any individual any more than 'Coriscus' would be predicated of Socrates or Plato. So 'Coriscus is 'a third man' other than man' is not
true unless man is a sort of thing. When I say: 'Coriscus himself is
man', I am accepting sort of thing as subordinated to this individual thing, so I am changing sort of thing into this individual
thing by concluding: 'therefore Corsicus is other than himself'. For
all paralogisms of word-figure are contrary to rules of inference, as
was said. But if man were this particular thing, this would follow
validly:

> 'Coriscus is 'a third man' other than man
>   but Coriscus himself is man
>   therefore he is 'a third man' other than himself;'

but the minor would be false, as this one is:

> 'Coriscus is 'a third man' other than Plato,
> granted there are three;
>   but Coriscus is Plato
>   therefore Coriscus is 'a third man' other than himself'

follows validly, but the minor is false. Aristotle mentions another
paralogism like this:[58]

> 'Coriscus is different from Coriscus the musician
>   but Coriscus the musician is Coriscus
>   therefore Coriscus is different from Coriscus'.

The first 'Coriscus' signifies this individual. The second, 'Coriscus
the musician', signifies of some sort. Since the difference of plain
Coriscus to Coriscus-as-musician is signified, as the quality of being
the musician Coriscus is signified, not the Coriscus who is this
individual, concluding to the otherness of Coriscus changes of some
sort into this individual. And so the inference is invalid.

98 Notice that in the first paralogism, what genus or species
is, is labelled what sort of thing. For genus or species, as common,
has the nature what sort of. But as predicated in what, it

58: Soph. El. 17, 175b 21-22.

signifies **what**. So too for **what sort of thing**, since it is common
and predicated in **what**. But in the second paralogism, Aristotle[59]
labels **'Coriscus the musician'** as **what sort of thing**, so **musician**
which is a quality, means **what sort**. The subject of that quality,
Coriscus, Aristotle calls **what**, so Coriscus the musician is **a sort
of thing**. Notice how Aristotle extends **what sort of thing** to these
two, since in the predicament of substance, only genera and species
mean **what sort of thing**.[60]   So there he takes **what sort of thing**
properly, here by extended denomination. In the same way, **what
sort of thing** is interpreted here as **this individual:**

> **'Socrates is an animal**
> **Plato is an animal**
and so on for individuals;
> **therefore every man is an animal'**.

Since **animal** is **what sort of thing**, and as it signifies the same
thing as **'Socrates'**, it seems to have the mode of **this particular
thing**. So concluding: **'therefore every man is an animal'** changes
the mode truly in **animal** (i.e., **what sort of thing**) into one
seemingly there (i.e., **this particular thing**). And so it does not
follow. But if that seeming mode were truly there, it would follow
validly, since then **animal** would be **this individual** simply, as in:

> **'Socrates is Socrates**
> **Socrates is Plato, Socrates is Cicero**
and so on for individuals;
> **therefore Socrates is every man'**

follows validly. Propositional falsity is no barrier to an argument's
validity.

99 They and those like them are wont to label this paralogism
a shift **'from from several determinate suppositions to a single
determinate'**, since **'animal'** has determinate supposition both in
premises and conclusion. But it is nothing, since going from one
determinate supposition to another produces no fallacy unless some
other defect accompanies it. As here:

> **'a white animal moves**
> **a white animal runs**
> **therefore a white animal both moves and runs';**

59: Soph. El. 22, 179a 1-2.
60: Categ. 5, 3b 13-16, p. 52.

in premises and conclusion, **'animal'** has determinate supposition. Similarly, wherever they say a shift is made from simple to personal supposition, that either does not produce Fallacy of Word-figure, or **what sort of thing** should be interpreted as **this particular thing,** as

> **'man is a species**
> **this man is a man**
> **therefore this man is a species',**

since **'man'** signifies **what sort of thing** and **'this man'** signifies **'this particular thing',** as is clear enough from what was said. And this:

> **'every man is an animal**
> **therefore every man is this animal';**

and this as well:

> **'every animate body aside from an animal is insensitive**
> **therefore aside from this animal';**

for in both, **'animal'** signifies **what sort of thing,** while **'this animal'** signifies **this particular thing;** so **what sort of thing** is interpreted as **this particular thing.**

100 Notice also that different genera, as found simply in the same word (<u>dictio</u>) are principles of deceiving on the basis of equivocation, as:

> **'a priest celebrates Mass**
> **a woman is a priest**
> **therefore a woman celebrates Mass'.**

Diverse genera, not only as in the same but different words (<u>dictio</u>), such that one has its own proper genus and seemingly has the genus of the other, are principles of deceiving on the basis of Fallacy of Word-figure as to the first mode, as was clear above.

This fallacy has been diffusely discussed because of its many difficulties.

ON EXTRALINGUISTIC FALLACIES

101 A fallacy is called extralinguistic (extra dictionem) if its plausible cause and cause of non-existence is in a thing (in re). Through this it differs from linguistic (in dictione) fallacies. They are the ones with their plausible cause in expression (dictione) and their cause of non-existence in a thing.

There are seven nonlinguistic fallacies: The first is **Accident,** the second **After a fashion and simply** (secundum quid et simpliciter), the third **Ignorance of the point in Question** (ignorantia elenchi), the fourth **Begging the Question** or **Search for what was originally conceded** (petitio ejus quod erat in principio), the fifth **Consequence,** the sixth **Non-cause as cause,** and the seventh, **Many questions as a single one.**

ON ACCIDENT

102 We must first discuss Fallacy of Accident. Aristotle posits[61] this sort of nature[62] for it: 'Fallacy of Accident arises when someone claims that any (attribute) belongs to a thing and its accident in like manner.' As in:

> 'man is a species
>   Socrates is a man
>   therefore Socrates is a species';

where **man** is subject and **Socrates** its Accident; and the claim is that 'species' belongs to both **man** and **Socrates** in like manner, for **species** belongs to both as an accident belongs to its subject.

103 Notice that wherever there is a Fallacy of Accident, a double sort of accident is required: one an accident of the subject, the other assigned being-in to the thing that is subject and its accident. Each is assigned in the common nature of paralogisms of accident just mentioned. So if someone asks how 'accident' is to be taken here, reply that the question itself is ambiguous because of that two-sided sort of accident always required for a paralogism on the basis of Accident. So if the question is about that accident assigned being-in to both, say Accident in that sense is not what

---

61: Soph. El. 5, 166b28-30.
62: rationem; here: 'definition'.

Porphyry takes as one of the five predicables, nor what Aristotle takes as one of the four predicates in Topics[63]. Nor is it Accident distinguished as an opposite to Substance, when we say: 'whatever is, is either Substance, Accident, or the Creator of Substance and Accident.' That accident is the same as 'non-necessary in consequence', for 'non-necessary' is said ambiguously. One way is in being predicate or subject, like 'Socrates is a man' or 'an animal is a substance'. It depends on whether the higher is in a way an accident of its inferior, or the converse when an inferior is an accident of its superior: 'something non-necessary' is not taken that way here. The other way, it is non-necessary in consequence, as we said; that is how 'an accident that is assigned being-in to both' is taken here. So accident taken this way is opposed to what 'happen of necessity' is. I do not mean 'happen of necessity' as an inferential necessity is caused by quality, quantity and order of propositions, - what is opposed to that necessity is labelled 'useless selection' in Prior Analytics[64] - but I do mean 'happen of necessity' insofar as inferential necessity is caused by relationships of Topic, as in dialectics, or by cause or effect, as in demonstrations. To this inferential necessity is opposed accident assigned being-in to both, because that way 'happen of necessity' is predicated ambiguously. So 'accident' this way is the same as 'non-necessary in consequence' as opposed to that inferential necessity we mentioned.

If one inquires about that accident which is an accident of the thing that is subject, I say it is extraneous or diverse in respect to some third thing. So 'man' as standing under the predicate 'species', has all inferiors as its accidents and all superiors similarly; so from both sides it is an accident, if any one of them is an accident. As in:

'man is a species
   man is a substance
   therefore a substance is a species'

or:

'man is a species
   Socrates is a man
   therefore Socrates is a species';

this way, both being superior and being inferior is an accident of man with respect to some third thing.

63: Topica I 5, 102b 4-7, et passim.
64: Anal. Priora I 28, 44b26; cf. Scholia in Anal Priora I, ad loc., p. 317, ed. Minio-Paluello.

104 Notice also that some have said the accident required for this fallacy was of an intermediate sort, partly the same as, and partly different from, the extremes. They were wrong in two ways. First, since in any syllogism, the middle term should be partly the same and partly different from each extreme. They were also wrong since they were supposing that a single mode of accident is required for this fallacy, which is false, since, as we have said, a double kind of accident is always required.

105 Note too that a double identity of middle term is required in any valid syllogism. One tolerates diversity within itself - and this identity is that of the middle term with respect to extremes, as we said - the other identity is that of the middle in itself as the repeated middle term in the premises, or as it stands in its nature of repeated middle. Given that the middle term is to be repeated in the premises, it should be simply the same. It is against this identity in the middle term that this fallacy offends.

On Causes and Modes of Accident

106 Now we have seen the common nature of paralogisms of Accident and that a two-fold sort of accident is always required for such paralogisms and how two modes of accident are and are not to be taken there, and that a two-fold identity is required in any syllogism, causes and modes of Accident are now to be discussed.

The motive principle of a Fallacy of Accident is the partial identity of the middle term as repeated in the premises. I say **'as repeated in the premises'** so its partial identitity as middle term itself to extremes be not understood, but itself as repeated. The deficient principle is diversity of a repeated middle term on the basis of definition. For instance:

> **'man is a species**
>   Socrates is a man
>   **therefore Socrates is a species';**

here an accident as middle term (**'man'**) is substantially the same in the premises, as repeated. But it is not identical as to definition, since **'man'** is subject in the major for what is common in itself, not as it is in Socrates or based on the comparison it has to its inferiors - but in the minor proposition, it is predicated of Socrates on the basis of the latter comparison, rather than the former. So it is identical in substance, diverse in definition, as repeated. But when I say:

'every man runs
    Socrates is a man
    therefore Socrates runs',

this is a valid syllogism, since 'run' is predicated of man on the
basis of how 'man' compares to its inferiors. So the middle term is
not taken in diverse definitions, as when subordinated to a species.

107 If anyone objects that the middle term is taken on the
basis of different accidental comparisons, therefore it is an accident
in this fallacy, say this does not follow. Although a middle term
may be taken in different accidental comparisons, this is not
because it is others' accident, but because other things are its
accidents: just as being a species is an accident of **man** and
Socrates is an accident of man differently, as was said before.

108 Modes of this fallacy are distinguished from the aspect of
accidents of a subject: they can be antecedent, consequent, or
convertible. In one way, an inferior is its superior's accident,
Aristotle says in his general solution of paralogisms of Accident,[65]
that Socrates is accidental to **man**. In Second Topics[66], he says
being equilateral is as accidental to a triangle as being an isosceles
is; an equilateral has three equal sides, an isosceles only two, while
a quadrilateral has all sides of different length. A superior is its
inferior's accident differently. So in his chapter on reduction to
Ignoring the Point, Aristotle says being a figure is accidental to a
triangle,[67] and in the beginning of his earlier Metaphysics[68], that
man is accidental to Socrates. 'Accident' is taken a third way on
the basis of one convertible being accidental to its matching
convertible, as will be clear later[89]. That is why I say that
sometimes a superior is an accident of its inferior, sometimes an
inferior of its superior, sometimes one convertible is an accident of
its matching convertible.

Understand things in similar fashion about antecedent and
consequent and convertible, whether they are predicables or not,
since this fallacy is an accident in predicables and nonpredicables.

65: Soph. El. 5, 166b35-36.
66: Topica II 3, 110b 24-25.
67: Topica II 3, 110b 24-24, p. 35.
68: Metaph. I 1, 981a 19-20, p.35.

On the first Mode

109   The first mode of the Fallacy of Accident is when an antecedent is an accident of its antecedent. As in:

> 'man is a species
>   Socrates is a man
>   therefore Socrates is a species'

or:

> 'an animal is an ass
>   a man is an animal
>   therefore a man is an ass'

or:

> 'an animal is running
>   a man is an animal
>   therefore a man is running

or:

'every triangle has three angles equal to two right angles
    an isoceles is a triangle
therefore an isosceles has three angles equal to two right angles'
or:

> 'every metal is natural
>   but every cast statue is metal
>   therefore every cast statue is natural'

or:

> 'all stones or wood are natural
>   but a house is made of stones and wood
>   therefore every house is natural'.

In the first paralogism, **Socrates**, which is **man's** antecedent, is its accident and **species** is assigned being-in to both. In the second, **man** is an accident to **animal** and **ass** is assigned being-in to both. It would be similar if **animal** were predicated of both, in which case the paralogism would be made in the second figure, as:

> 'an ass is an animal
>   a man is an animal
>   therefore a man is an ass'.

In the next paralogism **man** is an accident to **animal** and **run** is assigned being-in to both. In the fourth, **isosceles** is accidental to **triangle** and **having three sides** is assigned being-in to both.

69:   below, p. 132 ff.

110 Notice that in the paralogism, whether a dialectician or logician (demonstrator) prove 'having, three angles, etc.' about an isosceles triangle as about an adequate or convertible subject, it is still a sophistry of Accident. But if each proves possession of three sides about an isosceles as of a particular subject through a suitable middle term, one through a dialectical middle term, the other by a demonstrative one, it will still be a valid syllogism for both: a good dialectical syllogism for one, a valid particular demonstration for the other.

111 Notice that if 'triangle' is taken as predicable of an isosceles triangle, it is a dialectical middle term; if taken as containing the proximate cause of the capacity (passio) of 'having three sides', and made middle term to prove that capacity about an isosceles as of a particular subject, it is a demonstrative middle term, and for that reason, a particular demonstration. So the same thing, taken on the basis of different definitions, can be a dialectical or a demonstrative middle term. So one claiming that in the paralogism cited there is a Fallacy of Accident for logical demonstrators but a valid syllogism for dialecticians, is saying nothing. Even though 'triangle' be taken as containing the proximate and immediate cause of that capacity, it is still a Fallacy of Accident, as long as the same capacity is proven of an isosceles triangle as of a proper subject. It is obvious that a middle term so taken is not just dialectical. So it should be understood as we have said.

112 So too, **cast statue** is as accidental to **metal** as **home** is to **wood** and **stones,** insofar as the middle term stands under the predicate 'be natural' or 'be from nature'. In all these, antecedent is accidental to consequent, but in the last two, 'antecedent' and 'consequent' are not taken peculiarly in predication: **metal** is not predicated of a cast statue as a Peculiarity, nor are **stones** and **wood** of a house. If one object that there is an accident in this:

'every animal runs
    every man is an animal
  therefore every man runs',

since **man** is accidental to **animal,** and **run** assigned being-in to both, say as before, that there is no accident here, since **animal** is the subject of **run** discretely and expressly in the major for any inferior, and by the same token, **animal** is predicated of **man** in the minor by comparison with everything contained under **man.** The middle term is thus substantially identical and taken on the basis of the same comparison, so the middle term is taken on the basis of a single form, not different ones.

On the second Mode

113 The second mode of the Fallacy of Accident occurs when a consequent is accidental to its antecedent, for example:

> 'man is a species
>   man is a substance
>   therefore a substance is a species';

and:

> 'every triangle has three angles equal to two right angles
>   but every triangle is a figure
>   therefore a figure has three angles, etc.';

or:

> 'a doctor is healing Socrates
>   but Socrates is a man
>   therefore a doctor is healing Man';

> 'Socrates is a monk
>   Socrates is white
>   therefore Socrates is a White Monk[70]';

> 'I know Coriscus
>   and Coriscus is coming
>   therefore I know the one who is coming';

> 'every house is an artifact
>   every house is made of stones and wood
>   therefore stones and wood are artifacts'.

In the first, **substance** is accidental to **man** and **species** assigned being-in to both as to its proper, adequate subject. So it is a sophism of Accident.

In the second, **figure** is accidental to **triangle**. But **having three** etc. is assigned being-in to both as to a proper, adequate subject. So it is a similar fallacy.

In the next, **homo** is accidental to **Socrates**; for every change and all operations have to do with singulars. That is why a doctor heals Man only by accident in healing just Socrates or Plato.

70: A 'White Monk' is a Cistercian or Premonstratensian (Norbertine) Monk; a 'Black Monk' is a Dominican.

In the next, **being a monk** is accidental to **Socrates** and **white** assigned being-in to both. But **to be a monk** is a common accident and so it has the nature of a consequent, so a consequent is accidental to its antecedent. So too, **coming** is accidental to **Coriscus** and **being known by me** assigned being-in to each. In the last one, **stones** and **wood** are accidental to **house** as standing under the predicate **'be an artifact'** or **'be due to art'**. For stones and wood are neither artificial things nor due to some art; indeed they are natural things, but their being squared or gilded comes from an art. So they are accidents with respect to that predicate.

In all the above in the second mode, a consequent is accident to an antecedent.

On the third Mode

114 The third mode of the Fallacy of Accident occurs when one convertible is accident to its matching converitible, as in:

> 'man is a species
>   what can laugh is a man
>   therefore what can laugh is a species';

man is subject of **species** essentially, not by the nature whereby it can laugh; so **what can laugh** is accidental to **man** with respect to the predicate **'species'**. Again:

> 'to be able to laugh is a Peculiarity
>   a man is able to laugh
>   therefore man is a Peculiarity';

man is here accidental to **able to laugh,** since **able to laugh** is a subject of the concept **Peculiarity** (<u>proprium</u>) in such a way that it is not accidental by the nature of **man.** That way **man** is accidental to **able to laugh,** and that way one convertible is accidental to another convertible. So too here:

> 'a father is in a superordinate position
>   therefore so is a son',

insofar as **father** stands under that predicate, **son** is accidental to it and so **father** is subject and **son** accidental to its subject and **be in a superordinate position** is an accident assigned being-in to both. It is thus non-necessary insofar as **son** followed upon **father,** and so non-necessary in consequence. So too here:

'that which is a father is naturally prior to a son
therefore a father is naturally prior to a son'.

In this, the subject of paternity is the thing that is subject, (i.e., **that which is a father)** and **father** is accidental to the thing that is subject, and **to be naturally prior to a son** is assigned being-in to both.

115 Notice that this convertibility is different from those discussed above, since **'father'** is convertible with **'that which is father'** / the subject of paternity   just like a relation with its peculiar subject in which it has being or becoming when it is itself compared to another. **'Able to laugh'** is not paired with **'man'** that way, but as a peculiar capacity (passio) with its peculiar subject. Nor are **'father'** and **'son'** paired by either of the modes mentioned, but as one correlative with another. Many and diverse are the causes of convertibility.

From all this it is obvious that one convertible is an accident of its match on the basis of some third thing.

116 Notice that wherever a Fallacy of Word-figure is found, an accident is always involved but not the converse. That comes about by diverse principles and diverse natures accompanying each other. Take **to see:** this has two different pairings or two diverse respects accompanying it: **to see** is paired with eye as its organ and with color as its object; the two respects are always found together in the same act of seeing, though they are diverse. So too where there is a Fallacy of Word-figure: a mode of signifying is paired with a word (dictio) and belongs to it as instrument or sign; it is also paired with the thing signified, and is its object or significate. It is also its subject.

I understand this of a mode of signifying as appropriate to all modes of word-figure / all its species, namely according as this mode of signifying has these two diverse respects. That is why I say that if this mode of signifying were the motive principle, to the extent that it is in its sign which is a word (dictio), then there is linguistic (in dictione) deception, so a Fallacy of Word-figure. But if **'mode of signifying'** is taken on the basis of the other pairing, namely as paired with a thing to which it belongs as to a subject, and this way is made the motive principle, then there is extralinguistic (extra dictionem) deception, and thus it is an accident. So wherever there is Fallacy of Word-figure, there an accident is always found, but not the converse. A thing's nature does not depend on that of a word (dictio), while a word's nature does depend on the nature of a thing, since a word is a sign of a thing and related to it purposively. Perfection comes from purpose and fulfillment in what pertain to purpose, but not the other way around; for which reason there cannot be the nature of a word (<u>dictio</u>) without the nature of a thing.

117 Notice that wherever there is Fallacy of Accident, I say the middle term / that of which it is truly predicated that being-in is assigned to both, is **the thing that is subject;** and that the minor extremity / what is an extremity on the part of the minor is **an accident of the thing that is subject** (whether it can be subject or predicate of the middle term or not); and that the major extremity / an extremity on the part of the Major, I say is **an accident assigned being-in to both.** This is the other sort of accident that is non-necessary in consequence.

118 This is not contrary to what Aristotle says in Second Elenchi,[71] that sometimes what is in an accident is predicated of the subject. So it seems that we do not demonstrate something sophistically about accident only through the thing that is subject, but also through its accident. For I am saying that some paralogisms of Accident include only one part of a contradiction (as is clear in the above) while others have both parts. And this both implicitly and explicitly, as in:

'I know Coriscus
    I have no knowledge about the one coming
 therefore I know and I have no knowledge about the same person';

this conclusion has an implicit contradiction and takes one part from the side of the subject, the other from the side of an accidental. But when I say:

    'I know Coriscus
        and I do not know the one coming
        therefore I know and I do not know the same person',

the contradiction is explicit. In those with both parts of a contradicition,[72] it seems to be what Aristotle is saying. In the same place, he says on some occasions it seems to be so and they state it, but in other cases they do not say. In those which conclude to one part of a contradiction, it is always demonstrated through the

---

71:   <u>Soph. El.</u> 24, 179a 27-29.
72:   <u>Soph. El.</u> 24, 179a29-30.

thing that is subject that something suits an accident, or whether some terms are taken predicatively or not.

119 It might be solved another way - one I think better, though the first one is true - by saying there is nothing to those further objections, since in any such paralogism there is virtually a pair. So one should understand a third proposition in the premises, as follows:

'I know Coriscus
   I have no knowledge about the one who is coming
and Coriscus is the one who is coming
      therefore I know and I have no knowledge about the same person';

and they are put together as:

   'I know Coriscus
      Coriscus is that one who is coming
      therefore I know that one who is coming';

Again:

'I have no knowledge about the one coming
   and the one coming is that person who is coming
therefore I have no knowledge about that person who is coming
therefore I know and I have no knowledge about the same person'.

In the first paralogism, through 'Coriscus', which is the thing that is subject, it is demonstrated that that person who is coming is known to me, since that knowledge pertains to the minor extremity and is accidental to Coriscus to the extent that 'Coriscus' is subject of 'that person who is coming'. In the second, it is demonstrated through 'the one coming', the thing that is subject, that 'that person who is coming' is unknown to me and so the one coming is both the thing that is subject and the middle term; 'that person who is coming' is the major extremity and 'I have no knowledge about' the minor extremity, an accident to the one coming to the extent that 'the one coming' stands under that predicate.

So it is universally clear what should be assigned as the thing that is subject and what should be assigned as accident to the thing that is subject and what should be assigned as the accident which is assigned being-in to both.

ON THE FALLACY AFTER-A-FASHION AND SIMPLY

On the Definition of these Terms

120 We now take up the Fallacy **After-a-Fashion and Simply** (secundum quid et simpliciter). First notice that **'after-a-fashion'** is used two ways. **'After-a-fashion'** diminishes its whole in one way as **'white-footed'** (albus pedem) diminishes **'something white'** (album) simply taken, and **'dead man'** does **'man'**. Through this sort of **after-a-fashion,** the Fallacy of **After-a-fashion and Simply** arises.

The other way, **'after-a-fashion'** does not diminish its whole but simply posits it and makes an inference, as in **'curly headed'; therefore curly',** or **'snub nosed; therefore snubbed'.** This is in any form and in any accident denominating a whole by its part, like curly, which denominates a man by his head; snubness or aquilinity are only in a nose yet a man is said to be snubnosed or aquiline because of them; blindness is in the eyes and by it, a man is said to be blind; knowledge and virtue are in the soul as in a subject and thereby a man is said to be knowledgable or having virtues; and so for any other similar things that denominate a whole by a part.

All other forms and accidents of any sort are forms and accidents of a whole itself in such a way as not to pertain only to a part - none of these, I say, can give a name to a whole unless they are in that whole simply. It is in such as these that the fallacy **After-a-fashion and Simply** falls, since a determination arising in that sort as to part or as to some other respect, diminish the whole simply. That kind of **'after-a-fashion'** is taken here, not the other kind that does not diminish.

From this it is clear that **'after-a-fashion'** as taken here is said to be a determination diminishing the nature of what it is adjoined to. An undiminished thing is called one **'simply',** whether it is accident or substance, like **'(something) white', '(something) black', 'animal', 'man'.**

On Causes and Modes of this Fallacy

121 The motive cause of this fallacy is the partial identity of the same thing diminishing **after-a-fashion,** compared to itself **simply** said. The cause of non-existence is their difference.

This fallacy arises in as many ways as adding a determination to something diminishes it.

On the first Mode

122 First, on the basis of a part diminishing in mode. Like:

'he is a dead man
    therefore he is a man';

this does not follow because 'dead' diminishes the nature of 'man' itself. And

'a chimera is a matter of opinion
    therefore there is a chimera';

for 'matter of opinion' [or 'famous' : opinabilis] diminishes 'to be'. And:

'there is a pictured animal or a pictured eye
    therefore there is an animal or an eye';

'pictured' diminishes the nature of these things. Aristotle forms these paralogisms as follows:[73]

'what is not is a matter of opinion
like the chimera;
    therefore what is not, is'.

You can form all the others the same way, like:

'what is not a man is a dead man
    therefore what is not a man is a man'

'what is not an animal is a pictured animal
    therefore what is not an animal is an animal'.

On the second Mode

124 The second mode is based on integral part. Like:

73: Soph. El. 5, 167a 1-2.

'an Ethiopian is white as to the teeth
therefore an Ethiopian is white'.

On the third Mode

125 The third mode comes from things which are relative (ad aliquid). Like:

'riches are not good for the foolish man or the wastrel
therefore riches are not good';

even though they may not be good compared to something (ad aliquid), they are still good in themselves.

And:

'an egg is potentially an animal
therefore an egg is an animal';

every potency is such relative to something, since it is related to the actuality by which it is perfected.

On the fourth Mode

125 The fourth mode has to do with a Topic. Like:

'it is good to honor your father in Trivallis
therefore it is good to honor your father'

and:

'it is helpful to use a diet in hospitals
therefore it is helpful to use a diet';

though it might be expedient there, it is not expedient simply.

On the fifth Mode

126 The fifth mode has to do with when (quando). Like:

'he fasts during Lent
therefore he fasts';

and:

'it is helpful for someone to take medicine when ill
therefore it is helpful for someone to take medicine';

127 Note that wherever a fallacy of fashion and simply is found, it is understood as and is a double contradiction, one in the

conclusion, which is a true contradiction, the other in the premises, which is a diminished contradiction. The respondent says an Ethiopian is not white; his opponent says he is white as to the teeth; so he does not contradict him except **after-a-fashion.** And from that **after-a-fashion** contradiction, he infers a true one, as follows:

'therefore an Ethiopian is both white and not white';

so it offends against **After-a-fashion and Simply,** because a genuine contradiction does not follow from a contradiction **after-a-fashion.** All others are dealt with the same way.

128 That is why Aristotle gives a general solution for all paralogisms of this fallacy,[74] namely, to consider a conclusion as to contradiction, that is, to compare the contradiction of a correct conclusion to a contradiction in the premises, which is a contradiction **after-a-fashion.** That is why the one does not follow from the other.

129 Notice that it is the same fallacy to go from **After-a-fashion** to **Simply** as to go from **Simply,** negatively taken, to **After-a-fashion** itself, negated as far as its terms go. Like:

'it is not a man
    therefore it is not a dead man';
or:
'he is not white
    therefore he is not white as to the teeth',

for the motive principle remains the same, as does the defective principle: neither **fashion** nor **simply** is motive, but the partial match of the one with the other is.

130 Note also that you should not label things in which contraries seem equally to be-in as diverse parts from the other contrary. So if a shield is half white, half black, you ought not say, 'the shield is black or white', but 'partly thus and partly so'. That is why this argument is invalid:

'there is no color except whiteness, blackness or the intermediate
    color;
therefore nothing is colored except something white,
    or black, or colored by the intermediate color',

74: Soph. El. 25, 180a 23-31.

some colored things are tinted with a single color, some with several. That argument only holds for monochrome things. That is why the argument is null, since it does not hold universally. Even allowing a shield is not tinted by an intermediate color, it still does not follow that it is white or black. But this would be a valid argument:

'nothing is a color except black, white or the intermediate color;
     therefore nothing is colored except something white
     or black or something colored by that intermediate color,
     or partly white, partly black, partly colored by that
     middle color or by intermediate colors'.

So too in all contrary forms having a middle and inhering according to diverse parts, as something blackly white (album nigrum) so too, something coldly hot, softly hard, and whatever others that are-in the same whole according to different parts.

ON IGNORING REFUTING EVIDENCE

On Refutation

131 A refutation (elenchus) is a syllogism of contradiction of one and the same thing, not just of a name, but of both a thing and its name, not of a synomym, but of the same thing, derived from what have been necessarily granted, aside from the original point at issue, on the same basis, as identically related, in the same way, and at the same time.[75]   There are two things in this definition of 'refutation': 'syllogism' and 'contradiction'. For a refutation is nothing other than a syllogism whose conclusion contradicts the conclusion of another syllogism. A refutation is then two syllogisms contradicting each other, or whose conclusion contradicts a proposition previously assumed. A refutation is then a syllogism of one thing with its contradiction. So a refutation is always a syllogism with its contradiction.

132 In the definition of 'refutation' just given, some elements are included by reason of syllogism, some by reason of contradiction, some for both reasons. These are included by reason of syllogism: 'from what have been necessarily granted', 'aside from the original point at issue', which remove the fallacy of assuming what was to be proven (petitio ejus quod erat in principio), as will be clear

75: Soph. El. 5, 167a 23-27.

later.[76]   By reason of contradiction, these are posited: **'of one'** and **'the same'**,   that is, of the one and the same subject and predicate.   Unless it were the same subject and the same predicate, it would not be a contradiction, as in **'an Ethiopian is black'**, **'an Ethiopian is not black as to the teeth'** the predicate is not the same; while in **'no dead man runs'**, **'some man runs'**, the subject is not the same. The expressions **'on the same basis'** (secundum idem), **'with identical relation'** (ad idem), **'in the same way'** (similiter) and **'at the same time** (in eodem tempore) are also included there by reason of contradiction. Against these particulars the fallacy called **Ignoring the Point in Question** (Ignorantia Elenchi) also offends, it being one of thirteen mutually opposed fallacies, for in another way, Ignorantia Elenchi offends against all these particulars included in its definition, such that all fallacies reduce to this one, as will be clear later.[77]   For both reasons, these expressions are included: **not just of name only but of name and thing'** and **'not of a synonym, but of the same name'**, for both in a syllogism as well as in a contradiction it is required that a name be one thing and a thing something else. So this is not a contradiction: **'Marcus is running, 'Tullius is not running'**, because the same name does not occur there, just a synomym; nor is: **'every dog is able to bark'**, **'a certain dog is not able to bark'**, for we do not have the same objects here. But in:

> **'every sword cuts**
> **a particular instrument is a blade**
> **therefore a particular instrument cuts'**

there is no syllogism, since the same name is not repeated as the middle term, just a synomym.

On Ignorance

132 bis **'Ignorance'** is said in several ways. One is negative ignorance, the way a child lying in the crib is ignorant of all sciences.   This is called negative ignorance because it affirms nothing; the one who has this knows nothing. Another is dispositional ignorance: this is when one already knows a bit about a thing, but does not know it as it is. This again is said ambiguously, in one way called simple (that concerns principles or premised propositions) the other composite or multiple, and this is about conclusions. That is how Aristotle distinguishes Ignorance in the

76:   p. 145 f below.
77:   below, p. 159 ff.

First book of Posterior Analytics when he deals with pseudo-syllog-isms.[78]

133 You should understand further that each of these (simple ignorance and the one that is composite or multiple) is still ambiguous. Simple dispositional ignorance can be about principles themselves or about premised propositions, by apprehending them contrarily, as in accepting those that are false. The other way, simple ignorance can be about premised propositions, knowing something about them correctly, without recognizing their whole substance or power. So too, composite or multiple ignorance is ambiguous as to conclusions, as when they were to be taken contrarily, as in falsity, or if they were imperfectly known.

On Ignorantia Elenchi

134 Having seen what a refutation is and how many ways 'ignorance' is used, one must know that 'Ignoring the Point in Question' (ignorantia elenchi) is taken here with reference to dispositional, not negative ignorance. It is not about that sort of dispositional ignorance which is multiple or composite, but the simple one. Here, 'ignoring the point in question' should be taken by reason of the perfection of refutation and of its complement. That perfection is effected through determinations which are Peculiarities of a contradiction, i.e., those noted by the expressions 'with identical relation' (ad idem), 'on the same basis' (secundum idem), 'in the same way' (similiter), and 'at the same time' (in eodem tempore). It is further clear that dispositional ignorance should be taken here as simple, because it is a principle of arguing and as such should be paired as a principle is to a conclusion. So by this simple ignorance, later composite or multiple ignorance is caused, since the respondent is deceived through it by arguing sophistically.

On the Causes and Modes of this Fallacy

The cause of this fallacy's plausibility is the compatibility of two things taken after-a-fashion to two taken simply; the cause of its falsity is their diversity.

There are four modes of this fallacy.

78: Post. An. I 16, 79b 23-25, Jacobi's translation, Minio Paluello's edition, p. 34.

On the first Mode

135　The first mode is contrary to the particular **'with identic-al relation'** (<u>ad</u> <u>idem</u>).　For example:

> **'two is a double of one**
> **but two is not a double of three**
> **therefore a double and a non–double are the same'**

does not follow because **a double** is not taken with identical relation in both premises.

On the second Mode

136　The second mode offends against the particular **'on the same basis'** (<u>secundum</u> <u>idem</u>).　For example:

> **'this is double that in length**
> **this is not double that in breadth**
> **therefore this is double and not double'**

does not follow because **'double'** is not taken on the same basis, though double is predicated with respect to the same thing.

On the third Mode

137　The third mode is contrary to the particular **'in the same way'** (<u>similiter</u>).

> **'man is a species**
> **no man is a species**
> **therefore the same thing is a species and not a species';**

there is no contradiction in the premises, because the term **'man'** is not taken the same way.　In one it is taken for its inferiors, but in the other it is not, but for itself.

On the fourth Mode

138　The fourth mode is contrary to the particular, **'at the same time'** (<u>in</u> <u>eodem</u> <u>tempore</u>).　For example:

> **'my hand is closed at one time**
> **and it is not closed at another time**
> **therefore it is closed and it is not closed'.**

139 Notice that in this fallacy, even though there is a true contradiction in the conclusion, and another seeming one in the premises, as mentioned in the fallacy **After-a-fashion and Simply,**[79] this fallacy differs from that one, because this has a seeming contradiction in the premises with a defect in both parts of the contradiction, as paralogisms of this fallacy show. But a fallacy **After-a-fashion and Simply** has a seeming contradiction offending only in one part. This one's solution differs from that one's, because Aristotle[80] teaches with respect to both that we solve by considering the conclusion as a contradiction, i.e., by considering the true contradiction of a conclusion in contrast to seeming contradiction in the premises. Here we proceed by considering a true contradiction in contrast to the seeming one because of diminution of both parts, there, in contrast to the seeming one due to diminution only of the one.

140 If one objects that **fashion and simply** should be part of this fallacy, since a shift is made there from one taken **after-a-fashion** to one taken **simply,** while here the shift is from a pair taken **after-a-fashion** to a pair taken **simply,** so there really should not be two fallacies because a part is not numerically identical with its whole -, say neither is a part of the other, indeed they are fallacies divided on opposing grounds, since it is not **fashion** and **simply** themselves which constitute the fallacy **After-a-fashion and Simply,** but the relation of the one to the other. Just as species and genus are not a Topic but a relationship of the one thing to another. Even though 'man' is not numerically identical with 'animal', (being part of it), the relations are yet numerically identical among themselves. For one of these relationships is a generic Topic, while the other is a specific Topic. In the same way, the relationship of one thing taken **after-a-fashion** to a another thing taken **simply** is different from the relation of a pair taken **after-a-fashion** to another pair taken **simply,** even though an **after-a-fashion** unit is part of a pair, and a unit taken **simply** is part of a pair.

So these two fallacies will be specifically different. Similarly, though half a line is not numerically identical with a whole one, being part of it, the relationships are numerically identical. For the relationship of a whole line to its half is a double, while the relationship of a half to a whole line is subdouble or half.

ON ASSUMING THE POINT AT ISSUE

On its Definition

141 Determination about the seeking of what is in principle (petitio ejus quod est in principio : 'begging the question' : 'assuming the point at issue') is made according to truth in Prior Analytics[81] and according to opinion in Topics.[82]   We treat here of assuming the point at issue the second way.

It should be known that seeking what is a matter of principle ('begging the question', 'assuming the point at issue') as taken here, is when a conclusion that should be proven is sought for in the premises. Since therefore the same thing, under the same name, cannot be proven of itself (for a proof of something is always different from what is to be proven); but the same thing, under the same name is neither something different nor does it seem to be different; therefore the same thing under the same name cannot be proven by itself.   That is why what induces and what has been induced cannot be of the same sort, as

> 'a man runs
>   therefore a man runs'.

Therefore in such as these there can be no seeking for what is a root cause (quod est in principio). An argument like this is ridiculous, falls under no art and assumes what is a root cause. It is one thing to look for a principle and another to look for that which is in principle, since to presume a principle is when the same thing is inquired about under the same name, as in

> 'a man runs
>   therefore a man runs',

which produces no fallacy, because it is not contained under any species of argumentation, neither according to truth nor according to plausibility.

On Causes and Modes of this Fallacy

142 What causes the plausibility of the fallacy of assuming the point at issue is the seeming diversity of a conclusion from its premises; what makes it false is their identity.

That which is in principle is sought in five ways, as the end of the Eighth Book of the Topics[83] has it.

On the first Mode

143 The first is when the thing defined is sought in its definition, or the converse. As if there were a doubt about whether a man is running and this were assumed:

> 'a rational, mortal animal is running
> therefore a man is running'.

there is no proof here: since one of these was doubted, the other is necessarily to be doubted. It is the same if one assumes the first, then looks for the other in it.

On the second Mode

144 The second mode is when a particular is sought for in a universal. As if it should be proven that there is a single discipline concerned with all contraries, and the proof assumes this:

> 'of all opposites, there is the same discipline
> therefore there is the same discipline of all opposites'.

here the proof seeks a conclusion in the premises.

On the third Mode

145 The third mode occurs conversely when a universal is sought in particulars. As if it were to be proven that there is a single discipline concerned with all contraries, and these are assumed:

> 'of all opposites, there is the same discipline
> of all privative opposites there is the same discipline
> and so of the others;
> therefore of all opposites, there is the same discipline'.

81: Anal. Prior. II 16, 64b 28ff.
82: Topica VIII 13, 162b 31ff.
83: Topica VIII 13, 162b34-35.

On the fourth Mode

146 The fourth mode is when something conjoined is assumed in things that have been divided. As if it were to be proven that medicine has to do with one who is sick as well as with one who is in good health, and these be assumed:

> 'medicine is a science of the sick
>   medicine is a science of the ill
> therefore medicine is a science of the sick and the ill'.

On the fifth Mode

147 The fifth mode is when one correlative is sought in the other. As if it were to be proven that Socrates is the father of Plato, and these are assumed:

> 'Plato is the son of Socrates
>   therefore Socrates is the father of Plato',

here, what ought to be proven is sought.

148 One should know that this fallacy does not impede a demonstrative (<u>inferens</u>) syllogism, but a dialectic (<u>probantem</u>) one. Syllogisms are either demonatrative only, or demonstrative and dialectical.

149 Again: One should know there are two ways of knowing, one that goes from the conceptually prior to the conceptually subsequent, and this way is called conceptual; the other proceeds from the sensibly prior to the sensibly subsequent, and this way is called sensible. Those called conceptually prior are what are by their essence (<u>natura</u>); those called sensibly prior are things more pervious to the senses.

Therefore I say that in any of the paralogisms cited, there is a dialectical Topic in one mode, a sophistical one in another. For if something apt to be proven one way is primarily proven that same way, the argument is valid, and a dialectical Topic is there. But if something apt to be proven in one of those ways is proven primarily in another (and that will be through what is subsequent in that same way), then it is a sophistical Topic and the point in question will be assumed. This is easy to see in any of the paralogisms quoted, for anyone taking thought.

ON THE FALLACY OF CONSEQUENT

On Consequence

150 A Consequence is either simple or composite. Simple consequence like: **'if it is a man, it is an animal'** or **'if he is an adulterer, he is sleekly dressed** or a night prowler'; and so of other circumstances. A composite consequence is on the basis of oppositions. That is in contraries or contradictories, as in second Topics.[84]

151 A consequence that is composite / based on oppositions, has two species. One in a thing itself, the other the converse.

152 Consequence in a thing itself is when, from an antecedent's opposite, a consequent's opposite follows. For example: **'if it is justice, it is a virtue; therefore if it is injustice, it is a vice'**; here from an opposite of the antecedent **'injustice'** follows a consequent's opposite, **'vice'**. There is consequence in a thing itself in almost all contraries.

153 Contrary consequence is when, from a consequent's opposite, an opposite of the antecedent follows. Like **'if it is a man, it is an animal; therefore if it is a non-animal, it is a non-man'**. Here, from the consequent's opposite **'non-animal'**, follows an opposite of the antecedent, **'non-man'**. In contradictories, there can only be contrary consequence.

154 Again: There are two species of simple consequence. One on a Topic-relational basis. Like **'if it is a man, it is an animal'**; Here this is a relation from species. The other is on the basis of circumstances. That type is expected in Rhetoric.

155 Just as **'consequence'** is taken commonly for all those consequences, **'consequent'** is taken commonly insofar as one sophistical Topic is said to be based on a consequent. That Topic is called consequent-based rather than antecedent-based because in it, a consequent is made the principle of inferring on the basis that the consequent is affirmed in the antecedent, but the sophistical Topic is given its name from what induces rather than from what has been induced, as it is in dialectic.

84: <u>Topica</u> II 8, 113b 15ff.

On Causes and Modes of this Fallacy

156 The motive principle of a fallacy of **consequent** is the fit
of a valid consequence has with its converse. The deficient principle
is falsity of the converse. Aristotle touches briefly on that double
cause when he says[85] 'because they think a consequence convertible', which it is not. That he says **'consequence'** suggests valid
consequence, which is the motive principle for believing its converse; that he says **'is convertible'** suggests its converse. This is
false consequence, the principle of deficiency.

Aristotle mentions three modes of consequence.[86]

On the first Mode

157 The first mode is when a consequence is made on the basis
of Topical relationships. Like

'if it is a man it is an animal
therefore if it is an animal it is a man';

this is from affirmation of a consequent, so there it is a fallacy of
consequent. So too here:

'if it is not an animal, it is not a man
therefore if it is not a man, it is not an animal';

is likewise from affirmation of a consequent. So too here:

'if it is honey, it is tawny
therefore if it is tawny, it is honey
but gall is tawny
therefore gall is honey'.

so too here:

'if it is raining, the ground is drenched
therefore if the ground is drenched, it is raining'.

In all of the above, some think a consequence convertible which is
not. So they offend against the fallacy of consequent.

On the second Mode

158 The second mode is when a consequence is thought to be convertible because of some circumstances inherent in a person, as happens in Rhetoric. For example:

if he is an adulterer, he is sleekly dressed or **a night prowler**

and so for other circumstances;

therefore if he is sleekly dressed or **a night prowler, he is an adulterer;**

this is a fallacy of **consequent,** for if he is an adulterer, he has some of an adulterer's circumstances, but not the converse, as in **'if it is a man, it is colored'** and not the converse. So too here:

**'if he has stolen something, he has neither earned nor borrowed it
so if he has neither earned or borrowed it, he has stolen it'.**

This does not follow; for they think a consequence convertible which is not.

On the third Mode

159 The third mode of the fallacy of **consequent** occurs when they think a consequence is convertible which is made on the basis of oppositions. For example:

**'if it is made, it has a source
therefore if it is not made, it has no source
but the world is not made, that is, generated
therefore the world has no source
therefore the world is infinite in duration, thus the world is eternal';**

Mellisus[87] offended against the fallacy of consequent in the first deduction, for the correct consequence is this one:

'if it is made, it has a source'

85: Soph. El. 5, 167b 1-2.
86: Soph. El. 5, 167b 1-20.
87: Melissos of Samos, 5th cent. B.C.; (cf. Arist. Soph. El. 6, 168b 35-40).

whatever is generated has a source, since from nothing, something is not made; so if something is made, it is made from something; therefore if it is made, it has a source. But this does not follow:

'if it is not made, it has no source'.

This argues from negation of the antecedent and posits consequence in the thing itself in contradictorily opposed things, since in them, a contrary consequence is to be affirmed. For example:

'if it is made, it has a source
therefore if it does not have a source, it is not made';

then it follows validly. So too, this is a fallacy of **consequent**:

'if it is a man, it is an animal
therefore if it is not a man, it is not an animal'

from negation of the antecedent. Thus it is a fallacy of consequence in the thing itself, though it should be from the contrary; for in contradictories, it is not licit to argue consequence in a thing itself.

160 From what was said it is clear that wherever there is a fallacy of **consequent**, there is a double consequence. That is clear from the fact that wherever Aristotle speaks of a **consequent**, he always forms word-groups of a **consequent** in double consequence,[88] as in 'if this exists, that exists'; and when that exists, it is thought this exists.

161 Again: Substantial to any paralogism, linguistic as well as nonlinguistic, are its motive and defective principles. Therefore if in a fallacy of consequent, correct consequence is the motive principle, and false consequence the defective one, wherever there is a paralogism of consequent, double consequence is necessarily present.

162 Again on the same point: It is impossible for any consequence to be converted unless there be a pair of them. For if a consequence is converted, one has the converted consequence and that into which it is converted. Therefore there must be a pair of consequences, wherever there is a fallacy of **consequent**, if the cause Aristotle assigns is correct.

88: <u>Soph</u>. <u>El</u>. 5, 167b 1ff.; 6, 168b 27ff.

163 Again: That is clearly proven by the solution Aristotle sets down in Second Elenchi for paralogisms of consequent.[89] There he says that there are two sorts of consequence: one where a universal follows upon a particular, as in **'if it is a man, it is an animal'**, the one we earlier called simple.[90] The other he says is based on oppositions, which we called composite. This is the division of consequence we set down in the beginning.[91] In both, one solves by demonstrating that that one consequence is converted into another. Therefore, if his solution is universal, there is necessarily a twofold consequence wherever there is a fallacy of **consequent**, namely, what is converted, and what it is converted into. We concede all these points. So in arguments like: **'an animal is running; therefore a man is running'**, or **'a man is running; therefore Socrates is running'** and in all like them, there is not a Fallacy of Consequent, but one of Accident, as was earlier[92] clarified in word-groups of the Fallacy of Accident.

ON THE FALLACY OF
NON-CAUSE AS CAUSE

On two kinds of Syllogism

164 Syllogisms are of two types, demonstrative and contradictory. A demonstrative syllogism is one that has only one conclusion. An impossible syllogism is one which leads syllogistically to an impossible conclusion, and for this reason one of the premises, which is the cause of that impossible conclusion, is invalidated. So such a syllogism always has two conclusions. For example, if we ask: **'is a man an ass ?'** and that is conceded, an counterargument is:

**'no ass is a rational, mortal animal
    a man is an ass
therefore a man is not a rational, mortal animal
    but this is impossible
therefore a man is not an ass'**;

This syllogism is in the Fourth Figure of the First Mood.

89: Soph. El. 28, 181a 23-27.
90: p. 149 above.
91: p. 129 ff.
92: p. 129 ff.

On the Fallacy of Non-cause as Cause

165 We should note that the Fallacy of **Non-cause as Cause**
always occurs in impossible syllogisms. Moreover the fallacy of non-
cause as cause occurs when a non-cause is supposed to be the reason
why something impossible seems to follow, and what appears to be a
cause is later invalidated. For example, if we ask: **'is Brunellus a
man ?'** and that is conceded, the contrary argument is:

> **'no ass is a rational, mortal animal
>   a man is an ass and Brunellus is a man
> therefore a man is not a rational, mortal animal
>   but this is impossible
> therefore Brunellus is not a man'.**

In this argumentation there is a fallacy of **non-cause as cause,** for
what is invalidated is what seems to be a cause of the impossible and
really is not, namely, **'Brunellus is a man',** and without that premise
a contradiction follows from the other premises. It will be a syllogism in the fourth figure of the first mood, as we said earlier.

On the Causes of this Fallacy

166   The reason why this fallacy appears plausible is a
resemblance between what seems to be the cause and what is not
the cause, on account of some resemblance in some term signifying
the same thing. This is clear, since premises are the cause of a conclusion, because they share some term. So a proposition that does
not effect an inference (and so is not a cause), appears to be a
cause of the conclusion if it shares some term with one of the
premises; so what is a non-cause is taken as a cause. The motive
principle in this fallacy is a resemblance between causes in some
term.

167 The cause of falsity / or the defective principle is the
diversity of a proposition that is a non-cause compared to the cause
of the conclusion itself.   Aristotle gives an example of this
fallacy:[93]

> **'are soul and life the same thing ?';**

93: Soph. El. 5, 167b 27-31.

if this is conceded, a counterargument is:

> 'death and life are contraries
>   generation and corruption are contraries
> but death is corruption
>   therefore life is generation
> hence to live is to be generated;

This is contradictory: one who is living is not being generated, but one who has been generated;

> therefore soul and life are not the same thing';

in this final conclusion there is an offence involving non-cause as cause. Without it, the contradiction follows from the other premises. So one ought not deny that part, namely **'soul and life are the same thing'**, but this one: **'death and life are contraries'.**

In all of these, what is not a cause seems to be one, since it has something in common with terms in other propositions from which a contradiction follows.

168 From what has been said it is clear that this fallacy does not occur in a demonstrative syllogism. For example:

> 'every man is running
>   Socrates is a man and the sun is in Cancer
> therefore Socrates is running'

this is   **non-cause as cause,** since the proposition   **'the sun is in Cancer'** is not a cause nor does it seem to be one.

169 Notice that   **'death and life are contraries'** is ambiguous. Yet it is false in both senses. In one way, death is a change by which the soul is freed from the body, and that way, death and life are not contraries, since they are simultaneously in the same thing. As long as that change or dissolution is going on, a man is still living and will continue to live until that dissolution comes to a stop. So this way, it is necessary that death and life are simultaneously in the same thing. That is why they cannot be contraries in this way. But in another way,   **'death'** is taken, not for the very change of separation, but for the endpoint of that separation or dissolution, in which the soul is not being separated from the body, but has already been separated. Death is not contrary to life this way, but they are opposed privatively in a irreversible order with respect to the same thing, like sight and blindness with respect to the eye. So the proposition cited is false in both ways.

170 Again: 'Death is corruption' is ambiguous, since if 'death' is taken the first way, it is true; when the soul is freed from the body, a man corrupts. But if 'death' is taken the second way, it is false, since so taken, death is not corruption, but an end point of corruption.

So it is clear what propositions are to be invalidated in the premises and how they are to be distinguished.

ON THE FALLACY OF MANY QUESTIONS AS ONE

On Statement, Proposition, Interrogation and Conclusion

171 Statement, proposition, question, and conclusion are the same thing subtantially, but they differ by functions (rationibus) peculiar to each. For example, the word-group 'every man runs', as signifying that a thing does or does not exist, is called a statement; the same word-group, as put in premises to prove something, is a proposition; with a mode of interrogation added, it is a question, as in 'is every man running?'; as proven by another, that identical word-group is a conclusion.

172 In terms of those peculiar functions, they can be defined in the following ways. A **statement** is a word-group indicative of something insofar as it signifies that things do or do not exist. A **proposition** is an indicative word-group that is probative of another. An **interrogation** is an indicative word-group taken under the mode of asking a question. A **conclusion** is an indicative word-group proven by one or more middle terms. But since a statement is divided into one and many, as are a proposition and a question, it should be known that the unity from which a statement or a proposition is said to be one differs from the unity from which an interrogation is said to be one.

173 To make this obvious, notice that there are several modes of unity taken simply, on the basis of which a proposition and a statement is said to be one. There is a sort of thing that is a unit

simply, signified by several names, derived from several things signified by several names. Take a definition, like: 'rational mortal animal'. Here there are several things from which a unit results. There is one sort of unit simply that is one and under one name. This is subdivided into five parts. The first is something that is one proportionally, the sort predicated on the basis of prior and subsequent, as 'being' is of all beings and 'healthy' of all healthy things, and 'good' of all good things, as is clear in the Topics.[94] The second mode is something that is one by genus, like **soul** or **color**. The third mode is something that is one by species, like **man, whiteness**. The fourth is something that is numerically one, like Socrates or Plato. The fifth and last is something that is one by accident. I call something one by accident, accidentally one; one by genus, generically one, and one by species, specifically one.

174 So I say 'unity' taken commonly for all those modes of unity, makes both a statement and a proposition one, when one of those unities is subject and another predicate, as in: 'a stone is a rational mortal animal'; 'a man is a rational mortal animal'; 'a stone is a being'; 'a stone is an animal'; 'a man is an animal'; 'an ass is a man'; 'Socrates is a man'; 'Socrates is Socrates'; 'Socrates is Plato'; 'a man is able to laugh'; 'a man is white'. If one of the unities mentioned is not there, there will not be one statement, but many, and then many things are predicated of one, or one thing predicated of many, or many of many out of which there is no unit. The unity by which a question is said to be one is not that mentioned above, but the unity of an interrogative mode added to the unity which makes a proposition one, as in 'is a man an animal?': here, one of the unities mentioned above is subject, (since it is a specific unity), another is predicate, (since it is a generic unity), and to these unities is added the unity of a mode of questioning. This unity, which is that of an interrogative mode, is not unity simply taken, but unity taken after-a-fashion. That unity on the basis of which a proposition is one and a statement is one, is unity simply taken. So it is clear when a question is one. It is also clear that for a single question, a double unity is required, namely the unity of a thing divided earlier - and this is quasi-material in a single question -, and the unity of an interrogative mode, and that is completive of an interrogation.

175 A question is many when, in an interrogation, the unity of question mode remains, and what makes a proposition one (which was unity simply taken), is lacking. Since the unity of a mode of

94: Topica I 15, 107a 5-12, p. 24.

questioning remains, it is called an interrogation; since the other unity, simply taken, is lacking, it is called many. So these two, **question** and **many**, are well joined to each other, even though the lack of concord between substantive and adjective is evident.

On the Causes and Modes of this Fallacy

176 Having seen how statement, proposition, question and conclusion resemble and differ from each other, and in how many modes 'one simply' is predicated, when a statement is one or many, as well as proposition and interrogation, and on what basis **'many question'** is well said - we must now discuss causes and modes of the fallacy based on **Many Question as One.**

The plausible cause or motive principle of this fallacy is the unity of the mode of questioning; the cause of its falsity is a lack or privation of the unity of a single proposition. Unity **after-a-fashion** claims to be unity **simply,** so it conceals a defect and makes what does not exist seem to exist.

There are two modes of this fallacy.

On the first Mode

177 The first is when in singular number, several things are subject or predicate, like **'isn't he and he a man ?'** (after we have pointed to Socrates and Brunellus). If we answer yes, **'therefore Brunellus is a man';** if no, **'therefore Socrates is not a man'.** Answering a many question with a one response is invalid, and the reply should have been: **'true for one, false for the other'.**

On the second Mode

178 The second arises when several things are subject or predicate in the plural, like **'are those things good ?'** after pointing to a good and a bad thing. If the answer is **'good',** one can conclude, **'then the bad is good';** if **'bad',** **'then the good is not good'.** The answer should have been: **'one is good and the other is not good'.** But one conceding that definitions are given indifferently in the plural or singular, like **'a blind thing is naturally apt to see and doesn't'** and **'blind things are naturally apt to see and do not',** will not escape refutation. Having proven one is blind and another sighted, one could argue as follows:

**'those are naturally apt to see and not seeing
therefore they are blind'**

This way both will be blind. If it is said they are sighted, the argument concludes, **'therefore both are sighted; therefore the blind one sees'.** It would not be said one is sighted and the other is not, but a single response will be given because of the original concession that definitions were given indifferently in the plural and singular. That way one only answer is given.

ON REDUCTION OF ALL FALLACIES

On two kinds of Ignoring the Point at Issue

179 A double distinction of Ignorance of the Point in Question (ignorantia elenchi : 'ignoring a refutation or the point at issue') is usually made, as specifically one of the thirteen fallacies, yet generically the one to which all thirteen reduce.   One way Ignorance of the Point in Question is distinguished as specific is, that it is caused by ignorance of the differences **same relations, same basis, same way,** and **same time.** That way ignoring the point at issue is contrary to the completive form of a refutation, since those differences are completive of contradiction and so of a refutation, contradiction itself being completive of a refutation. But as Ignorance of the Point in Question is commonly caused by ignorance of all differences posited in the definition of a refutation, it is thus generic, and that way, all fallacies reduce to it.

Another way the distinction is made is that Ignorance of the Point in Question is always contrary to all the differences of a refutation, but in different ways, since in one way it is autonomous, in another, different from a consequent. In the first way, there is a single principle of deception from one opposite divided against the others; the second way it is generic to all. One is said to ignore refutation from a consequent when, since there is one name, he believes there is one thing, though there is no one thing. Since he believes there is one thing, he believes from the consequent that there is one term; and from the consequent that there is one middle term; and consequently one syllogism. And then further through this, he believes that there is a single refutation. In this way, Ignorance of the Point in Question is from a consequent.

Another way, the point at issue is ignored in itself and is ignored in its parts from the consequent, when first it is believed that there is a refutation when there is none. Believing there is a refutation, one believes all differences of a refutation are present.

That way a refutation is overlooked first, its parts or all its differences are overlooked as a consequence. In this way it is specific, as happens in one way when going from defining things (as from a genus and differences) to the thing defined, and conversely from the thing defined to those that define it. Though the second distinction is more subtle than the first, the third is more probable and I believe it more to be true.

On generic Reduction

180 Reduction of paralogisms as well as fallacious refutations to Ignorance of the Point in Question is of two sorts, generic and specific. Generic reduction is in the fact that all are unmodified. But 'lack of modification' is ambiguous, since its opposite, modification, is ambiguous. Just as syllogistic necessity is ambiguous: one sort is caused by quantity, quality, order of propositions and terms of a syllogism; so too modification, as syllogistic moods are determined in Prior Analytics.[95] Lack of modification opposed to modification is to be determined in Prior Analytics, where it is called a useless selection.[96] Syllogistic necessity caused in a specific syllogism is different. This necessity too is ambiguous, since one is caused by Topical relationships, as in a dialectic syllogism, the other by pairing cause to effect, as in a demonstrative syllogism. In the same way, modification owed a specific syllogism is ambiguous. But this is nothing other than inferential necessity through Topical relationships as far as a dialectical syllogism is concerned, or pairing cause to effect in a demonstrative one. Lack of modification as opposed to modification caused by source topical is discussed in the Elenchi,[97] since another sort of modification lack (which has to do with the relation of cause to effect or the converse), is determined in the Posterior Analytics, since it is a pseudo-syllogism.[98] So when Aristotle says they are all unmodified, understand that for the modification lack which has to with with modification caused by Topical relationships and not about others.[99]

95: Anal. Prior. I 4-22.
96: ibid. I 28, 44b26.
97: Soph. El. 6, 168a 21ff.
98: Anal. Post. I 2, 71b9ff.
99: Soph. El. 6, 168a 18-21.

On specific Reduction

181 Specific reduction is to demonstrate how, through each sophistical Topic, common differences of syllogisms and contradictions are ignored, or differences peculiar to each. Through this, a refutation is further ignored, because just as a difference added to a genus constitutes a species, a contradiction added to a syllogism constitutes a refutation. Therefore a contradiction is the complement of a syllogism. So any difference of a refutation is either common to a syllogism and a contradiction, or what is a peculiarity of the former is a peculiarity of the latter. Therefore, through ignorance of them, Ignorance of the Point in Question arises.

182 Therefore Aristotle reduces apparent syllogisms and refutations to ignorance of the point at issue, saying 'equivocation, word-group and similar formation are reduced in that they are ambiguous'.[100] He posits a double defect in term, syllogism and contradiction, and for that reason, in a refutation. How ambiguity is in word-figure was already discussed.[101] Anyone can see that in equivocation and amphiboly. But composition, division and accent reduce in that there is a different, not the same, word-group or name. A word-group had to be somehow referentially the same, if either a refutation or syllogism were to arise.

183 He next reduces seeming syllogisms and extralinguistic refutations to ignorance of the point in question, saying: 'those connected with Accident are clear, once syllogism has been defined'.[102] For they pose a defect in the particular 'happening of necessity' put into the definition of a syllogism. Thus a defect of Accident is clear. In terms of this fallacy, specialists and the all-knowing are refuted by the ignorant. On the basis of the fallacy of Accident they produce apparent syllogisms against the wise. Those that are fallacies **after-a-fashion and simply** are reduced, because affirmation and negation do not concern the same thing, as in 'an Ethiopian is white as to the teeth', 'an Ethiopian is not white'.

184 Then he reduces those which are fallacies on the basis of ignorance of the point in question insofar as it is specific, saying: 'clearest of all are the already cited fallacies based on ignorance of the point in question, which is why they are called that.'[103]

100: Soph. El. 6, 168a 24-25.
101: p. 115 ff. above.
102: Soph. El. 6, 168a 34-35.

185 He later reduces others, saying, 'paralogisms that are such because the original point in question is assumed and those of non-cause posited as cause are obvious by definition; a conclusion should arise of necessity, from the fact that what were not in non-causes would be so, and again a conclusion should follow without including what was in principle, which those do not have which are based on seeking what was in principle.'[104]

186 He later reduces Fallacies of Consequent, saying, 'fall-acies connected with the consequent are reduced like those of accid-ent, for a consequent is part of accident'.[105]   That way, when a fallacy of Accident is reduced, so is one of Consequence. That a consequent is part of accident is clear from what we have said of the latter, since as was said,[106] in one way, an antecedent is accident to its consequent, in another, a consequent is accident to its antecedent, and in a third, one is convertible with the other. For that reason, accident is common to what antecedes, follows upon, and converts with it.   A consequent / that which follows is thus necessarily part of accident, since antecedent is common to these three.

187 But notice that one Topic is not part of another. It cannot be said the sophistical Topic as to consequent is a subjective or integral part of the sophistical Topic as to accident. So understand that a consequent is part of accident from the side of the terms in which it arises, not from the side of those sophistical relationships or sophistical Topics. Just as the Topic from species is not part of the Topic from genus, but those things of which these are relation-ships are so constituted that one is part of the other. So a conse-quent is a quasi subjective part of an accident from the side of those things in which they arise, and not from the side of those sophistical relationships. This is what Aristotle proves according to which a consequent is part of accident, when he says 'for a consequent is an accident'.[107]   It is true likewise that an antecedent is an accident and likewise that a convertible is an accident, as was said in the tract on accident.[108]

103:   Soph. El. 6, 168b 17-18.
104:   Soph. El. 6, 168b 22-26.
105:   Soph. El. 7, 169b6-7.
106:   Soph. El. 6, 168b 28.
107:   Soph. El. 6, 168b 28.
108:   p. 129 ff.

188 The fallacy of **Consequent** has another reduction peculiar to itself. It posits a defect against the syllogistic difference **'things posited'**. This is clear, since affirming the greater does not affirm the less, as **'animal'** does not affirm **'man'**. A consequent does not affirm its antecedent, since it is greater, but the converse. So since the difference **'things posited'** speaks of the order of premises to conclusion based on Topical relationships (sophistical Topics determined in the Elenchi being contrary to a syllogism through Topic-relationships), where there is a consequent, there is no order of premises to conclusion on the basis of some Topic-relationships. Because where there is a **consequent,** the difference **'things posited'** is not found. So through this **'things posited'** difference, the fallacy of **consequent** is of itself reduced, positing as it does a defect in that difference.

Notice too, as often touched upon, that 'posit' is ambiguous in a syllogism. One sort of positing is through quantity, quality and the order of propositions and terms. That is how the difference **'things posited'** is taken in Prior Analytics.[109] A different sort of positing in a syllogism is that through Topic-relationships; that is the sort found in a dialectical syllogism. The sophistical source **according to the consequent** is counter to this positing.

189 Those producing a fallacy because they make many questions as one are reduced because they posit a defect contrary to the unity of a proposition. A proposition is a unit about one thing, since the definition of 'one only' is identical with that of 'thing taken simply', like that 'man' and 'man only', and so of others. So if one only proposition is what signifies one thing of one thing, it will be a proposition simply, which signifies one thing of one thing. This is the source from parts sufficiently enumerated.

190 Having concluded generic, then specific reduction on the ing basis of differences of refutation and contradition, Aristotle next determines which sophistical Topics are reduced from the aspect of contradiction and which from the aspect of syllogism, saying:[110] 'therefore those that are word-based are reduced since there is an apparent contradiction, which is peculiar to refutation; the others are reduced according to the definition of a syllogism'.

Let these remarks on fallacies and on their reduction suffice.

109:   Anal, Priora I 1, 24b 18-19.
110:   Soph. El. 6, 169a 19-21.

TRACT VIII

ON RELATIVES

On two kinds of Relative

1 There are two kinds of Relatives: one for which existing is somehow to-be-to-another,[1] so one of the ten Predicaments. The other is what recalls something gone before, since as Priscian Major has it,[2] relation is a recalling of what is past. In **'Socrates, the one who is debating, is running'**, the relative **'who'** (qui) effects recall of Socrates, who is what is past. Omitting relatives in the first mode, we now have those of the second in mind.

On Substantive Relatives

2 Some relatives recall a substance, like **'(the one) who'** (qui), **'(that one) who'** (ille), **'(an other one')** (alius), some recall an accident, like **'(the kind) who'** (talis), **'(such) that'** (qualis), **'as many (as)'** (tantus), **'so much (as)'** (quantus). A substantive relative is one that recalls what is numerically identical with its antecedent, like **'(the one) who'** (qui), **'(that) one who'** (ille). Again: Some substantive relatives recall an identity, like **'(the one) who'** (qui), **'(that) one who'** (ille); others recall something diverse, like **'(the first) one'** (alter), **'(the) other (one) who'** (reliquus) and the like.

On Identical Relatives

3 A Relative of Identity is what recalls and stands for the same thing. In **'Socrates, the one who is debating, is running'**, the relative **'who'** recalls and stands for Socrates.

Some relatives of identity are nouns, like **'who'** (qui), **'which'** (quod); some pronouns, like **'(that) one'** (ille), **'(the) same (one)'** (idem); some reciprocal, like **'(of) oneself'** (sui), **'(to) oneself'**

1: cf. Aristot. Categ. 7, 8a31-32, editio compos, p. 62.
2: Inst. gramm. XVII.56. p. 141.

(sibi), 'oneself' (se), 'by oneself' (a se); others non-reciprocal, like 'who' (qui), 'that' (ille), 'same' (idem). A reciprocal is so-called, not because it is what-is-undergoing-something (patiens), but because it superimposes a patient mode on agent substance. Being a patient is one thing, mode of patient another, as is clear from the fact that a nominative can be a patient, like 'Socrates is being struck'. But a nominative cannot have the mode of patient. That is why mode of patient is always in oblique cases. It is thus clear that patient is one thing and mode of patient another.

Questions

4 If asked what a reciprocal relative adds to an agent, say it adds substantial identity to an agent and puts it under the mode of patient, as in 'Socrates sees himself'. A substance previously under the mode of agent is put under the mode of patient, as in the pronoun 'himself' (se). So a reciprocal can be defined as follows: a reciprocal is what signifies an agent substance under a patient mode.

5 Again: If asked why the pronoun '(of) oneself' (sui), '(to) oneself' (sibi), 'oneself' (se), '(by) oneself' (a se) lacks a nominative, say the solution is already obvious from what was said: an agent cannot be signified as a patient, nor under the mode of patient, except in oblique cases. But the nominative means mode of agent. For that reason, the nature of nominative is repugnant to the nature of the pronoun '(of) oneself' (sui), '(to) oneself' (sibi), 'oneself' (se), '(by) oneself' (a se). For that reason, that pronoun cannot have an agent nominative.

6 From what was said it is clear that all relatives of identity recall a substance identical with its antecedent and that they recall and stand for the numerically same thing. It is also clear from this, that more certainty is effected by a relative of identity than by its antecedent substituted for a relative. In 'a man is running, a man is debating', it is dubious whether the same man is spoken of or not. But in saying: 'a man is running and that is the one who is debating', it is certain that the same man is spoken of. This is clear by what Priscian has in his Minor,[3] that in saying: 'Ajax came to Troy, Ajax fought bravely' it is dubious whether it is to be understood of the same person. But if one says: 'Ajax came to Troy and the same one fought bravely', it is understood to be about the same one. So it is obvious that more certainty is effected by a relative of identity than by its antecedent substituted for a relative.

3: Inst. gramm. XVII 56, p. 142.7-11.

Doubts

7 A doubt usually raised about relatives of identity is whether deception resulting from diverse relation is one based on Equivocation, Amphiboly, or some other fallacy. In **'a man sees an ass who is rational'** (homo videt asinum qui est rationalis) the relative **'who'** can be referred to the term **'man'** or the term **'ass'**. There are thus diverse statements there. Equivocation is wont to be commonly assigned.

There are counterarguments: The noun **'who'** (qui),[4] as a relative, signifies a single thing as equally related to every object that exists under the mode of substance, as in **'a man who runs'**, **'a color which is in a body'**, **'a place which contains a thing located'**, etc. Therefore deception from diverse relation is not a fallacy of equivocation. Again: The noun **'who'** as a relative, signifies substance indeterminately. But that substance is naturally apt to be determined just as well by one antecedent as by another. Therefore since substance taken indeterminately as such is a unit, able to recall any antecedent whatever, therefore the signification of the relative **'qui'** will be unitary. Therefore it is not equivocation. Again: The nature of any antecedent at all, as it is in a thing related, is unitary, namely, this thing that is recalled. Therefore all antecedents of a relative, on the basis of a relative noun, share a single name and a single nature. Therefore a relative is univocal insofar as recalling a thing gone before. Therefore particular relatives, like **'who'** (qui), **'that'** (ille), **'other'** (alius), insofar as recalling their antecedents, are not equivocal.

If one object that the relative **'who'** (qui) is of one nature as taken in its antecedent **'man'** and of another as taken in the antecedent **'ass'**, as in the word-group above, therefore the noun is common but has diverse natures, therefore it is equivocal - say that argument is invalid. It could be proven in the same way that any univocal is equivocal, as **'animal'**, taken as a man or as in a man, has a one nature, and as it is in a horse or is a horse, another nature. So the noun **'animal'** is common yet not equivocal, but univocal.

8 Solve this briefly by saying that just as univocals are said to have the same nature, not of themselves, but in one using them univocally, like **'man'**, **'cow'**, **'horse'** and the like in **'animal'**, so too,

---

4: English prefers 'a man who...', 'an ass which...' [fpd]

all relatives ought to have the same nature, not of themselves, but in one using them to recall, or in what they recall, and that they also have the same name. Univocals are therefore used univocally by that fact. But his objection is about the nature of relative things as such, so we concede the objector's contentions. I thus concede that deception effected by diversity of relation is not equivocation. Again: That sort of deception is in the ordering of words (dictio) among themselves. Therefore it is in a word-group, since a word ordering is nothing other than a word-group. Therefore it is not equivocation, since equivocation is to be found only in a single word.

9 Again: I prove there is no amphiboly here, since wherever amphiboly occurs there is a construction of one unit with another unit, like the word-group **'Aristotle's book'** for the first mode; in **'plow sand'** (litus aratur) for the second, and **'knowing age'** (scit saeculum) for the third. So it is clear inductively through all the modes of amphiboly, that wherever it exists, there is a construction of one thing only with another single thing. But wherever a fallacy of diverse relation arises, it is not a construction of one thing only with another single thing, indeed it is a construction of one thing with diverse things. Therefore deception from diverse relation does not produce Amphiboly. Which we concede.

Again: Wherever there is deception from the fact that some word (dictio) can be related to different things, there is a fallacy of composition and division. But deception from diverse relation arises from the fact that some word can be related to different things. Therefore deception from diverse relation is a fallacy of composition or division. And this we again concede.

On Relatives of Diversity

10 Next about Relatives of Diversity. A Relative of Diversity is what stands for something other than what it recalls, as in **'Socrates is running and another is debating'** (Sortes currit et alius disputat). The relative **'another'** (alius) recalls Socrates and stands for someone other than Socrates, for the sense is **'Socrates is running and someone other than Socrates is debating'** (Sortes currit et alius a Sorte disputat). And in this way it recalls Socrates to mind.

On a rule about a Relative of Diversity

11 This sort of rule is given for a relative of diversity:

If a relative of diversity is added
to a superior and to an inferior,
what is added to the superior is made
inferior, and what is added to the
inferior is made superior.

For example, 'something other than animal; therefore something other than man' (<u>aliud</u> <u>ab</u> <u>animali</u>; <u>ergo</u> <u>aliud</u> <u>ab</u> <u>homine</u>). This is a Topic from Species, since in 'something other than animal', the relative of diversity ('something other than') is added to 'animal', which is superior to **man**, and in 'something other than man' it is added to the inferior, namely 'man'. For that reason, 'something other than animal' is inferior to 'something other than man'. And for that reason, it is a Topic from Species or Subjective Part.

On a rule about a Relative of Identity given by predecessors

12 A rule like this about a relative of identity is wont to be given by earlier scholars.

No proposition begun by a relative
has a contradictory.

They give a reason like this: in 'every man is running and he is debating' (<u>omnis</u> <u>homo</u> <u>currit</u> <u>et</u> <u>ille</u> <u>disputat</u>), the relative 'he' (<u>ille</u>) has respect to the antecedent 'man' because of the dependency of its relation. When negation comes to a proposition beginning with a relative, expressed as follows: 'he is not debating' (<u>ille</u> <u>non</u> <u>disputat</u>), then that negation negates the verb which follows, and does not negate the respect of relation the relative has to its antecedent. Therefore the negation does not negate anything the affirmation affirms. Therefore it does not contradict it. Therefore, since this is the case in any proposition beginning with a relative, no proposition beginning with a relative has a contradictory.

Objections

13 An objection is made against this. Whatever may negate may also affirm something about any supposit. But a verb may make a negation of any supposit, and so may make an affirmation. Therefore it may do that of a supposit that is a relative word (dictio). Therefore any proposition beginning with a relative has a contradictory. Again: Any proposition or statement that is unitary has a contradictory. But every proposition beginning with a relative, as long as no equivocal word nor several subjects or predicates are in it, is unitary. Therefore every proposition beginning with a relative has a contradictory. Again: Aristotle, in the first book of On Interpretation,[5] says a negation is opposed to any affirmation, and the converse. Therefore an affirmation beginning with a relative.

We concede this, saying the rule quoted above is false.

14 We respond to their reason that a relative is paired both with its antecedent and with the verb of which it is subject. Since an affirmation and negation is a sentence affirming or denying one thing of another (that is, a predicate of a subject), I say that, just as is clear by the definition of affirmation and negation given, affirmation and negation regard only the pairing of subject to predicate. Therefore in a proposition beginning with a relative, a contradiction is taken only by pairing a subject to a predicate. Therefore only by pairing a relative to the verb of which it is the subject, not by pairing a relative to its antecedent. This way it is inappropriate to deny the respect which a relative has to its antecedent, since that respect is not there because of the nature of affirmation, nor because of the dependence of subject-as-subject, but because of a dependence of that which is the subject. For subject-as-subject is one thing, that which is the subject another, just as predicate-as-predicate is one thing, and that which is the predicate another. So whatever is affirmed in a proposition beginning with a relative is denied in its contradictory. And the contradictory of 'he is debating' (ille disputat) is: 'it is not he debating' (non ille disputat), with the negative preposed to the relative.

5: De interp. 6, 17a31-33.

On a certain rule about a
Relative of Identity

15 A rule like this about a Relative of Identity is given:

every non-reciprocal relative of identit should have the same supposition as its antecedent.

In **'every man is running and he is Socrates'** (<u>omnis homo currit et ille est Sortes</u>), the relative **'he'** (<u>ille</u>) stands for every man, and the sense is: **'that one is Socrates'**, that is, **every man is Socrates.** But I say **'non-reciprocal'**, because in saying **'every man is seeing himself'** (<u>omnis homo videt se</u>), the sense is not **'every man is seeing every man'.** So in place of the reciprocal relative **'himself'** (<u>se</u>), it is illicit to put its antecedent; but in place of another, it is licit.

On Relatives of Accident

16 Having discussed substantive relatives, we now must take up Accidental Relatives. A Relative of Accident is what recalls the same thing by way of denomination, as **'(being) that sort'** (<u>tale</u>), **'(being) which sort'** (<u>quale</u>) and the like. So this is a difference between a substantive and an accidental relative, that a relative of substance recalls the univocal thing or recalls by its mode, which is **'(being) something'** (<u>quid</u>), like **'whiteness which is in a wall', 'color that is in a body'**, and so of the others - while a relative of accident is what recalls the thing by mode of denomination, as **'Socrates is white and Plato is that sort'** (<u>Sortes est albus et talis est Plato</u>).

Another difference between them is that a substantial relative recalls a numerically identical thing, while an accidental relative recalls a specifically identical thing, as in **'Socrates is white and Plato is that sort'**, since a numerically identical accident cannot exist in different subjects, but a specifically identical accident can.

On division of a Relative of Accident

17 Accidental Relative is divided, since a relative of identity like **'(being) that sort'** (<u>talis</u>) is one thing, while a relative of diversity like **'(being) of another sort'** (<u>alteriusmodi</u>) is another. A Relative of Identity in Accidents is what recalls a specifically identical accident and stands for one and the same species, as in **'Socrates is white, and Plato is that sort'.** A Relative of Diversity in Accidents is what recalls a specifically identical Quality and stands for a specifically different quality, as in **'Socrates is white and Plato is of another sort'** (<u>Sortes</u> <u>est</u> <u>albus</u> <u>et</u> <u>alteriusmodi</u> <u>est</u> <u>Plato</u>).

A relative of substantial identity differs from one of accidental identity, because a relative of substantial identity recalls a numerically identical substance, while a relative of accidental identity does not recall a numerically identical accident, but rather one specifically identical.

On Relatives of Accidental Identity

18 Again: One kind of Relative of Identity in Accidents is a Relative of Quality, like **'that sort'** (<u>talis</u>), **'what sort'** (<u>qualis</u>); another is a Relative of Quantity, like **'(so) many as'** (<u>tantus</u>), **'(so) much as'** (<u>quantus</u>).   Again: Relatives of Quantity are either of continuous quantity, like **'(so) many as'** (<u>quantus</u>) or Relatives of Number, like **'(so) many (as)'** (<u>tot</u>), **'(so) often (as)'** (<u>totidem</u>). Again: some Relatives of Number are nouns, like **'(so) many (as)'** (<u>tot</u>), some adverbs, like **'so often as'** (<u>toties</u>).

On the words (<u>dictio</u>) such, so great, so many, as often, so often

19 Note that **'such'** (<u>talis</u>), **'so great'** (<u>tantus</u>) **'so many'** (<u>tot</u>), and **'so often as'** (<u>totidem</u>) can be relatives, demonstratives, or responsives. Said of things present, they are demonstratives (e.g., pointing to a lake and saying **'just like the Nile'** (<u>talis</u> <u>est</u> <u>Nilus</u>) or to Hercules, with **'Plato is as big as he is'** (<u>tantus</u> <u>est</u> <u>Plato</u>) and so on. If not said of things present, i.e. by pointing at things that are here, they are relatives or responsives.   The latter are properly responsive when answering a preceding question, like **'he is the sort that Plato is'** (<u>talis</u> <u>est</u> <u>qualis</u> <u>est</u> <u>Plato</u>) in answer to **'what sort of a person is Socrates ?'** (<u>qualis</u> <u>est</u> <u>Sortes</u> ?). They are relatives when proferred though no question has been put, as in **'The way Plato is, is the way Socrates was'** (<u>qualis</u> <u>est</u> <u>Plato</u>, <u>talis</u> <u>fuit</u> <u>Sortes</u>), and when adjective nouns of Special Accidents are mentioned, as in **'An Ethiopian is black and such is a crow'** (<u>Ethiops</u> <u>est</u> <u>niger</u> <u>et</u> <u>talis</u> <u>est</u> <u>corvus</u>)   or **'Socrates was white and such was Plato'** (<u>Sortes</u> <u>fuit</u> <u>albus</u> <u>et</u> <u>talis</u> <u>est</u> <u>Plato</u>).

And this should suffice about relatives.

TRACT IX

ON EXTENSIONS

On Personal Supposition

1 Personal Supposition is the acceptance of a common term for its inferiors. One sort is determinate and the other diffuse, as was clear above.[1] Again: There is another division of personal supposition: one restricted, the other extended. So Restriction and Extension have to do with Personal Supposition.

On Restriction and Extension

2 Restriction is the narrowing of a common term from a larger to a smaller supposition. In **'a white man is running'** the adjective **'white'** restricts **'man'** to standing for whites.

Extension is the broadening of a common term from a smaller to a larger supposition. In **'a man can be the Antichrist'**, the term **'man'** not only stands for those who exist, but also for those who will, and so it is extended to men in the future. I say **'of a common term'**, since a discrete term like **'Socrates'** is neither restricted nor extended.

On the Division of Extension

3 One type of Extension is effected by a verb, like **'can'** in **'a man can be the Antichrist'**; by a noun, as in **'for a man to be the Antichrist is a possibility'** (<u>hominem</u> <u>esse</u> <u>Antichristum</u> <u>est</u> <u>poss-ibile</u>); by a participle, as in **'a man enabled to be the Antichrist'** (<u>homo</u> <u>est</u> <u>potens</u> <u>esse</u> <u>Antichristus</u>); by an adverb, as in **'a man is necessarily an animal'**. Here, **'man'** is extended not only for present time, but also for the future. For that reason, another division of extension follows: one with respect to supposits, as in **'a man can**

1: p. 71.

be the Antichrist', another with respect to time, as in 'a man is necessarily an animal', as was said.

A Sophism

4 In connection with what was said, this sophism is questioned: 'the impossible can be true'. Proof: What is or will be impossible can be true, as for the Antichrist not to have been (Antichristum non fuisse) will be impossible after his time, yet it can be true now, since it is true. Therefore the impossible can be true. Counterargument: Whatever can be true, is possible. But the impossible can be true. Therefore the impossible is possible. The argument is in the third mood of the first figure. But the conclusion is false. Therefore one of the premises is false. Not the major. So the minor. But this is the first. Therefore the first is false.

Solution: The first ('the impossible can be true') is simply false. Its proof offends by Fallacy of Accident. When I say 'what is or will be the impossible', I am talking about two things, namely the subject of that impossibility, and impossibility itself, that which is itself impossible. But for what is or will be the impossible, impossibility or the impossible is an accident. So what is or will be impossible is the subject matter and the impossible is its accident, and 'can be true' is assigned being-in to each. As here:

'for the Antichrist not to have been will be the impossible
    but for the Antichrist not to have been can be true
  therefore the impossible can be true';

this is invalid, since for the Antichrist not to have been is the subject and the impossible is its accident and can be true is assigned being-in to both.

On two Rules

5 About Extension effected by reason of supposits, there is a rule like this:

a common term which is subject of a verb having ability to extend, of itself or from another, is extended to those things which can be under the form of the subject term

In **'a man is able to be white'** (<u>homo</u> <u>potest</u> <u>esse</u> <u>albus</u>), the term **'man'** not only stands for present men, but is also extended to all who will exist. I say **'of itself'** because the verbal **'is able to be'** (<u>potest</u>) has of itself the nature of extending. I say **'from another'** because the participial **'having ability'** (<u>potens</u>) and the nominal **'possibile'** (<u>possibile</u>) confer ability to extend upon the verb to which they are adjoined, as in **'a human is enabled to be white'** (<u>homo</u> <u>est</u> <u>potens</u> <u>esse</u> <u>albus</u>), or **'that an animal be white is possible'** (<u>animal</u> <u>possibile</u> <u>est</u> <u>esse</u> <u>album</u>).

6 About Extension effected by reason of tense, there is rule like this:

> a common term, serving as subject or appositive of a verb having ability to extend as to time, stands for those things which are and which will always be.

In **'a man is necessarily an animal'**, both **'man'** and **'animal'** are taken for things that are and always will be.

Let these remarks suffice about Extensions.

TRACT X

ON APPELLATIONS

On the Definition of Appellation

1 Appellation is the acceptance of a term for an existent thing. I say **'for an existent thing'** because a term signifying a non-being like **'Caesar'**, **'Antichrist'** and **'chimera'** does not call up anything (<u>non</u> <u>appellat</u>), and so on for the others.

Appellation differs from Supposition and from Signification, since Appellation has only to do with an existent thing, while Signification and Supposition concern both the existent and non-existent. **'Antichrist'** signifies the Antichrist, and stands for the Antichrist, but calls nothing up, but **'man'** signifies **man,** and of its nature, stands for both existents as well as non-existents, and calls up only existent men.

On the Division of Appellation

2 One sort of Appellation is that of a common term like **'man'**. Another is that of a singular term like **'Socrates'**. A singular term signifies, stands for, and calls up the same thing, because it signifies an existent thing, like **'Peter'** or **'John'**.

On the Appellation of a Common Term

3 Again: one sort of common term Appellation is that of a common term for the-thing-itself-in-common, as when a common term has simple supposition, as in **'man is a species'**, or **'animal is a genus'**. A common term then signifies, stands for, and calls up the same thing, as **'man'** signifies man-in-common, and stands for man-in-common, and calls up man-in-common.

4 The Appellation of a common term for its inferiors is another sort, as when a common term has Personal Supposition. In **'man runs'**, **'man'** does not then signify, stand for, or call up the same thing, but signifies **'man'** in common, stands for particular men, and calls up particular, existent men.

Let these remarks about Appellations suffice.

TRACT XI

ON RESTRICTIONS

On the definition of Restriction

1 Having discussed Extensions and Appellations, we must now take up Restrictions. Restriction is the narrowing of a common term from a larger to a smaller supposition, as said before.[1]

On the Division of Restriction

2 One kind of Restriction is effected by a noun. In **'a white man'**, the term **'man'** does not stand for blacks, nor for those of a color in between, but is restricted to whites. Another is effected by a verb. In **'a man is running'**, the term **'man'** stands for men in the present. Another is effected by a participle. In **'a man running is debating'**, the term **'man'** stands for men running. Another is by a restrictive relative clause (implicatio). In **'the man who is white is running'** the **'who is white'** restricts **'man'** to whites.

On Restriction effected by a Noun

3 Again: One sort of nominal restriction is effected by an inferior put next to a superior. In **'animal-man'** the term **'animal'** stands only for animals that are men. Another is by a difference added to a genus, a difference that is essential since it is constitutive of a species. In **'rational animal'**, the term **'animal'** stands for rationals only. Another sort is by an accidental Adjective. In **'a white man'**, the term **'man'** stands for whites only.

On a rule about Restriction effected by a Noun

4 A rule like this about Restriction by a noun, taken commonly, is given:

1: p. 172 above.

every noun not diminishing, nor having
ability of extending, adjoined from the
same word-group-part to a common term,
restricts that term to standing for those
things its signification demands.

This is clear in the examples cited above. For **'man'** by its signification restricts **'animal'** to animals that are men in **'animal-
man'**, and **'white'** restricts men by its signification to white men
in **'white man'**. I say **'not diminishing'** to exclude nominals diminishing the nature of an adjunct, like **'dead'**, **'corrupt'** and the like:
they do not restrict but rather destroy what they are adjoined to. I
say **'nor having ability of extending'** to exclude extensive words
(dictiones) like **'possible'**, **'capable'** and their like, which do not
restrict, but rather extend.

5 Note that the less always restricts the more common. That
is the case with **'white man'**, since **'man'** is found in men white,
black and in between, but **'white'** is not. To that extent, **'man'** is
the more and **'white'** the less common, so **'white'** restricts man.
But as **'white'** is found in men as well as in brute animals and stones
while **'man'** is not, **'white'** is the more and **'man'** the less
common. So **'man'** restricts **'white'** to the whiteness existing in
men in **'white man'**. And **'man'** stands only for white men and
'white' is narrowed to whiteness in men. In this way, each narrows
the other, but as to different things.

On a rule about a Restricted Term

6 Again: A rule like this is given about a restricted term:

if a universal marker comes next to a
restricted term, it does not distribute
it, except for those to which it is
restricted.

Take **'every white man is running'** for example: since **'man'** is
restricted to white men, it cannot be distributed except for white
men.

On another rule about Restriction

7 Again: Another rule like this is given about Restriction:

nothing posited from the predicate
side can restrict a common term

posited from the subject side as
to its principal signification.

In 'a man is white', the term 'white' posited in the predicate
cannot restrict 'man' posited in the subject to whites. For if it
were restricted to whites, therefore (by the preceding rule) 'if a
universal marker comes next to it', it would only distribute it for
whites. So in 'every man is white', the term 'man' is taken only
for whites. Its sense is thus: 'every white man is white'. So these
are equipollent: 'every man is white' and 'every white man is
white'. Therefore if the first is true, so is the second; and if one is
false, so is the other. This is true: 'every white man is white'.
Therefore this will be true as well: 'every man is white'. But it is
false. Therefore the first one is false as well. Therefore in 'every
man is white', the term 'white' is not restricted to whites. And
that is how this rule is clear.

I say 'as to its principal signification', because a predicate
restricts its subject as to consignification. In 'a citizen is white'
(albus) the term 'citizen' is restricted to males and not whites, so
'white' restricts it as to consignification, which is gender, and not as
to its principal signification.

On two rules about Restriction effected
by a Restrictive Relative Clause (implicatio)

8 Again: A rule like this is given about Restriction by an
Restrictive Relative Clause (implicatio):

every implication immediately adjoined
to a common term restricts it just as
its adjective does.

In 'a man who is white is running', the term 'man' is restricted to
whites by the restrictive relative clause (implicatio) 'who is white'.

9 Again: A rule like this is given about the same Restriction:

as often as a universal marker and an
implication are placed in the same
locution, the word-group is ambiguous.

This is from the fact that the marker can precede an implication and
thus distribute a common term for any of its suppLsits, as in 'every
man is running who is white'. Or the Implication can come first and

restrict the common term, then the universal marker that comes after it does not distribute that term except for those to which it is restricted, as in **'every man, who is white, is running'**. It is then equipollent to: **'every white man is running'**.

On some rules about Restriction
effected by a Verb

10 Next, on restriction effected by the verb, about which several rules are given. The first is like this:

> a common term standing as subject or coming next to a present tense verb taken simply, not having ability to extend of itself nor from another, is restricted to standing for what are under the form of the subject term.

I say **'of a common term'** because a discrete term is neither restricted nor extended. I say **'present tense'** to exclude verbs in other tenses, because a common term has different supposition with them. I say **'taken simply'** to exclude diminishers like **'it is thinkable'** or **'unthinkable'**. I say **'not having ability to extend'**, to exclude extensive verbs like **'is able to'**. I say **'neither of itself or from another'**, because in saying **'is able to'** or **'is possible to'**, even though the verb **'is'** does not of itself extend, it does have extensive potential through its adjuncts. I say **'under the form of the subject term'**, because **'man'** stands for what are under humanity, and **'animal'** for what are under animality, in **'a man is an animal'**.

11 Again: Another such rule is given:

> a common term, standing as subject or coming next to a past verb simply taken but not having ability to extend of itself nor from another, is restricted to standing for those things which are or were under the form of the subject term.

In **'a man was an animal'**, the term **'man'** stands for those who are or were men, if those who are men were men in the past, and **'animal'** stands for those who are or were animals.

12 Again: Another rule:

a common term standing as subject or
coming next to a future verb etc.,
stands for those things which are or
will be under the form of the subject
term, if those things that are, will be
in the future.

As in **'a man will be an animal'**.

13 From what was said it is clear that a verb restricts as to
consignification, which is time, and not as to its Signification.[2]

A Sophism

14 On the basis of all that, inquiry is made of this sophism:
'every animal was in Noah's ark. Proof: Man was in Noahs' ark;
Horse and Cow were in Noah's ark, and so on for each one. Therefore every animal was in Noah's ark.

Counterargument: Every kind of animal was in Noah's ark.
Caesar was an animal. Therefore Caesar was in Noah's ark. But
that is false. Therefore one of the premises is false. Not the minor.
Therefore the major. I prove the first premise is false, for there is a
rule[3] that a common term standing for something, or coming next to
a verb, etc., is restricted to standing for what are, or were, or will
be, under the form of the subject term. Another rule[4] is: if a universal Marker accompanies a restricted term, it distributes it for
everything to which it is restricted. So in **'every animal was in
Noah's ark'**, the term **'animal'** stands for every animal that existed
in the past. But there existed many animals in the past which were
not in Noah's ark. Therefore the first premise is false.

Again to the same point: In the proposition: **'every animal
which then existed, was in Noah's ark'**, the term **'animal'** is more
restricted than in **'every animal was in Noah's ark'**, because in
'every animal was in Noah's ark', the term **'animal'** is restricted to
what existed in the past simply, while in the former it is restricted
only to those which were in that past by the implication put there.

2: See below, p. 182.
3: See above, p. 180.
4: See above, p. 178.

Therefore since only those which existed in that past were in Noah's ark, and not others, this **'every animal was in Noah's ark'** should be false, since in it, more than that are stood for.

Solution: Some say **'every animal was in Noah's ark'** is ambiguous because there can be distribution for singulars within genera, or for genera of singulars. In the first way it is false, since when distribution is for singulars of genera, distribution is then for all individuals under the genus and species. Then it would be appropriate for all individuals contained under **animal** to have been in Noah's ark. And that is false. But when distribution is made for genera of singulars, there is only distribution for genera or species. But there was no species of animal which would not have been in Noah's ark. And in that way, the first premise is true.

I do not agree with that solution, because animal species were not of themselves in Noah's ark, only individuals. So it did not have truth at that time except for single members of genera, that is, for individuals, not for genera of singulars. So I say the first premise simply taken is false, and concede all arguments for this. But the proof offends by Fallacy of Consequent from Insufficient Enumeration, because it does not accept all parts of the distribution which are in the subject of the proposition **'every animal was in Noah's ark'**.

Question

15 It is usually asked whether terms are restricted in a negative the same way they are in an affirmative proposition. It seems they are not. Some say **'be'** restricts to existents, and **'not be'** to non-existents. Again: It seems every negative in which **'be'** is simply negated, is therefore false, if terms are restricted similarly in affirmative and negative. In **'there is a rose'**, the term **'rose'** is restricted to existents. Therefore, if in **'a rose there is not'** it is similarly restricted to existents, its sense is **'a rose which there is, is not'**. This is false. Therefore so is **'a rose there is not'**. So any negative in which **'be'** simply taken is negated, is false. But that is false. So it seems that terms are not restricted the same way in the affirmative and negative.

I prove they are similarly restricted: if in **'there is a man'**, the term **'man'** is restricted to existents, and in **'there is not a man'** to non-existents, both are therefore true, since of existents, **'be'** is truly predicated; of non-existents, truly denied. Therefore two contradictories are simultaneously true. Which is impossible. Therefore what it follows from is impossible, namely, that terms are not restricted the same way in the affirmative and negative.

Again: There is a rule that

> every verb simply taken, lacking abil-
> ity of itself or from another to extend,
> restricts its subject term as to its
> consignification (which is time), not as
> to its signification.

Therefore Tense is the cause of that restriction. But tense remains identical in affirmative and negative opposites, as in **'there is a rose,** '**there is not a rose'.** Therefore for the same things, restriction is effected in both.

And we concede these arguments.

16 To the first objection, say the verb **'be'** no more restricts to existents than **'run'** restricts to runners, since no verb restricts its subject term as to its signification, but as to consignification, which is time. So it does not restrict to existent, but to present, supposits. Present supposits can be in some terms, whether existents or nonexistents. In **'it is assertable',** the term **'assertable'** stands both for existents and non-existents. All assertions false in the present, are present but non-existents, since no false thing is.[5] In this way, **'be'** does not restrict to things existent but to things present. So in like fashion, **'not be'** does not restrict to non-existents, but to things present, since tense is the same in both, and that is the cause of Restriction.

17 To the second, say the form of a common term is ambiguous: one kind is that only realized in existent things, like **'humanity',** the form of a man, and **'animality',** that of an animal. In such terms, all present supposits are existents. The other is form of a common term realized both in existents and non-existents, like **'assertability',** which is an assertable form, since some assertables are existents, like **'God exists'** and all true, others are non-existents, like **'man is an ass'** and all false. In such as these, when a common term is restricted to things present, it is restricted to existents and non-existents as well. So the sense of the proposition **'a rose there is not'** is not: **'a rose which there is, is not',** but rather, **'a rose, taken presently, there is not'.**

5: i.e., exists.

On Restriction effected by Usage

It is commonly held that another sort of restriction is effected by usage. For example, **'there is nothing in the box'**,[6] though the box is full of air, since the term **'nothing'** by usage stands for solid or firm things. And **'the king is coming'** stands for the king of one's own country, and **'teacher is lecturing'**, for one's own teacher.

On Restriction effected by a verb's Transitivity

19 It is also commonly held that there is another kind of restriction effected of the transitivity of a verb. In **'Socrates feeds man'**, the term **'man'** stands for someone other than Socrates by virtue of the transitivity of the verb, since giver and receiver are of themselves diverse. So feeder and fed should be different. If then they are sometimes the same, this is by the accident that one and the same thing is subject of the two, just as Duke and Bishop are indentical by accident. So they say this does not follow:

'Socrates feeds himself
  and he himself is a man
  therefore he feeds man'.

Here there is a Fallacy of Accident, since the pronoun **'himself'** cannot stand for someone different from Socrates, but **'man'** can.

And let these suffice on Restrictions.

6:   trunk, strong-box, coffer.

TRACT XII

ON DISTRIBUTIONS

On the Definition of Distribution

1 Distribution is the multiplication of a common term effected by a universal marker (signum). In 'every man', the term 'man' is distributed or diffused for any of its inferiors by the marker 'every' (omnis), and that is the way multiplication of a common term occurs. I say 'of a common term' because a singular term cannot be distributed. That is why 'every Socrates', 'every Plato', and their like are incongruous. Solecism in word-group-parts (partes orationis) is also found there.

On Universal Markers

2 Some universal markers are distributive of Substance, such as 'every (one)', 'not a (one)' (nullus) and the like. Others distributive of Accidents, such as 'of whatever kind' (qualiscumque), 'of however many' (quantuscumque). A marker distributive of substance is one distributing things defined through the mode 'what' (quid), such as 'every (one)', 'not a (one)' (nullus) as in 'every whiteness' and 'every blackness'. So 'substance' is taken commonly with respect to things of whatever kind, when 'a marker distributive of substance' is used. A marker distributive of accident is what distributes things defined through the mode of an accident, as through the mode of 'what kind' (qualis) or 'how many' (quanti), as in 'of whatever kind' or 'of however many'.

On markers distributive of Substance

3 Again: Some markers distributive of substance are distributive of Integral Parts, like 'whole' (totus), others of Subjective Parts, like 'every (one)', 'not a (one)' (nullus), 'either (one)' (uterque). Again: some markers distributive of subjective parts are distributive of pairs, like 'either', 'neither' and their like; others of several things, like 'every', 'not a' and their like.

On the marker 'every'

4 We must first discuss markers distributive of substance and first among them, the marker **'every'** (omnis). Note that in plural number it is taken two ways: collectively, as in **'all (omnes) the apostles are (the) twelve'**, where **'therefore these are (the) twelve'** does not follow, even if some have been pointed out. It is also taken distributively or divisively, as in **'all men naturally desire to know'**.[1]

What it may signify

5 It is then asked what the marker **'every'** signifies. It seems to signify nothing, since every thing is either universal or singular. But the marker **'every'** signifies neither a universal nor a singular. Therefore the marker **'every'** signifies not a thing. Again to the same point: **'every'** is not predicable of one nor of several. Therefore it is neither universal nor singular. And so it signifies nothing.

On the contrary: Depending on whether a thing exists or not, a word-group is said to be true or false.[2] Therefore if **'every'** signifies nothing, neither truth nor falsity is caused in a word-group by putting it in or taking it out. This is true: **'an animal is a man'**; therefore so is **'every animal is a man'**; but that is false; therefore so is the first, namely that **'every'** signifies nothing.

Solution: Say to the first, that **'every'** does not signify something as a universal, but that something is taken universally[3] for it signifies that a common term is taken for every one, as in **'every man'**. This way, **'every'** signifies a kind of thing. But 'thing' (res) is ambiguous: one kind of thing is what can be made subject or predicate, like **'man'** or **'animal'**, **'runs'** or **'debates'**. It is to this thing that one objects first and it is true that **'every'** signifies nothing, since every thing of that sort is either universal or singular and **'every'** signifies neither a universal nor a singular. But there is a different kind of thing: the disposition of a thing that can be made a subject or a predicate. That is the sort of thing the marker **'every'** signifies. Truth or falsity in a word-group is caused both by this as well as by that other sort of thing.

1: Cf. Arist., Metaph. I 1, 980a1.
2: Cf. Arist., Categ. 5, 4b9-10, p.54.
3: Cf. Arist., De interpr. 7, 17b11-12 and 10, 20a9-10.

6 It is objected that 'every' does not signify a disposition of a subject, because in every syllogism, the middle term should be repeated with its dispositions in the minor proposition. Therefore we should syllogize as follows:

'every man is an animal;
  Socrates is every man;
therefore Socrates is an animal',

since **'every'** is a disposition of the subject in the major proposition; therefore it should be repeated in the minor. But that is false; therefore **'every'** is not a disposition of the subject.

Solution: Just as **'predicate'** means two things (what is the predicate and predicate-as-predicate), **'subject'** means two things as well: (what is the subject, and subject-as-subject). Accordingly, disposition of subject is ambiguous. One kind of subject-disposition is what it is subject of, like **'white'**, **'black'** and other independent dispositions. These are the ones that should be repeated in the minor with the middle term. But the other is a disposition of subject-as-subject, like **'every'**, **'not a'** and all markers, whether universal or particular. Dispositions of that sort ought not be repeated in the minor proposition with the middle term, since they are respective; they dispose a subject as paired with a predicate. In **'every white man is running'**, the disposition **'white'** should be repeated, because it is independent and thus pertains to what the subject is. But the disposition **'every'** ought not be repeated, because it is respective of subject to predicate, and so pertains to subject-as-subject. Therefore we ought to say something like:

'every white man runs
  Socrates is a white man
therefore Socrates runs'

not

'Socrates is every white man.'

W h e t h e r i t d e m a n d s t h r e e A p p e l l a t e s

7 Having discussed what the marker **'every'** signifies, and what sort of disposition it signifies, it is next asked whether it demands three appellates. It seems that it does, since every perfection is in threes, as the beginning of On heaven and earth[4] has

---

4: Arist., De coelo I 1, 268a11.

it. Therefore what is perfect is in threes; but entire (omne) and
perfect (perfectum) are the same, as it says in the same place;[5]
therefore the entire is in threes; therefore 'every' requires three
appellates.

Again to the same point: Aristotle says there[6] that we do not
say 'all men' but 'two men' of a pair, Of at least three, we do
say 'all men; therefore 'every' (omnes) needs three appellates.

On the contrary: In any demonstration, all propositions are
universal; but demonstrations are made about the sun and moon; so
one ought to say 'every sun' and 'every moon'; but 'sun' has only a
unique supposit; so too does 'moon'; therefore 'every' does not
need three appellates.

Likewise to the same point: 'Everything deprived of light by
earth's interposition is wanting'. This proposition is conceded by all,
since held by an authority.[7]   It is also universal. But what is
'deprived of light by earth's interposition' has but a unique supposit,
namely this single moon. Therefore 'every' does not always demand
three appellates.

Likewise to the same point: ' 'Every' signifies that it is universally taken'.[8]   But this 'universally taken' is a mode peculiar to
the universal itself. A peculiarity, however, is diversified according
to diversification of its subject: if man is taken simply, risible is
taken simply; if man is diminished, risible is diminished too; if
man is dead, risible is dead as well. But the universal is found
sometimes in several things, like man, horse and lion, sometimes
in one only, like sun and moon. Therefore 'every' sometimes is
found in several things, sometimes in one only. Therefore 'every'
sometimes needs three appellates, sometimes one only.

Again to the same point: Form is ambiguous: the one kind is a
material form (as my soul is my body's form and yours is that of your
body) and that form is a part and not predicated of what it is the
form of. The other is a form which is a predicable form, so all
superiors, like genera and species and differences, are called forms

5: ibid., 268a20-21.
6: ibid., 268a16-19.
7: Cf. Arist., Anal. Post. II 2, 90a16; Boeth., De top. diff. I,
     1181 A 3.
8: See above, p. 186-7.

of their inferiors, like **'man'**, **'horse'**, **'animal'** and their like. But individuals of this predicable form are its matter. Therefore since form exceeds its matter by neither of the modes mentioned, nor is exceeded by it, therefore no universal exceeds its individuals nor is exceeded by them. Therefore since **'every'** means equation of a universal with its individuals, like **'every man'**, it is then appropriate that, since the **'sun'** (and **'moon'**, having but a unique individual) is truly said to be **'every sun'**, so too **'every moon'** and **'every phoenix'**.

We concede that, saying the above propositions are true: **'every'** does not always demand three appellates, but when adjoined to a universal term having several supposits, **'every'** does need to have several. But when conjoined with a universal term having one only individual, it needs but one supposit.

As to the first objection (that every thing's perfection is in threes), say it is true. The three are: the substance of a thing, its potential, and its operation. Aristotle touches on the three in the words: 'a nature aptly designed works so'. By saying **'nature'**, he touches on a thing's substance; in **'apt'**, its potential; by **'works so'**, its due operation. So a man is said to be perfect since he has a man's substance, potential, and the operation due him. So too, the marker **'every'** has a universal marker's substance and potential, since it is distributive, and it has its operation when it distributes. In these three its perfection lies.

To the second objection, say **'man'** and **'men'** differ because **'man'** means species itself as such, which is predicable of many, while **'men'** in the plural means species, not as such, but as actually multiplied by individuals' numerically diverse matters. So **'every'** in the plural, by reason of the multiplicion effected by diverse matters, demands at least three appellates. In the singular, since **'every'** regards species as such and not individuals' matter, it only demands an essence naturally apt to be predicated of several, whether actually shared in by several or by one only. For that reason it sometimes demands three appellates, sometimes one only, depending on the nature of the universal to which it is adjoined.

On a rule about what was discussed

8 There are some who say **'every'** always needs at least three appellates, and they give a rule like this:

9:   where ? Perhaps in some comment in the <u>De coelo</u>.

as often as a universal affirmative
marker is added to a common term
lacking a sufficiency of appellates,
an appeal is made to a non-being.

Take **'every phoenix'**: since the term **'phoenix'** has but a single
existent supposit, its marker **'every'** appeals to non-existent
phoenices. For that reason, **'every phoenix'** has the sense: **'some
phoenix and two other phoenices which do not exist'**. So they say
these two propositions **'every phoenix exists'** and **'some phoenix
does not exist'** are at the same time false yet not contradictories,
since in the negative one, **'a phoenix which does exist'** is stood for
and in the affirmative, **'two phoenices which do not exist'**, is stood
for. That way the subject is not the same in both.

On its Refutation

9 This can be refuted in several ways. First, because this
incongruity follows from the falsehood they posit: **'every'** would[10]
need at least three appellates, which has been shown above[10] to be
false. Second: Aristotle[11] holds that a proposition in which a
universal, universally taken, is subject of a predicate, contradicts
the proposition where the same universal, not universally taken, is
subject of the same predicate. These are of that sort: **'every
phoenix exists'** and **'some phoenix does not exist'**. Therefore they
are contradictories. Which they deny. So their rule is false.

Again to the same point: the rule[12] is:

a common term as subject of, or coming
next to, a verb in the present tense,
simply taken, and not having ability of
extending of itself nor from another,
is restricted to standing for what are
under the form of the subject term.

Therefore in **'a phoenix exists'**, the term **'phoenix'** is restricted to
standing for one phoenix only, since there is but a unique supposit
there. Therefore by another rule given earlier,[13] if a universal

10: Above, p. 189.
11: De interpr. 7, 17b16-18.
12: See above, p. 180.
13: Above, p. 178-9.

marker is added to it, it does not distribute it except for a unique supposit. Therefore there will be no appeal to non-existent phoenices. Their rule is thus fallacious and founded on a fallacy. Which we concede.

A S o p h i s m

10 On the basis of what was said above, the sophism is questioned: **'every man exists and anything differing from him is non-man'.** (<u>omnis</u> <u>homo</u> <u>est</u> et <u>quodlibet</u> <u>differens</u> ab <u>illo</u> est <u>non-homo</u>). Proof: This is the sort of copulative in which each part is true. Therefore the whole itself is true. Counterargument: Every man exists and anything differing from him is non-man. Therefore Socrates exists and anything differing from him is non-man. This is false, since this is the sort of copulative in which one part is false; therefore it is itself false.

Solution: **'Differing from every man'** is less than **'differing from Socrates'**, because **'differing from every man'** stands only for things other than man, while **'differing from Socrates'** stands for the same things, and for all men other than Socrates as well. So this follows validly: **'differing from every man, therefore differing from Socrates'**. It is the Topic from Species or Subjective Part. So if a universal marker is added, there is a shift from inferior to superior with distribution. That way a Fallacy of Consequent occurs in the proof, based on one sort of shift. Shift is ambiguous in proof. This follows validly: **'every man, therefore Socrates'**, and is the Topic of a Whole in Quantity. But this does not: **'anything different from every man; therefore anything different from Socrates';** here there is a **Fallacy of Consequent,** as was said; so too in: **'every man; therefore every animal'.**

A n o t h e r S o p h i s m

11 This sophism is likewise questioned: **'every man and (an) other man exist'** (<u>omnis</u> <u>homo</u> et alius <u>homo</u> <u>sunt</u>). Proof: Socrates and an other man exist, Plato and an other man exist, and so on for the others; therefore every man and an other man exist. Counterargument: The relative **'(an) other'** is a relative of diversity; therefore it stands for something differing from every man; but there is not a man other than every man; therefore the first is false.

Solution: The first is false and the proof offends by Fallacy of Word Figure, shifting from several determinates to a single determinate. For the term **'(an) other'** has determinate supposition in the premises as well as conclusion. Again: The proof offends by the Fallacy of Accident, since, though **'Socrates'** and **'Plato'** and **'Cicero'** infer **'every man'** of themselves, yet as conjoined with **'(an) other man'**, they cannot infer **'every man'** in **'every man and (an) other man exist'**. Just as I know Coriscus in himself, but not under the accident **'to come'**.

On a certain rule

12 So a rule like this is given:

as often as one follows upon another, conversely or not, should something suit the one in such a way as not to suit the other, and an inference is drawn from the one it does suit about the one it does not, - there is always a Fallacy of Accident.

For example: This follows validly: **'it is a man, therefore it is a substance'**. And species suits man in a way it does not suit substance. So if from **'man'** an inference is drawn about substance, it will be a Fallacy of Accident. Like: **'man is a species; therefore substance is a species'**; and: **'risibility is a peculiarity; therefore man is a peculiarity'**; and: **'the house is worth a hundred marks; 'therefore so are the walls'**. Some of these follow conversely, like **'man'** and **'risible'**, but some do not.

Another Sophism

13 Again: This sophism is questioned: **'every man is every man'**. Proof: Socrates is Socrates; Plato is Plato; Cicero is Cicero, and so on for singulars; therefore every man is every man. Or thus: Boethius[14] says no proposition is truer than the one in which the same thing is predicated of itself. Therefore no proposition is truer than this one. Counterargument: Its contradictory (**'some man is not every man'**) is true. Therefore it is itself false. Again to the same point: Every man is every man; but Socrates is a man; therefore Socrates is every man. But the conclusion is false. Therefore so is the first, from which it follows.

14: Cf. In Arist. Periherm. ed. 1, p. 215.18-20; ed. 2, p. 480.7-9.

Solution: The first is simply false. And proof offends by the Fallacy of Consequent from Insufficient Enumeration, since along with what it does take up, it should also take up these from the side of subject: 'Socrates is every man', 'Plato is every man' and so for the others; and these also from the side of predicate: 'every man is Socrates', 'every man is Plato', and so for singulars. It omits all these, so offends by the Fallacy of Insufficient Enumeration. As to the other, say the same thing is not predicated of itself, but that 'every man' is predicated of man taken for any part of himself.

O n   t h e   m a r k e r   ' n o t   a   (o n e) '   (<u>n u l l u s</u>)
W h a t   i t   m a y   s i g n i f y

14 Next on the marker **'not a (one)'** (<u>nullus</u>) which signifies negatively universally.[15]   So it signifies the same thing as the marker **'every'** with negation added later. Therefore **'not every'** ('<u>omnis</u> <u>non</u>') and **'not a (one)'** ('<u>nullus</u>') are equipollent.

O n   a   R u l e

15 For the marker **'not a (one)'** a rule like this is given:

> a s   o f e n   a s   t h e   m a r k e r   **' n o t   a   (o n e) '**   i s
a d j o i n e d   i m m e d i a t e l y   t o   a   c o m m o n   t e r m ,
i t   d i f f u s e s   i t   d i s t r i b u t i v e l y   a n d   m o b -
i l e l y ;   a n d   s i m i l a r l y ,   a   t e r m   t o   w h i c h
i t   i s   m e d i a t e l y   a d j o i n e d .

For example, **'no man is an ass'** (<u>mullus</u> <u>homo</u> <u>est</u> <u>asinus</u>). So descent can be made below a subject as follows: **'therefore Socrates is not an ass, nor is Plato'** and so on of the others; below a predicate as follows: **'no man is an ass;   therefore no man is Brunellus nor Fanellus'**, and so on for the others.

A   S o p h i s m

16 This sophism is questioned on the basis of what was said: **'no one man is every man'** (<u>mullus</u> <u>homo</u> <u>est</u> <u>omnis</u> <u>homo</u>). Proof: Socrates is not every man, Plato is not every man, and so on of the others;   therefore no one man is every man. Or as follows: its contradictory (**'some man is every man'**) is false; so it is true. Counterargument: an opposite is predicated of an opposite there,

---

15:   Cf. above, p. 186-7.

since **'every'** and **'not a (one)'** are opposites. Therefore the locution is false.

Solution: The first is true simply taken. Respond to the refutation by refuting it, because there, an opposite is not predicated of an opposite, but **'to be every man'** is removed from **'every man'** for any supposit of 'every man', and that is true.

On the marker 'nothing' (nichil) What it may signify

17 Next about the marker **'nothing'**, which signifies the same as the marker **'not a (one)'** (nullus) and in addition, signifies the term receiving its distribution, since **'nothing'** (nichil) signifies **'not a thing'** (nullam rem); for **'not a (one)'** (nullum) is a universal marker with negation, while **'thing'** (res) is the term receiving its distribution.

A Sophism

18 Accordingly, this sophism is questioned: **'one who is seeing nothing is seeing something'** (nichil videns est aliquid videns). Proof: One who is not seeing this thing is one who is seeing something, for one who is not seeing Socrates is one who is seeing Plato; one who is not seeing that thing is one who is seeing something, and so on for singulars; therefore one who is seeing nothing is one who is seeing something. Counterargument: Here, opposite is predicated of opposite, since **'to see something'** (aliquid videre) is under what **'to see nothing'** (nihil videre) is under. Therefore the locution is impossible.

Some make a distinction about **'one who is seeing nothing is one who is seeing something'** from the fact that the word (dictio) **'nothing'** can be in the accusative case, with the sense: **'one who is seeing not a thing is one who is seeing something'** (nullam rem videns est aliquid videns). Or it can be in the nominative case, with the sense: **'no thing that is seeing is a thing that is seeing something'** (nulla res videns est aliquid videns). On that basis they posit amphiboly there from diversity of case. But this is no solution, because it is false in both senses.

Others make a distinction about **'one who is seeing nothing is one who is seeing something'** on the basis that the negation found within the term **'nothing'** can negate the participle placed first, and then its sense is: **'one who is not seeing any thing is one who is** seeing something' (quamlibet rem non videns est aliquid videns), and this way it is divided. Or it can negate the verb 'is' (est) with the sense: 'one who is seeing any thing is one who is not seeing something' (quamlibet rem videns non est aliquid videns), and this way it is composite, since the negation is put into a more due position. But this again is no solution, for it is false in either sense, since opposites are affirmed about the same thing.

So say the first is simply false and proof offends by the Fallacy of Word Figure going from several determinates to a single determinate of the term '(one) seeing' (videns). For in the premises it has determinate supposition, as it does in the conclusion, since both the premises as well as the conclusion are nonfinite. It also offends by the Fallacy of Accident, since see (videre) fits all premises as such, not just as unified in this whole, '(one) seeing nothing'. For this reason, whole is accidental to parts and to see something (videre aliquid) is assigned to-be-in in each of them.

19 Note that all the premises are ambiguous, since negation can determine the verb or the participle, as said before.[16] That is why predecessors held that the premises, but not the conclusion, were ambiguous, because of a rule like this they gave:

as often as negation and distribution are included within a single term, whatever the one concerns, so does the other.

So, since distribution placed in an oblique cannot extend to the verb in the sentence cited above, neither can negation.

Some other Sophisms

20 Again: A judgement about these sophisms is completely identical:

'one having no head is one having some head' (nullum caput habens est aliquod caput habens)

'one differing from no man is one differing from some man' (a nullo homine differens est ab aliquo homine differens)

16: Above, p. 194 f.

'one having no eye is one having some eye'
(nullum oculum habens est aliquem oculum habens)

'you are someone or other or one differing from someone or other'
(tu es quilibet vel differens a quolibet)

'you are every man or one differing from every man'
(tu es omnis homo vel differens ab omni homine)

On markers distributive of Two

21 Next on markers distributive of two. These include: 'both / either' (uterque), 'neither' (neuter) and their like. They differ from such as 'every', 'not a (one)' and their like, mentioned above, since they distribute for all individuals of a common term, but 'both / either' and 'neither' distribute solely for pairs pointed out, such as 'either of these', 'neither of these'.

A Sophism

22 On the basis of what was said, question is made of this sophism: 'what is stated by both / either of these is true' (ab utroque istorum enuntiatum est verum) given that Socrates says 'God exists', that Plato says 'a man is an animal' and that they both say 'a man is an ass', and that the latter two are picked out by the pronoun 'these' (isti). Proof of the first: What is stated by Socrates is true; what is stated by Plato is true; therefore what is stated by both of them is true. Counterargument: What is stated by either of these is true; but nothing is stated by both of these except that a man is an ass; therefore that a man is an ass is true.

Solution: The first is true and the refutation offends by the Fallacy of Accident, because on Aristotle's authority,[17] this proposition is put as true: 'there is one and the same study of all contraries', yet no particular study is of all contraries except study in general, so this is a Fallacy of Accident:

'There is one and the same study of all contraries
but there is no study except this or that study,
and so on for the others;
therefore this or that study is of all contraries'

Which is false. And similarly,

'man is a species
  but no man exists except Socrates or Plato or Cicero
and so of each one
  therefore Socrates is a species or Plato or Cicero (is)'

This is accidental, as was clear in the Fallacy of Accident.[18] So too in what was proposed, since the word (dictio) 'stated' and the word (dictio) 'true' are taken for the same thing in general. And that way what is stated by either is true. That is why 'stated' is not taken for a particular statement by either of them. That is why **a particular statement by either / both of these** is accidental to **what is stated by either / both**, as an inferior is to its superior, and **to be true** is assigned being-in to both. And I call 'superior' in general, everything greater, whether it be essential or accidental.

But some say the first is simply false and **'what is stated by either / both'** is taken for a particular statement by either of them, and that 'true' is taken for a particular truth as well. The proof offends by the Fallacy of Word Figure, going from several, to a single determinate of the term **'what is stated'**, and the same for the term **'true'**.

But the first solution is better and more subtle.

Another Sophism

23 Again: Question is made of this sophism: **'having neither eye you can see'** (habendo neutrum oculum tu potes videre). Proof: Not having the right eye, you can see; not having the left eye, you can see; therefore having neither eye, you can see. Counterargument: having neither eye you can see. Therefore while you have neither eye, or if you have neither eye, or because you have neither eye, you can see. Which is false. For a gerund ending in -do is to be interpreted by while or by if or by because. But it is false in any way. Therefore the first is simply false.

Solution: The first is simply false, and proof offends by the Fallacy of Accident, since ability to see suits parts as such, insofar as they are divided. It does not suit them insofar as they are united within their whole / does not suit the whole itself; for a whole is identical with all parts united at once. By a rule cited earlier,[19]

17:   Topica I, 14 105b5, p. 20 (and elsewhere).
18: ·Above, p. 129 ff.

since whole follows upon parts, and ability to see suits parts, not whole, if an inference is made about a whole on the basis of parts, it is consequently a Fallacy of Accident.

Whether Negation has ability to distribute

24 Having discussed signs distributive of subjective parts, it is next asked whether negation has the ability distribute or diffuse. It seems it does, for Aristotle[20] says in First Perihermenias that these two are Contradictory: 'man is just' - 'non-man is just'. Therefore the first is universal, since a common term is the subject. But only if 'non-man is just' is universal. Therefore the term 'man' is distributed. But there is nothing there by which it is distributed except negation. Therefore it is distributed by negation.

On the contrary: If negation has ability to distribute, then just as 'every Socrates' is incongruous, so too is 'non-Socrates'. Which is false, since even though a distributive marker cannot be added to a singular term, negation can be validly added to it. Again: Wherever distribution is found, there is a common term taken universally. Therefore it is fitting that a word (dictio) signifying universally be there. But a universal marker signifies universally, while negation does not. Therefore negation does not have ability to distribute.

We concede that, saying negation does not diffuse, only negates, what it finds. So adjoined to a common term, it negates it, but once a superior is negated, removal of any inferior follows, for superior destroyed, any inferior is destroyed, just as if a genus is destroyed, so too is any species of it. That way negation does not diffuse but negates what it finds, whether it be a universal or a singular.

The solution to the objection is now clear, for the fact that 'non-man is just' is universal is not because of the nature of distribution found in negation, but because man in common is negated, and once that is removed, so is any inferior.

19:   See above, p. 195.
20:   De interpr. 10, 19b27-28.

On Distribution of an Aptitude

25 Again: Potential Distribution is often posited, as in **'every man is afraid at sea'**, that is: **is naturally apt to be afraid at sea.**

On Accomodated Distribution

26 Again: Accomodated Distribution is often posited, as in **'the heavens cover all things'**, that is: **all things other than themselves;** and **'God created all things'**, that is: **all things other than Himself.**

But these two kinds of Distributions are not as proper as the ones discussed above.

On the marker '(the) whole (of)' (totus)

27 Next, on the marker **'(the) whole (of)'** (totus), which is distributive of integral parts. This is clear in **'(the) whole (of) Socrates is white'**, with the sense: **'Socrates is white as to any part of him'.** So from **'(the) whole (of) Socrates is white'** two propositions immediately follow: **'Socrates, as to any part of him, is white'**, and **'any part of Socrates is white'.** Proof: In the proposition: **'the whole (of) Socrates is white'**, Socrates as such is the subject of whiteness, while his parts are subjects of whiteness, not as such, but insofar as they are parts of his whole. But insofar as they belong to the whole, they belong to the form of the whole. Therefore they are not subjects of whiteness except by means of the whole. Therefore this follows initially: **'Socrates as to any part of him is white'**, and subsequently: **'any part of Socrates is white'.**

Again: In **'the whole (of) Socrates is white'**, a whole is a subject of whiteness directly,[21] parts indirectly,[22] because in what is a whole, parts are understood indirectly; in what is a part, the whole is taken indirectly. This is clear by the definition of what a whole is. As a house consists of wall, roof and foundation. Socrates consists of parts of that sort. Therefore what a whole is gives us to understand its indirect parts. Therefore upon: **'(the) whole (of)**

21: **'directly'** translates in rectitudine. Nominative case is is casus rectus (fpd).
22: **'indirectly'** translates in obliquitate. A non-nominative case is a casus obliquus (fpd).

Socrates is white', this follows immediately: 'Socrates as to any part of him is white'; and subsequently: 'any part of Socrates is white'.

Again to the same point: Whatever is a a part has no existence except in its whole, for it has no perfection except from that whole. Therefore it is not subject of anything except through its whole. Therefore upon: '(the) whole (of) Socrates etc.', there immediately follows: 'Socrates, as to any part of him, etc.' and subsequently: 'any part of Socrates etc.'

A Sophism

28 According to what was said, this sophism is questioned: '(the) whole (of) Socrates is less than Socrates' (totus Sortes est minor Sorte). Proof: Any part of Socrates is less than Socrates. Therefore Socrates, as to any part of him, is less than Socrates. Therefore (the) whole (of) Socrates is less than Socrates. Counter-argument: (The) whole (of) Socrates is less than Socrates. But (the) whole (of) Socrates is Socrates. Therefore Socrates is less than Socrates. Which is false.

Solution: The first, '(the) whole (of) Socrates is less than Socrates', is true and the refutation offends by the Fallacy of Accident, since in '(the) whole (of) Socrates is less than Socrates', a predicate is attributed to parts it truly suits, though it does not suit the whole. Therefore this is simply false: 'Socrates is less than Socrates'. Therefore, if an inference is drawn about a whole through parts, it will be a Fallacy of Accident. Therefore (the) whole (of) Socrates is the thing that is subject and **Socrates** is its accident and **to be less than Socrates** is assigned to-be-in to both. The refutation also offends by the Fallacy of Simply and After-a-Fashion, since '(the) whole (of) Socrates is less than Socrates' does not posit that Socrates is less than Socrates simply, but less as to his parts; that way it posits Socrates is less than Socrates after-a-fashion. And that way, since an inference is drawn simply as follows: 'therefore Socrates is less than Socrates', it offends by the Fallacy of After-a-Fashion and Simply. Just like: 'Socrates is less than Socrates as to his foot; therefore Socrates is less than Socrates'.

29 Again: Since sometimes '(the) whole (of) Socrates, therefore Socrates' follows, as in '(the) whole (of) Socrates is white, therefore Socrates is white', and sometimes it does not, one asks when it does.

Say there are some accidents which indifferently suit whole
and part, such as **white** and **black, hot, cold, to increase** and **to
decrease** and their like. In such as these, **'(the) whole (of) Socrates
is white; therefore Socrates'**, follows validly, as in **'(the) whole (of)
Socrates is white;   therefore Socrates is white'**,   and so of the
others. But there are other accidents which fit parts and not the
whole and conversely, the whole and not parts, such as **totality,
majority, minority** and **paucity**. In such as these, **'(the) whole (of)
Socrates exists, therefore Socrates exists'** does not follow.

On markers distributive of Accidents

30 Next, on markers distributive of accidents.   First among
these to be discussed are markers distributive of quality.

On markers distributive of Quality

31 A marker said to be distributive of quality which distributes a thing defined by the mode of quality, such as **'(of) any kind'**
(qualelibet), the particular of which is **'(of) some kind'** (aliquale).

It is objected that since an accident is multiplied when its
subject is multiplied, therefore since markers distributive of
substance distribute or multiply a subject, it is appropriate that they
distribute or multiply the accident itself.   Therefore markers
distributive of quality are superfluous.

Say accidental multiplication is ambiguous. One way, accident
is multiplied numerically;   and this multiplication is effected by
markers distributive of substance, as in **'every man is white'**.   The
other way, accident is multiplied specifically;   and this is effected
by markers distributive of accident, as in **'a thing of any kind runs'**,
that is, **'a thing having a quality of any kind runs'**.

A Sophism

32 Based on what was said above, question is made of this
sophism: **'anything of any kind knows about anything of that kind
that it is itself of the kind which it is itself'** (quodlibet qualelibet de
quolibet tali scit ipsum esse tale quale ipsum est). Assume Socrates
knows grammar, dialectic and rhetoric, that Plato and Cicero do
too, and that they know that they possess them;   then let there be
another three men, of whom the first knows one of those studies, the
second a different one, and the last the third, and that these men do
not know they possess those studies, and of the others, they know

nothing; but the others know about themselves and about these; and that there are no more men nor qualities.

Proof of the first: This thing of any kind knows, about anything of that kind, that it is itself of the kind which that is; that thing of any kind, etc.; and so of the third. And there are no more. Therefore anything of any kind knows about anything of that kind etc. Counterargument: anything of any kind etc.; therefore anything grammatical knows of any thing of that kind etc..

Solution: The first is true and refutation offends by Fallacy of Consequent, going from inferior to superior with distribution, since **'anything'** stands for three only, but **'anything grammatical'** stands for that same three as well as for the one who possesses only grammar; and in that way **'something grammatical'** is in more than **'of any kind'**. As a result, if distribution is added as follows: **'anything of any kind; therefore anything grammatical'** a **Fallacy of Consequent** arises, as in **'every man, therefore every animal'**. So too in the ablative, as in **'about anything of any kind; therefore about anything grammatical'** (de quolibet qualelibet; ergo de quolibet grammatico), since it speaks of anything of that kind.

O n   m a r k e r s   d i s t r i b u t i v e   o f   Q u a n t i t y

33 Next on markers distributive of quantity. They distribute a thing defined by a mode of Quantity.

A   S o p h i s m

34 Accordingly this sophism is questioned: **'As many times as you have been a Parisian, you have been a man'** (quotienscumque fuisti Parisius, fuisti homo). Proof: you have been a Parisian one time, and that time you have been a man; another time you have been a Parisian, etc. and so on of the others; therefore the first is true. Counterargument: As many times as you have been a Parisian, you have been a man; but you have been a Parisian twice; therefore you have been a man twice. Which is false, since the word (dictio) **'twice'** posits an interruption of the act to which it is adjoined; but the act of being a man was not interrupted in you.

Solution: The first is simply false. But solve the proof by denying the disjunction, because the second part of the copulative (**'that time you have been a man'**) is false. So far, you **'have been'** a man at no time, due to the fact that your life has not yet been cut off in such a way that you would start to live again and later it would be stopped. And that is what would be required for you to 'have been' a man twice, just as a race starts twice and ends twice, so someone could run twice.

On the word (dictio) 'twice'

35 Note that 'twice' (bis) does not imply an interruption in, but an end of, that act to which it is adjoined; but upon an end there does follow an interruption. If however a paralogism were formed as follows:

'whenever you have been a Parisian, you have been a man
   but twice you have been a Parisian
   therefore twice you have been a man',

then the first is true but the refutation offends by the Fallacy of Word Figure from Commutation of Predicament, since 'whenever' (quandocumque) is in the predicament 'When' while 'twice' means a mode of discrete quantity.

On the nominal 'infinite' (infinitum)

36 Next, on the nominal 'infinite'. This is said in five ways.[23] First, that is said to be infinite which cannot be penetrated, as voice is said to be infinite with respect to sight, because it is invisible, not naturally apt to be seen. Second, that is said to be infinite which has incomplete penetration because it has as yet not been gone through, yet is naturally apt to be penetrated, as when someone is going through a space and has not yet come to its end. Third, something is said to be infinite by addition, like an augmentable number, which is infinite by addition of a unit or another number. Fourth, something is called 'infinite' on the basis of division, like a continuum: every continuum can go on being divided infinitely. That is why it is defined by Aristotle[24] in VI Physics as follows: 'A continuum is divisible into ever divisibiles'. But in the fifth way, 'infinite' is said both ways, that is by addition and division, like time. For time is a continuum, and it is infinitely divisible, so infinite by division; and since one time comes after another, by the addition of one time to another, time is infinite by addition.

23:   Cf. Boethius, De divisionibus, 888 D9ff.; Arist., Physica III 4, 204a2-7 and Thomas Aquinas, In III Phys. lect. 7, c.
24:   Phys. VI, 3, 232b24-25.7

As to these three last significations, infinite is defined[25] as
follows: something infinite, in things accepting Quantity, is that
whose nature it is, always to take up something extra. So, if after
one part of line, another is accepted and after that, a third, and its
end can never be reached, a line would then said to be infinite.

37 It is customarily held that **'infinite'** is sometimes taken as
a common term,[26] and then the proposition **'infinites are finite'**
(infinita sunt finita) is equipollent to **'some infinites are finite'**
(aliqua infinita sunt finita). Sometimes it is taken for a distributive
marker, and then that proposition **'infinites are finite'** is equipollent
distributionally to: **'for one thing or another, many are finite'**
(quolibet plura sunt finita). This is proven as follows: for one, many
are finite, for two, many are finite, for three, many are finite and so
on of the others; therefore for one thing or another, many are
finite. It is said to constitute interscalar, or interrupted, or
discontinuous distribution, because the word **'many'** in the first
proposition stands for two and so on, in the second for three and so
on, thus always gradually, or ascending step by step. For that
reason, the word-group **'for one thing or another many'** constitutes
interscalar distribution, since what I say with **'for one thing or
another'** (quolibet) stands for some things, and what I say with
'many' stands for others, ascending numerically, as was said.

A S o p h i s m

38 Based on what was said above, this sophism is queried:
'infinites are finite' (infinita sunt finita). Proof: Two are finite,
three are finite, and so on to infinity; therefore infinites are
finite. Counterargument: Opposites are there predicated of opposites; therefore the expression is impossible.

It can also be proven as follows: for one thing or another,
many are finite; therefore infinites are finite.

Solution: Some make the distinction that **'infinite'** is equivocated into **'infinite-for-us'** and **'simply infinite'**. As a result, if
'infinite' is taken merely with reference to us, the first is true and
an opposite is not predicated of an opposite, since things that are
infinite as far as we are concerned, like stars or grains of sand, are
simply finite. But if **'infinite'** is taken simply, the first is false and

25: See Arist. Phys. III 6, 207a7.
26: Marginal note in the Cordoba manuscript: 'i.e., a term which is
     commonly related to all indefinites (infinita).'

an opposite is predicated of an opposite. Others make a distinction from the fact that 'infinite' can be a common term; that way the first is false; or it can be a syncategorematic word (<u>dictio</u>) which of itself entails distribution, as was said; and that way they hold it to be true.

But neither of those solutions is valid, for if each distinction were removed, and 'infinite' were taken simply and on the basis that it is a common term, proof and refutation of the sophism still remain. So say that the first is simply false and that the proof offends by the Fallacy of After-a-Fashion and Simply, since infinite by addition is infinite somehow or other, not simply infinite. So when it accepts numerical parts by addition, like two, three, four, it does not accept infinity simply, but somehow or other, or after-a-fashion; and for that reason one cannot infer infinite simply from them. In that way, since from **infinite After-a-Fashion** one concludes to **infinite Simply,** it offends on the basis of the Fallacy of After-a-Fashion and Simply.

And let what has been said about distributions suffice.

INDEX OF REFERENCES
(All reference numbers refer to pages)

102; 'posit' is ambiguous as
to quantity, quality and order
of propositions and terms
163; universal marker &
implication in same locution
make it ambiguous 179

amphiboly
principle of deception is from
a word-group simply one, yet
signifying several 90; its
plausibility: diversity of same
word-group 90; from amphi
(doubt) & bole (judgement)
or logos (speech) 90; (1)
word-group principally signifies more than one, like 'Aristotle's book' 90; (2) from
transfer: 'plough sand' transferred to 'waste time' 91;
(3) word-group signifies
several, each part only one:
'knowing age' 91; ambiguous
as to deception in word-group
simply identical or deception
caused in us 90; always
occurs in construction of one
unit with another unit 167;
from diversity of case 194

analogy
description of what is said
analogically can be validly
given 78

animal species
were not of themselves in
Noah's ark, only individuals
182

'animal'
signifies real & pictured; the
name is common, natures diverse 25; in 'animal is
genus' stands for anim-
al-in-general, not one of its
inferiors 70; diffused immobilely since descent below
it is not allowed 72; 'an-

imal' as superior restricted
by its inferior 'man' in 'animal-man' to animals that are
men 177; stands for those
who are or were animals in 'a
man was an animal' 180

answer
to 'what kind ?' is affirmative or negative 4; to 'what
number ?' is universal, particular, nonfinite or singular 4;
to 'what ?' must be categoric
or hypothetic 4; answering a
many question with one response is invalid 158

antecedent 9, 164, 165, 166,
168, 169, 170: the categoric
to which the conjunction 'if' is
immediately joined is called
the antecedent, the other, the
consequent 9; a substantive
relative is one that recalls
what is numerically identical
with its antecedent 164;
certainty is greater from a
relative of identity than from
an antecedent substituted for
a relative 165

Antichrist
signifies and stands for the
Antichrist but calls nothing
up 175

any one at all (quilibet) 4

'anything'
in this fallacy stands for three
things: 'anything grammatical' for more 202

apparent wisdom
acquired by arguments from
sophistical Topics 81

appellation 25
acceptance of a term for an
existent thing 175; one appellation of a common term:
thing-itself-in-common 175;

whole defined)' (5) (a) sub-
stantal: peculiarly (soul in
body), (b) accident (white in
wall); (6) something in goal
(virtue in beatitude); (8)
thing located in place (something in a vessel); (9) Boethius subdivides (5) as mentioned 26; mode of being-in as
accident in a subject one
thing, mode of being-in as
part in a whole another 28

beg question
begging question: conclusion
to be proven is sought for in
the premises 146

being
Being is predicated of these
ten, but said equivocally, so is
not a genus 18; though predicated according to a single
name of all things, it is not
predicated according to a
single nature 24; the nature
Being, said of a substance, is
Being in itself; as predicated
of the other 9 Predicaments,
'Being in another' 24;

bell 1

belong to 4

bishop
Duke and Bishop are identical
by accident 184

body 1, 30, 32, 36

Boethius 21, 26, 192

both (uterque) 4

'both'
is said of 2, 'all' of 3 188

boxer 32

'bread eating dog',
while materially identical,
may vary formally 99; 'bread
eating dog' has potential
polysemy since the definition
given suits it 99; 'bread'
may be subject to, or put next
to 'eating' in 'bread eating
dog' 99; has specific identity
in material division: like boy-
youth-man 100; always identical by perfection since this
word-group is completed by
the inflection found there
100

breath
first a syllable accident, then
a word accident 112

broaden 172

Brunellus 18

buba 2

case 2;
assigned a word so that one
word can be ordered to another 92; case-diversity
deceives by amphiboly, not
equivocation 92; accusative
case: amphiboly from 194;

case-ending 25, 35:
noun's accident insofar as
activity or passivity emanate
from nominative noun 97;
noun's accident as activity /
passivity pass into a noun as
in oblique cases 97; a noun-
accident compared to a verb
97; a relational accident -
disposition of substance in respect to an act 97; case-
endings and the like order
words to each other 97; deception from case-ending is
from word-ordering or word-
grouping: it results in amphiboly, not equivocation 97

case-forms
other than nominative are not
nouns for the dialectician 2;
those deriving from a base
form (principale) 67

identical) 8; universal affirmative is converted by accident into particular negative and universal negative into particular negative 8

convert 8

convertibly 31, 32, 34, 35, 36

coordinate

'two and three are five' is categoric when composite with a coordinate subject 98

copula

is clear by analyzing 'man runs' as 'man is running' 3

copulation

acceptance of an adjectival term for something 70

copulative 8

in which each part is true 191; in which one part is false 191

Coriscus

"a 'third man' other than man" is false unless 'man' is 'a sort of thing' 123; signifies 'this individual'; 'Coriscus the musician' signifies 'of some sort' 123

correlative 31

one correlative is sought in the other 148; seeking one correlative in the other does not impede demonstrative but dialectic syllogisms 148

corruption: going from being to non-being 36, 61

costume (habitus) 16, 36

creator

whatever exists is either substance, accident or the creator of substance and accident 127

crow 23

cubit 30, 36

curvature 32

de inesse (about Being-In) 12

de re

when a dictum stands for part of itself, word-groups are called de re 106; de re word-groups label a dictum's own subject 106

death

and life are contraries 155; is corruption 155; is not corruption but an end point in corruption 156

deception

effected by diversity of relation is not equivocation 167; from diverse relation is a fallacy of composition or division 167; from diversity of relation is in the ordering of words among themselves 167;

definite

'definite' distinguishes noun from nonfinites like non-man 2; 'definite' vs. non-finite like 'non-man' 2; vs. word-group whose parts are separate signs 2; vs. oblique cases 2; 'non-man' not a noun for dialecticians but a nonfinite noun 2; vs. non-significative expressions 2; 'without tense' vs. verb 2; non-nominatives are not nouns but cases or obliques for dialectician 2; conventionally significative vocal expression 2; lacks tense, separately significant parts and cases other than the nominative 2

definition

a word-group signifying what the essence of a thing is 22; it should consist of genus and differences 21; a statement signifying a thing's essence (quid est esse) 52; is of something said univocally, not analogically 78; of 'one only' identical with that of 'thing taken simply' 163

definition in thing defined 26, 28, 31, 32, 36

delight and sadden 33

demonstrative syllogism
involves reasoning from true and basic principles 77; only has one conclusion, contradictory always has two 153

demonstratives 4
said of things present 171

denominative
25, 32, 33: differ only by an ending from the noun basing their appellation 24; should agree with a univocal in its beginning 25; differ by caseending, which is material 25; differ by ending from base by which they have appellation 25

denominatively
'grammatical', 'strong', 'white' and their like are predicated senominatively 24

denote
a parallelism can be denoted with respect to the verb 'walk' 105

description 22
a word-group consisting of genus and peculiarity 54; a word-group signifying the being of a thing through accidentals 54

destroy
nominals like 'dead' and 'corrupt' destroy rather than restrict 178

determinate 172
called determinate though standing for all since only true if one is running 71

determine 4
in 'what one only can bear can bear man', 'only' can determine the verbs 'can' or 'bear' 106

dialectic: 1-14
art facilitating approach to principles of all methods 1; from 'dia' (two) and 'logos' (discourse) or 'lexis' (reasoning) 1; so discoursing or reasoning of a pair 1

dialectical disputation
collects contradictions from probable premises 77; 3 kinds like those of dialectic: discriminative, exercitative and doctrinal 79; tool: dialectical syllogism concluding from probable premises 77;

dialectical syllogisms
are not faulty for starting from false premises 77

dialectical topic:
proof is primarily given by an apt mode 148

dialectic
dialectic's end: opinion acquired by argments derived from dialectical Topics 81

dialectician(s)
admit only noun and verb as parts of the word-groups they study 3

dictum
(what was said) 12; as a unit, always subject of third-person verb 105; can stand for itself or part of itself as subject to some verb 104; may be a thing, but not 'thing' as taken here 106; a dictum's subject is not the dictum 106;

'unthinkable' 180

diminution: decrease in pre-existent quantity 36

discourse / sermo
cannot be held without vocal expressions 1

discrete quantity 30

discrete term
like 'Socrates' is neither restricted nor extended 172; neither restricted nor extended 180

disjunction 9

disposition 32
subject dispositions like 'white' should be repeated in the minor 187; like 'every' respective: dispose subject as paired with predicate, to subject-as-subject so ought not be repeated in minor 187; like 'white' independent; pertain to what the subject is 187

disputation
cannot be held without discourse 1; disputation, discourse, vocal expression and sound 1; activity of one person syllogizing with another as to a proposal to be demonstrated 76; requires: opponent, respondent, proposal, disputation and its instrument 76; disputation's difference, 'to be demonstrated', blends its activity & object 76; object: disputed facts 76; of 4 kinds: didactic, dialectical, tentative and sophistical 77; said analogically of four types 78; Aristotle does not define, just divides disputation in Elenchi 78; prime and secondary analogates vary 78

disputing 1

distinguish 2

distribute
in 'every man is an animal' by marker demand, the term 'man' is diffused / distributed for any of its supposits 71; 'man' as restricted to white men in 'every white man is running' cannot be distributed except for white men 178; a preceding marker can distribute a common term for any supposit 179

distribution:
multiplication of common term effected by universal marker 185; placed in an oblique cannot extend to the verb, nor can negation 195; wherever found, a common term is taken universally 198; accommodated often posited with 'all' 199; potential often posited with 'apt to' 199; interscalar, interrupted, or discontinuous 204

diverse 27
deception effected by diversity of relation is not equivocation 167; deception from diverse relation a fallacy of composition or division 167

diversity
relative of diversity in accidents recalls specifically identical quality and stands for specifically different quality 170

divided
'two are five and three are five' is copulative when divided 98; five are two and three' can be divided or composite 107

Equivocation
diverse natures of things united in same word, simply taken
83; principle of deficiency /
cause of non-existence / falsity: diversity of natures and
of things signified 83; motive principle / plausible cause:
unity of a word simply taken
83; can be taken in itself or
secondarily as having something in common with amphiboly 84; further requires our
inability to distinguish nominal natures 84; is from
word signification 89; same
word equally signifies (1)
diverse things (dog) 84; (2)
different things analogically
(health) 85; (3) from diverse
consignification ('suffering'
past and present) 87; from
metaphor reduces to equivocation (2) 86; divided by a
term's being major, minor or
middle accidental 89; 1st
two modes arise from signification, 3rd from consignification 89; in words from signification or consignification
89; equivocation or definition
better preserved where many
are equally signified than
when one is signified first,
then others 89; common
modes of equivocation and
amphiboly 92; (to signify
several things principally)
more appropriate to word
than word-group 96; deception from absolute accidents;
amphiboly: deception from
respective accidents 98;
equivocation, word-group and
similar formations reduced in
that they are ambiguous 161;

deception effected by diversity of relation is not equivocation 167
essence 22
Ethiopian 22
'every'
'every man runs', as proven
by another word-group, is a
conclusion 156; as put in
premises to prove something,
it is a proposition 156; as
signifying a thing ± exists, a
statement 156; a universal
marker distributive of substance, defined through the
mode 'what' 185; universal
marker distributive of substance 185; 'every Socrates'
is a solecism in word- group
parts 185; does not signify
something as a universal, but
that something is taken universally 186; in the plural is
taken collectively, distributively or divisively 186; not
predicable of one nor of several 186; signifies a common
term taken for every inferior 186; signifies disposition
of a thing that can be made
subject or predicate 186;
signifies not a thing, but a
kind of thing, which is ambiguous 186; if 'every' signifies
nothing, its ± presence ±
affects truth value little 186;
as disposition of subject in the
major, it should be repeated
in the minor 187; seems to
demand 3 appellates 187; as
'universally taken' a mode peculiar to the universal itself
188; sometimes found in several, sometimes only in one
188; adjoined to a term having several supposits 189;

'rational' in 'rational animal' to animals that are rational 177

genus in species 26, 28, 34, 36

geometrican
being a doctor or geometrician is in man, but not in every man 21

gerund
ending in -do interpreted by 'while' or 'if' or 'because' 197

grammar
not about all contraries, but the ± congruous 71; perfect tool a simple congruous sentence, figuratives are incomplete 76

grammarian 28, 32, 33, 35

grammatical
accident: non-present tense in the verb 2; 'grammatical', 'strong', 'white' and their like are predicated senominatively 24

greater:
(here) what surpasses another in power and ability 64

greater-less 30

groan 2

habit: 32, 36
a quality hard to change vs. disposition: a quality easy to change 32

have (habere)
27, 28, 32, 34, 35, 36, 37:
have armor on 25; shoes on 27; a possession like a house or field 37; a wife 37; bushel 'has' grains of wheat 37; flask 'has' wine 37

'healthy'
always signifies identical health, but by different modes 83; of an animal, signifies its subject, of urine a sign, of food, what effects it, of drink, what prepares for it 84; said first of an animal, then of what keeps it so: preposition 'in' first means relation of things to subject, then their relation to what they effect or conserve 87

hear 1

hearing and deafness 34

hot and cold 32

house
consists of wall, roof & foundation: Socrates has parts of that sort 199

hypothetic 4;
from 'hypos' (under) and 'thesis' (position) 8;

hypothetical 8

I = particular affirmative 47

identical 165, 170, 171
half a line is not numerically identical with a whole one, but relationships are numerically identical 145; numerically identical accident cannot exist in different subjects, specifically identical accidents can 170

identical numerically
numerically identical accident cannot exist in different subjects, specifically identical accidents can 170

identical specifically
numerically identical accident cannot exist in different subjects, specifically identical accidents can 170

identity, substantially
reciprocal relative adds substantial identity and mode of

imperfect tools for disputation 76

infer 192, 205

inference 192, 198, 200

inferior 19, 22-24, 177

inferior Position 31

'infinite'
said 5 ways: (1) what cannot be penetrated, (2) what can, but has not yet been gone through (3) by addition (4) by division (5) by both additition and division (203); as to las 3 significations, defined as: whose nature it is, always to take up something extra 204; customarily taken as common term 204; as distroibutive marker, makes proposition 'infinites are finite' distributionally equipollent to 'for one or another, infinites are finite 204; equivocated as 'infinite-for-us' and 'simply infinite 204; can be common term or syncategorematic word 205; 'infinite by addition' is infinite somehow or other, not simply 205

inflection
indicative, imperative & infinitival word-groups completed by own proper inflections 100

instrument 1

intergral Whole:
what is composed on quantitative parts 56

intensifie or diminished 29

interpretation:
exposition of one word by some other word 54;; (1): not converted like 'hurting the foot' (laedens pedem) 54; (2): converted, like lover of wis-

dom' (philosopher) 54

interrogation
indicative word-group taken under the mode of asking a question 156

interscalar
interscalar / interrupted distribution 204

introduction
prior to narration in a speech 35

inventor 2

'invite'
can be a word or a word-group 111

'is'
and 'lives' equal as potential 'verb simply', not in actuality 101; 'is' predicate of its subject 'whatever lives' in 'whatever lives always is' 101

'is'
taken by factual demand for as many essences as 'man' 71; verb 'is' does not extend of itself, but has that potential through its adjuncts 180

justice 32

knowing age 167

knowing
(1) conceptual: goes from conceptually prior to the conceptually subsequent 148; (2) sensible: goes from sensibly prior to sensibly subsequent 148; the conceptual is prior by essence, the sensible, prior by sensibles 148

knowledge 32

law
of contradictories 8; of subalternates 8; of subcontraries 8

leftwards 36

men in 'a man is running 177; restricted to standing for whites only by accidental adjective 'white' 177; restricted to whites by restrictive relative clause in 'the man who is white is running' 177; does not stand for blacks but restricted to whites in 'a white man' 177; as restricted to white men in 'every white man is running', cannot be distributed except for white men 178; found in men white, black and in between so more common than 'white' 178; restricted to whites by the implication in 'a man who is white is running' 179; stands for men who are or were men in 'a man was an animal' 180; is distributed / diffused for inferior by marker 'every' 185; means species as such: 'men' means species as actually multiplied 189

'man'

as a common term with personal supposition does not signify, stand for or call up the same thing in 'man runs' 176; as a common term with simple supposition signifies, stands for, and calls up man-in-common 175; signifies and stands for ± existent man but only calls up existents 175

Marcus-Tullius 18

mare

a particular mare is bred to a particular ass for the generation of a mule 23

marker(s)

(particular) include 'some one', 'a certin one', 'the first',

'the other' etc. 4; marker (signum) 4; if in S of proposition to be converted, must have all P in its scope and reduces that whole to S 8; universal markers include 'every', 'not a one', 'nothing', 'any', 'either', 'neither' 4; universal and particular markers (signa) are not terms 69; universal marker & implication in the same locution make it ambiguous 179; preceding marker can distribute a common term for any supposit 179; when 'marker distributive of substance' used, 'substance' is taken commonly for things of any kind 185; distributive of substance distributes things defined through the mode of 'what' (quid) 185; some distributive of substance are distributive of subjective parts ('not a [one]') 185; some of integral parts ('whole'); some distributive of subjective parts are distributive of several things ('every') 185; distributive of accident distributes things defined by mode of acciednet as though mode 'what kind' (qualis) 185; 'not a (one) (nullus) signifies negatively universally 193; 'not every' (omnis non) and 'not a (one)' (nullus) are equipollent 193; 'nothing' (nichil) signifies 'not a thing' (nullam rem) 194; 'of whatever kind' is a universal marker disrtibutive of accident 185; of pairs ('eihter', 'neither') 196; of quality distributes a thing defined by the

'suffering' consignifies present time & imperfect past 88; in present tense adjoined to active/passive verb vary in (con)signification 88; 'man' restricted by participle to men running in 'a man running is debating' 177

particular 4

marker 4; sought in universal 147

parts of speech / word-group

dialectician posits two (noun and verb): the rest are called syncategorematics 3

parts of word-group / speech

constitute   word-group's significate but retain their own proper significate 96

passion / passivity 18

passion / undergoing

an effect and consequence of action 34; passivity: a quality of Being Affected 30; peculiarity: undergoing something is not in an agent but in a patient 34; peculiarity: to be brought about by action 34

past 30

patient 34

is one thing, mode of patient another 165; nominative can be patient but cannot have the mode of patient 165; reciprocal relative adds substantial identity and mode of patient to agent 165

peculiar(ity) / proprium

17, 18, 21, 23,: what is always in each member and always only in a member 21; defined by Aristotle: what is in species alone, predicated conversely of that to which it is peculiar, and does not in-

dicate what the essence of a thing is 21-23; said four ways 21; defined fourth way, it is one of five predicables 22; vs. accident: peculiarity is predicated of only one species, accident of several 22; peculiarity vs. acc: accident is first in individuals, 2nd in genus and species; peculiarity is first in species, then in individuals 22

peculiarly / proprie 1

pendere

'pendere' has one perfection in the 2nd, another in 3rd conjugation 98; has different meanings by accent 110

perfect 3

a man is called 'perfect' who has man's due substance, potential & operation 189

perfection

is called an act(uality) 99; is in threes: entire and perfect are the same 187; a thing's perfection is in three things: its substance, potential and operation 189; a part has no being but in its whole, for it has no perfection except in that whole 200; every word-group taken as composite or divided: some difference is always to be found on the side of perfection, and thereby, of significates 98

personal supposition

acceptance of a common term for its inferiors; determinate or diffuse 71, 172

phoenix'

is restricted to one in 'a phoenix exists', so their rule is fallacious 190

place 30, 32, 34, 36
place in nature
  provides firm ground to natural things, as a Topic, it confirms arguments 52
plow sand 167
polysemy / multiple ambiguity
  Alexander says polysemy
  (multiple ambiguity) is actual,
  potential or imaginary 82;
  consists of both identity and
  diversity in a word-group 99;
  actual: one simply identical
  word(-group) signifies several
  things 82; actual polysemy is
  polysemy simply taken 116;
  it occurs in equivocation and
  amphiboly 82; **imaginary:**
  the same word has truly one,
  and seemingly another, mode
  of signifying 116; **potential:**
  when an identical word or
  word-group signifes different
  things depending on different
  perfections 98
Porphyry 19, 20, 22, 72, 127
posit(ing)
  ambiguous in syllogisms: one
  by quantity, quality and order
  of propositions and terms;
  the other which has to do with
  Topic-relationships 163
possess / have / habere
  (1) quality (virtue) (2) size
  (2 cubits) (3) have about the
  body (coat) (4) a member
  (finger) (5) have contained
  (flask has wine) (6) a possession (house) (7) a wife -
  furthest from posession 36-7
possibly 11
postposed 10
potential
  the potential a word-group
  has for diverse species from

its expression side is ordered
to its potential for diverse
significates 102-3; verb 'is'
does not extend of itself, but
has that potential through its
adjuncts 180
precede
  a preceding marker can distribute a common term for
  any supposit of it 179
Predicable
  17-24: predicable / universal:
  genus, species, difference,
  peculiarity (proprium) and
  accident 17; same as universal, but formally different 17; predicaebles are
  defined by being said, universals by being 17; predicated of several 17; all 5
  alike in being predicable of
  several 24
Predicament 19, 24, 25, 27, 36
predicate universally
  (dici de omni): when there is
  nothing under the subject
  etc. 38
predicate, a
  what is said of the other 3;
  predicate-as-predicate is one
  thing, that which is the predicate another 169; restricts
  its subject as to consignification, not as to principal
  signification 179;
predicate, to 17-24:
  in 3 ways: equivocally, univocally, denominatively 25;
  neither name nor nature of
  some things said of a subject
  are predicated 28; white
  may be predicated of a subject but whiteness never is
  28; 'white' as predicate of 'a
  man is white' cannot restrict

to recall 167; any proposition begun with a relative has a contradictory 169; relatives proferred when no question has been put 171; proferred when nouns of special accident are mentioned 171; rule about restriction by a restrictive relative clause 179

relative, substantial
substantial relative recalls a numerically identical thing; accidental relative recalls a specificaly identical thing 170

relatively opposed 34

relatives of accidental identity are relatives of quality or relatives of quantity (continuous or number) 171; or responsives not said of things present 171; recall identical or diverse substances 164; a substantive relative recalls the univocal thing or by its mode 'something' 170

relatives of identity
are nouns or ± reciprocal pronouns 164

remote
propositions' matter is three-fold: natural, contginent and remote 7

remove (deny) 4

represent 1

representation 69

repugnant 165

res (sense) 11

res: see thing

respect
of relative to antecedent is not there because of the nature of affirmation nor the dependence of subject-as-subject, but because of the

dependence of that which is the subject 169

respondent 1

responsive
proper responsives are answers to preceding questions 171

restrict
'citizen', in 'a citizen is white (albus)' is restricted as to consignification (here, gender) 179; 'man' is restricted to standing for whites only by the accidental adjective 'white' 177; 'man' and 'white' restrict each other in 'white man', but as to different things 178; 'man' as restricted to white men in 'every white man is running' cannot be distributed except for white men 178; 'man' does not stand for blacks but is restricted to whites in 'a white man' 177; 'man' is restricted by the participle to men running in 'a man running is debating' 177; 'man' is restricted by the verb to present men in 'a man is running' 177; 'man' is restricted to whites by the restrictive relative clause in 'the man who is white is running' 177; 'man' is restricted to whites by the implication in 'a man who is white is running' 179; 'white', as predicate of 'a man is white', cannot restrict 'man' as the subject to whites 179; 'white' in the predicate cannot restrict 'man' in the subject 179; another rule about restriction 178, 179; extensive

70; signification and supposition concern both existent and non-existents 175; verb restricts its supposit as to consignification, not as to signification 183

signification (principal)
predicate restricts its subject as to consignification, not as to principal signification 179; term restricts another as to consignification, not principal signification 179

significative
an expression is significative if it represents something when heard 1; conventional and simple (noun, verb) or complex (word-group) 2; distinguishes noun from non-significative expressions 2; naturally: represents the same to all (groans and barking) 2

'signify'
has to do with a vocal expression 70

signifying by convention represents something depending on its inventor's choice (man) 2

signum (marker) 3

simple
conventional expressions are noun and verb 2; simple conversion 8; simple suppostion 70; the Fallacy After-a-Fashion and Simply 137

simple supposition
acceptance of common term for a universal thing signified by it 70; that of a common term after an exceptive word like 'except' 70; that of a common term as subject or as affirmative predicate 70; in

subject or predicate 72; singular 4

singular term
one naturally apt to be predicated of on thing only 4; every change and all operations have to do with singulars 132; signifies, stands for, and calls up the same thing 175; cannot be distributed 185

size 36

snub-nosed 23

solecism
fault in constructing contrary to the rules of the art of grammar 80; 'man's runs' is a mistake of needed ending 97; positing a solecism destroys the nature of inference yet leaves seeming conclusion 118; 'question is many' lacks concord but is well joined 157

some (one) (aliquis) 4

son-father 28

sophistic Disputation
syllogizes from what seem, but are not, probable 78; is ordered to five goals: Refutation, Falsity, Paradox, Solecism & Trivialization 79; proximate goal: apparent wisdom 80

sophistical syllogism(s)
one that seems to be, but is not, a syllogism 78: divide like sophistical disputation 80

sophistical Topic(s)
thirteen fallacies: six linguistic, seven extralinguistic 81; proof is primarily in a non-apt mode 148

sophists
prefer to seem wise and not be to being wise without

of the minor 45;
3rd Mood of 2nd Figure reduces to 4th Mood of 1st Figure by simple conversion 43;
4th Mood of 2nd Figure reduces to 1st Mood of 1st Figure by reductio ad absurdum 44;
3rd Mood of 3rd Figure reduces to 3rd Mood of 1st Figure by simple conversion of the minor 45;
4th Mood of 3rd Figure reduces to 3rd Mood of 1st Figure by simple conversion of the minor 45;
5th Mood of 1st Figure proven through 1st Mood of 1st Figure 41
6th Mood reduces to 2nd by simple conversion of the conclusion 42

syncategorematic:
word-group-part not noun or verb 3; syncategorematics = 'consignificatives' 3; dialectician labels forms other than noun or verb, 'syncategorematics' 3
taken 17, 19, 21, 23, 24
in multiple ambiguity through adverbs 12; 'taken simply' excludes diminishers like 'unthinkable' 180; any negative where 'be' simply taken is negated is false 182

teeth 1
temporal adverb 11
temporal partial:
word signifying a bit of time adverbially 58
temporal totality:
word embracing every time adverbially 58
tenor same as accent 112

tense
distinguishes noun from verb 2; absolute accident of a word 97; 'man' stands for men who are or were men in 'a man was an animal' 180; common term has different supposition with verbs in different tenses 180; verbs in tenses other than present imply different suppositions 180; tense being identical in affirmative and negative, restriction identical 183; causes a verb's rectriction, but tense is identical in affirmatives and negatives 183;
tentative syllogism
tool: tentative syllogism (concluding from things probable to the respondent) 77; often called materially defective by objectors 77; argues from what seem true to the respondent & one pretending to have knowledge must know 77; argues from commonalities to commonalities or from commons to peculiars 79
term 69, 70, 71, 72, 73, 74: common one naturally apt to be predicated of several subjects 4; two propositions cannot be made from three terms without taking one twice 38; term taken twice subject in one and predicate in other or vice versa 38; term taken twice before conclusion called middle term 38; middle Term must never be put into the conclusion; 40; each unconstructed term signifies either substance, or

quality, or quantity, or relation, or action, or passivity, etc. 69; significatino of a term (here) is the convetional representation of a thing by a vocal expression 69; in 'white man', 'man' is an unconstructed term 69; term signifying a non-being does not call up (non appellat) anything 175; restricts another as to consignification, not principal signification 179; the form of a common term is ambiguous as to one realized only in existent or in existents as well as non-existents 183

the other (one) (reliquus) 4

thing (res)
peculiarity (proprium) is what is in species alone, predicated conversely with that to which it is peculiar, and does not indicate what the essence of a thing is 22; this particular thing (individual) 29; truth and falsity are in things as in a subject 29; a thing is cause of the truth of a proposition or sentence made about that thing itself 35; signified substantively or adjectivally 69; indifferently things themselves, their double mode and relations 83; things' double mode: consignification and signification 83; the thing signified which is the principle of truth and falsity 117; 'whiteness' as thing and mode of signifying 120; a fallacy is called extralinguistic if its plausible cause and cause of non-existence is in a thing 126; nature doesn't depend on

a word's, but a word's nature does depend on that of a thing 134; undiminished thing is one called 'simply' 137; same thing, under same name, cannot be proven of itself 146; thing defined sought in its definition 147; 'nothing' by usage stands for solid or firm things 184 a different kind of thing: the dispostion of a thing that can be made subject or predicate 186; truth and falsity in a word-group is cause both by this and that other sort of thing 186

thing present
demonstratives are said of things present 171

thing subjected
distinguish thing subjected from accident to thing subjected 136

throat 1

time
something is first said to be prior to another in time 35; those are said to be together whose generation is at the same time 35; a temporal totality is a word embracing every time adverbially, like 'always' 58

to 'stand for'
is one thing, 'make true for' another 71; see stand for

'to be said of a subject'
here: said of an inferior (animal of man) 26; see said of

to be-in
26, 29: taken as accident in a subject 26; as in a goal; as in a vessel; as in an efficient

warm and cool 33
what (essential) kind 19, 21,
21, 23
what (que) 4
what kind ? (qualis) 4
what number ? (quantus) 4
what sort of (quale) 33
'what sort of thing'
interpreted as 'this particular
thing' 122
when 16-21, 27, 29, 32-36
'whenever'
is in predicament 'When';
'twice' means discrete quantity 203
where 18, 27
white and black 34
'white'
is found in men, brute animals
and stone, so is more common
than 'man' in 'white man'
178; as predicate of 'a man
is white' it cannot restrict
'man' as subject to whites
179; in predicate cannot restrict 'man' in subject 179
'who'
as a relative signifies a single
thing existing through the
mode of substance 166; signifies substance indeterminately 166
whole
universal whole / genus 55;
integral: one composed of
parts that have quantity and a
part of it is called integral
56; in quantity: a universal
taken universally 57; in
mode: a universal taken without determination 58; in
place: a word embracing
every place adverbially 58;
if it is impossible for a whole
in quantity to be genus as

genus, it is not possible that a
common predicate term be
diffused 73; ability to see
suits parts as united within
their whole, not the whole itself 197; identical with all
parts united at once 197;
follows upon parts and ability
to see suits parts 198; subjected to whiteness directly,
parts indirectly 199; in what
is a whole, parts are understood indirectly 199; what a
whole is gives us to understand its indirect parts 199;
inference drawn about a
whole through parts is a fallacy of accident 200; some
accidents fit parts but not the
whole 201; some accidents
indifferently suit whole and
part 201
whole in place
a word embracing every place
adverbially 58
whole in quantity
a universal taken universally
57; ambiguous as to ± complete and ± diffused mobilely
73; results simply if common
term is multiplied simply 73;
somehow or other results if
common term are multiplied
somehow or other 73
wish 11
with respect to 16-21, 24
word(s) [dictio(nes)]
not so much a sign of many
things as a sign of signification or consignification 89;
word's principal signification
opposes its consignification &
metaphoric signification 97;
are signs of things 101; a
word has an accidental mode
of signifying a thing as an

individual 117; has an accidental mode of signifying what is principle of ± congruity, like gender 117; has an accidental mode of signifying due to the thing signified 117; here function as signs and instruments 119; taken as things rather than signs of things is fallacy of consequent, not word-figure 119; is a sign of a thing and related to it purposively 135; understood by vocalic boundary as signifying what, what sort, masculine, etc. 115; word's accidental mode of signifying should come last naturally, not temporally 115; 'twice' posits an interruption of act to which it is adjoined 202; does not imply an interruption in, but an end of, an act 203

word or word-group
'quies' can be a word or a word-group 110; word-groups ± do share equally in word-group identity 100; 'metuo' can be a word or a word-group 111

Word Figure 113
is a mode of signifying accidentally in a word 115; motive principle of fallacy: likeness of accidental mode of signifying 117; deficiency principle of Fallacy of Word-Figure: incompleteness or diminution of likeness 117; all word-figure fallacies are contrary to the rules of inference (e.g., which is middle term) 118; words taken as things rather than signs of things is a fallacy of consequent, not word-figure 119;

word meaning
convention is the remote, composition the proximate cause of word meaning 95

word-group (oratio): 166, 167
a constructed / complex expression 3; conventionally significative with separately meaningful parts 3; complete (perfect) or incomplete 3; perfect / complete generates complete sense in hearer's mind ('man is white') 3; complete is either indicative, imperative, optative or subjunctive 3; an incomplete generates incomplete sense ('white man' vs 'man is white') 3; only indicative said to be a proposition 3; need not be true in one, false in another composition, division or accent 102; can either be composed of different letters, syllables or words, or of the same in varied order 99; word-group identity is ambiguous as to identity of perfection or material 99; word-groups are composite when words ordered by their most due position 101; divided if not ordered according to most due position 101; concepts of simple words unanalyzable, those of composites, analyzable 94; word ordering is nothing other than a word-group 167; said to be ± true depending on whether a thing ± exists 186

'works'
in 'a nature aptly designed works so' touches on a thing's operation 189

INDEX OF SOPHISMS AND EXAMPLES

In the STUDIES IN THE HISTORY OF THE LANGUAGE SCIENCES (SiHoLS) series (Series Editor: E.F. Konrad Koerner) the following volumes have been published thus far, and will be published during 1990:

1. KOERNER, E.F. Konrad: *The Importance of Techmer's "Internationale Zeitschrift für Allgemeine Sprachwissenschaft" in the Development of General Linguistics.* Amsterdam, 1973.

2. TAYLOR, Daniel J.: *Declinatio: A Study of the Linguistic Theory of Marcus Terentius Varro.* Amsterdam, 1974. 2nd pr. 1989.

3. BENWARE, Wilbur A.: *The Study of Indo-European Vocalism; from the beginnings to Whitney and Scherer: A critical-historical account.* Amsterdam, 1974. t.o.p. 2nd pr. 1990.

4. BACHER, Wilhelm: *Die Anfänge der hebräischen Grammatik* (1895), together with *Die hebräische Sprachwissenschaft vom 10. bis zum 16. Jahrhundert* (1892). Amsterdam, 1974.

5. HUNT, R.W. (1908-1979): *The History of Grammar in the Middle Ages. Collected Papers.* Edited with an introduction, a select bibliography, and indices by G.L. Bursill-Hall. Amsterdam, 1980.

6. MILLER, Roy Andrew: *Studies in the Grammatical Tradition in Tibet.* Amsterdam, 1976.

7. PEDERSEN, Holger (1867-1953): *A Glance at the History of Linguistics, with particular regard to the historical study of phonology.* Amsterdam, 1983.

8. STENGEL, Edmund (1845-1935), (ed.): *Chronologisches Verzeichnis französischer Grammatiken vom Ende des 14. bis zum Ausgange des 18. Jahrhunderts, nebst Angabe der bisher ermittelten Fundorte derselben.* Amsterdam, 1976.

9. NIEDEREHE, Hans-Josef & Harald HAARMANN (with the assistance of Liliane Rouday), (eds): *In Memoriam Friedrich Diez: Akten des Kolloquiums zur Wissenschaftsgeschichte der Romanistik/Actes du Colloque sur l'Histoire des Etudes Romanes/Proceedings of the Colloquium for the History of Romance Studies, Trier, 2.-4. Okt. 1975).* Amsterdam, 1976.

10. KILBURY, James: *The Development of Morphophonemic Theory.* Amsterdam, 1976.

11. KOERNER, E.F. Konrad: *Western Histories of Linguistic Thought. An annotated chronological bibliography, 1822-1976.* Amsterdam, 1978.

12. PAULINUS a S. BARTHOLOMAEO (1749-1806): *Dissertation on the Sanskrit Language.* Transl., edited and introduced by Ludo Rocher. Amsterdam, 1977.

13. DRAKE, Glendon F.: *The Role of Prescriptivism in American Linguistics 1820-1970.* Amsterdam, 1977.

14. SIGERUS DE CORTRACO: *Summa modorum significandi; Sophismata.* New edition, on the basis of G. Wallerand's *editio prima,* with additions, critical notes, an index of terms, and an introd. by Jan Pinborg. Amsterdam, 1977.

15. PSEUDO-ALBERTUS MAGNUS: *Quaestiones Alberti de Modis significandi.* A critical edition, translation and commentary of the British Museum Inc. C.21.C.52 and the Cambridge Inc.5.J.3.7, by L.G. Kelly. Amsterdam, 1977.

16. PANCONCELLI-CALZIA, Giulio (1878-1966): *Geschichtszahlen der Phonetik* (1941), together with *Quellenatlas der Phonetik* (1940). New ed., with an introd. article and a bio-bibliographical account of Panconcelli-Calzia by Jens-Peter Köster. Amsterdam, n.y.p.

17. SALMON, Vivian: *The Study of Language in 17th-Century England.* Amsterdam, 1979. Second edition 1988.

18. HAYASHI, Tetsuro: *The Theory of English Lexicography 1530-1791*. Amsterdam, 1978.
19. KOERNER, E.F. Konrad: *Toward a Historiography of Linguistics. Selected Essays.* Foreword by R.H. Robins. Amsterdam, 1978.
20. KOERNER, E.F. Konrad (ed.): *Progress in Linguistic Historiography: Papers from the International Conference on the History of the Language Sciences, Ottawa, 28-31 August 1978.* Amsterdam, 1980.
21. DAVIS, Boyd H. & Raymond K. O'CAIN (eds): *First Person Singular. Papers from the Conference on an Oral Archive for the History of American Linguistics. (Charlotte, N.C., 9-10 March 1979).* Amsterdam, 1980.
22. McDERMOTT, A. Charlene Senape: *Godfrey of Fontaine's Abridgement of Boethius the Dane's 'Modi Significandi sive Quaestiones super Priscianum Maiorem.* A text edition with English transl. and introd. Amsterdam, 1980.
23. APOLLONIUS DYSCOLUS: *The Syntax of Apollonius Dyscolus.* Translated, and with commentary by Fred W. Householder. Amsterdam, 1981.
24. CARTER, M.. (ed.): *Arab Linguistics, an introductory classical text with translation and notes.* Amsterdam, 1981.
25. HYMES, Dell H.: *Essays in the History of Linguistic Anthropology.* Amsterdam, 1983.
26. KOERNER, Konrad, Hans-J. NIEDEREHE & R.H. ROBINS (eds): *Studies in Medieval Linguistic Thought,* dedicated to Geoffrey L. Bursill-Hall on the occasion of his 60th birthday on 15 May 1980. Amsterdam, 1980.
27. BREVA-CLARAMONTE, Manuel: *Sanctius' Theory of Language: A contribution to the history of Renaissance linguistics.* Amsterdam, 1983.
28. VERSTEEGH, Kees, Konrad KOERNER & Hans-J. NIEDEREHE (eds): *The History of Linguistics in the Near East.* Amsterdam, 1983.
29. ARENS, Hans: *Aristotle's Theory of Language and its Tradition.* Amsterdam, 1984.
30. GORDON, W. Terrence: *A History of Semantics.* Amsterdam, 1982.
31. CHRISTY, Craig: *Uniformitarianism in Linguistics.* Amsterdam 1983.
32. MANCHESTER, M.L.: *The Philosophical Foundations of Humboldt's Linguistic Doctrines.* Amsterdam 1985.
33. RAMAT, Paolo, Hans-Josef NIEDEREHE & E.F. Konrad KOERNER (eds): *The History of Linguistics in Italy.* Amsterdam, 1986.
34. QUILIS, Antonio & Hans J. NIEDEREHE (eds): *The History of Linguistics in Spain.* Amsterdam, 1986.
35. SALMON, Vivian & Edwina BURNESS (comps): *A Reader in the Language of Shakespearean Drama.* Amsterdam, 1987.
36. SAPIR, Edward: *Appraisals of his Life and Work.* Edited by Konrad Koerner. Amsterdam, 1984.
37. Ó MATHÚNA, Seán P.: *William Bathe, S.J., 1564-1614: a pioneer in linguistics.* Amsterdam, 1986.
38. AARSLEFF, Hans, Louis G. KELLY & Hans-Josef NIEDEREHE (eds): *Papers in the History of Linguistics. Proceedings of ICHoLS III, Princeton 1984.* Amsterdam, 1987.
39. PETRUS HISPANUS: *Summulae Logicales.* Translated and with an introduction by Francis P. Dinneen, S.J. Amsterdam, 1990.
40. HARTMANN, R.R.K. (ed.): *The History of Lexicography. Papers from the Dictionary Research Centre Seminar at Exeter, March 1986.* Amsterdam, 1986.

41. COWAN, William, Michael K. FOSTER & Konrad KOERNER (eds): *New Perspectivess in Language, Culture, and Personality. Proceedings of the Edward Sapir Centenary Conference (Ottawa, 1-3 October 1984)*. Amsterdam, 1986.

42. BUZZETTI, Dino & Maurizio FERRIANI (eds): *Speculative Grammar, Universal Grammar, and Philosophical Analysis of Language*. Amsterdam, 1987.

43. BURSILL-HALL, G. L., Sten EBBESEN & E.F. Konrad KOERNER (eds): *De Ortu Grammaticae. Studies in Medieval Grammar and Linguistic Theory in Memory of Jan Pinborg*. Amsterdam/Philadelphia, 1990. n.y.p.

44. AMSLER, Mark: *Etymology and Discourse in Late Antiquity and the Early Middle Ages*. Amsterdam/Philadelphia, 1989.

45. OWENS, Jonathan: *The Foundations of Grammar*. Amsterdam, 1987.

46. TAYLOR, Daniel (ed.): *The History of Linguistics in the Classical Period*. Amsterdam, 1987.

47. HALL, Robert A. jr. (ed.): *Leonard Bloomfield, Essays on his Life and Work*. Amsterdam, 1987.

48. FORMIGARI, Lia: *Language and Experience in 17th-century British Philosophy*. Amsterdam/Philadelphia, 1989.

49. DE MAURO, Tullio & Lia FORMIGARI (eds): *Leibniz, Humboldt, and the Origins of Comparativism. Proceedings of the international conference, Rome, 25-28 September 1986*. Amsterdam/Philadelphia, 1990.

50. KOERNER, Konrad: *Practicing Linguistic Historiography. Selected Essays*. Amsterdam/Philadelphia, 1989.

51. KOERNER, Konrad & Hans-Josef NIEDEREHE (eds): *History and Historiography of Linguistics*. Amsterdam/Philadelphia, 1990. n.y.p.

52. JUUL, Arne & Hans F. NIELSEN (eds): *Otto Jespersen: Facets of his Life and Work*. Amsterdam/Philadelphia, 1989.

53. OWENS, Jonathan: *Early Arabic Grammatical Theory. Heterogeneity and Standardization*. Amsterdam/Philadelphia, 1990. n.y.p.

54. ANTONSEN, Elmer H. (ed.) with James W. Marchand and Ladislav Zgusta: *The Grimm Brothers and the Germanic Past*. Amsterdam/Philadelphia, 1990. n.y.p.